Bloom's Literary Themes

Alienation
The American Dream
Civil Disobedience
Dark Humor
Death and Dying
Enslavement and Emancipation
Exploration and Colonization
The Grotesque
The Hero's Journey
Human Sexuality
The Labyrinth
Rebirth and Renewal
Sin and Redemption
The Sublime
The Taboo
The Trickster

DARK HUMOR

Bloom's Literary Themes

DARK HUMOR

Edited and with an introduction by
Harold Bloom
Sterling Professor of the Humanities
Yale University

Volume Editor
Blake Hobby

BLOOM'S
LITERARY CRITICISM
An imprint of Infobase Publishing

Bloom's Literary Themes: Dark Humor

Bloom's Literary Criticism
An imprint of Infobase Publishing
132 West 31st Street
New York NY 10001

Library of Congress Cataloging-in-Publication Data
    Bloom's literary themes. Dark humor / edited and with an introduction by Harold
Bloom ; volume editor, Blake Hobby.
        p. cm.
    Includes bibliographical references and index.
    ISBN 978-1-60413-440-7 (hc : alk. paper)   1. Black humor.   2. Humor in literature.
    I. Bloom, Harold. II. Hobby, Blake.   III. Title: Dark humor.
    PN56.H83B56 2010
    809.7—dc22
                                        2009038091

Bloom's Literary Criticism books are available at special discounts when purchased in
bulk quantities for businesses, associations, institutions, or sales promotions. Please call
our Special Sales Department in New York at (212) 967-8800 or (800) 322-8755.

You can find Bloom's Literary Criticism on the World Wide Web at
http://www.chelseahouse.com

Series design by Kerry Casey
Cover design by Takeshi Takahashi
Composition by IBT Global, Inc.
Cover printed by IBT Global, Inc., Troy NY
Book printed and bound by IBT Global, Inc., Troy NY
Date printed: January 2010
Printed in the United States of America

10 9 8 7 6 5 4 3 2 1

This book is printed on acid-free paper.

❧ *Contents* ❧

Series Introduction by Harold Bloom:
Themes and Metaphors   xi

Volume Introduction by Harold Bloom   xv

The Plays of Aristophanes   1
    "Aristophanes' Comic Apocalypse" by Louise Cowan,
      in *The Terrain of Comedy* (1984)

The Plays of Samuel Beckett and the Theatre of the Absurd   29
    "The Theatre of the Absurd" by Martin Esslin, in
      Theatre in the Twentieth Century (1956)

Catch-22 (Joseph Heller)   47
    "*Catch-22* and Angry Humor: A Study of the
      Normative Values of Satire" by James Nagel, in
      Studies in American Humor (1974)

Cat's Cradle (Kurt Vonnegut)   57
    "Dark Humor in *Cat's Cradle*" by Blake Hobby

A Clockwork Orange (Anthony Burgess)   67
    "*A Clockwork Orange* and the Metaphysics of Slapstick"
      by Matthew J. Bolton

On Dark Humor in Literature   79
    "The Comedy of Entropy: The Contexts of Black
      Humour" by Patrick O'Neill, in *Canadian Review of
      Comparative Literature (1983)*

Divine Comedy (Dante Alighieri)   105
   "Elements of Dark Humor in Dante's *Divine Comedy*"
   by Lauren P. De La Vars

The Dumbwaiter (Harold Pinter)   115
   "When Farce Turns into Something Else: Harold
   Pinter's *The Dumb Waiter*" by Scott Walters

The Stories of Nikolai Gogol and *Lolita*
(Vladimir Nabokov)   127
   "Observations on Black Humor in Gogol and
   Nabokov" by Woodin W. Rowe, in *The Slavic and East
   European Journal* (1974)

"A Good Man Is Hard to Find" (Flannery O'Connor)   139
   "Clichés, Superficial Story-Telling, and the Dark
   Humor of Flannery O'Connor's 'A Good Man Is
   Hard to Find'" by Robert C. Evans

Henry IV, Parts One and Two (William Shakespeare)   149
   "The Rejection of Falstaff" by A.C. Bradley, in *Oxford
   Lectures on Poetry* (1909)

"The Love Song of J. Alfred Prufrock"
(Thomas Stearns Eliot)   171
   "'Almost Ridiculous': Dark Humor in Eliot's 'The Love
   Song of J. Alfred Prufrock'" by Robert C. Evans

A Modest Proposal (Jonathan Swift)   181
   "Wood's Halfpence" by Leslie Stephen, in *Swift* (1882)

The Mysterious Stranger (Mark Twain)   197
   "*The Mysterious Stranger* and '3,000 Years Among the
   Microbes': Chimerical Realities and Nightmarish
   Transformations" by Patricia M. Mandia, in *Comedic
   Pathos: Black Humor in Twain's Fiction* (1991)

Reservation Blues (Sherman Alexie)   219
   "The Saddest Joke: Sherman Alexie's Blues" by James
   A. Crank

White Noise (Don DeLillo)   229
   "The Dark Humor of *White Noise*" by Joseph Dewey

Who's Afraid of Virginia Woolf? (Edward Albee)   241
   "Dark Humor in Edward Albee's *Who's Afraid of*
   Virginia Woolf?" by Kate Falvey

"The Yellow Wallpaper" (Charlotte Perkins Gilman)   251
   "'Too Terribly Good to Be Printed': Charlotte
   Gilman's 'The Yellow Wallpaper'" by Conrad
   Shumaker, in *American Literature* (1985)

Acknowledgments   263

Index   265

꧁ Series Introduction by Harold Bloom: ꧂
Themes and Metaphors

1. TOPOS AND TROPE

What we now call a theme or topic or subject initially was named a *topos*, ancient Greek for "place." Literary *topoi* are commonplaces, but also arguments or assertions. A topos can be regarded as literal when opposed to a trope or turning which is figurative and which can be a metaphor or some related departure from the literal: ironies, synecdoches (part for whole), metonymies (representations by contiguity) or hyperboles (overstatements). Themes and metaphors engender one another in all significant literary compositions.

As a theoretician of the relation between the matter and the rhetoric of high literature, I tend to define metaphor as a figure of desire rather than a figure of knowledge. We welcome literary metaphor because it enables fictions to persuade us of beautiful untrue things, as Oscar Wilde phrased it. Literary *topoi* can be regarded as places where we store information, in order to amplify the themes that interest us.

This series of volumes, *Bloom's Literary Themes*, offers students and general readers helpful essays on such perpetually crucial topics as the Hero's Journey, the Labyrinth, the Sublime, Death and Dying, the Taboo, the Trickster and many more. These subjects are chosen for their prevalence yet also for their centrality. They express the whole concern of human existence now in the twenty-first century of the Common Era. Some of the topics would have seemed odd at another time, another land: the American Dream, Enslavement and Emancipation, Civil Disobedience.

I suspect though that our current preoccupations would have existed always and everywhere, under other names. Tropes change across the centuries: the irony of one age is rarely the irony of another. But the themes of great literature, though immensely varied, undergo transmemberment and show up barely disguised in different contexts. The power of imaginative literature relies upon three constants: aesthetic splendor, cognitive power, wisdom. These are not bound by societal constraints or resentments, and ultimately are universals, and so not culture-bound. Shakespeare, except for the world's scriptures, is the one universal author, whether he is read and played in Bulgaria or Indonesia or wherever. His supremacy at creating human beings breaks through even the barrier of language and puts everyone on his stage. This means that the matter of his work has migrated everywhere, reinforcing the common places we all inhabit in his themes.

2. CONTEST AS BOTH THEME AND TROPE

Great writing or the Sublime rarely emanates directly from themes since all authors are mediated by forerunners and by contemporary rivals. Nietzsche enhanced our awareness of the agonistic foundations of ancient Greek literature and culture, from Hesiod's contest with Homer on to the Hellenistic critic Longinus in his treatise *On the Sublime*. Even Shakespeare had to begin by overcoming Christopher Marlowe, only a few months his senior. William Faulkner stemmed from the Polish-English novelist Joseph Conrad and our best living author of prose fiction, Philip Roth, is inconceivable without his descent from the major Jewish literary phenomenon of the twentieth century, Franz Kafka of Prague, who wrote the most lucid German since Goethe.

The contest with past achievement is the hidden theme of all major canonical literature in Western tradition. Literary influence is both an overwhelming metaphor for literature itself, and a common topic for all criticism, whether or not the critic knows her immersion in the incessant flood.

Every theme in this series touches upon a contest with anteriority, whether with the presence of death, the hero's quest, the overcoming of taboos, or all of the other concerns, volume by volume. From Monteverdi through Bach to Stravinsky, or from the Italian Renaissance through the agon of Matisse and Picasso, the history of all the arts demonstrates the same patterns as literature's thematic struggle with itself. Our country's great original art, jazz, is illuminated by what the great creators called "cutting contests," from Louis Armstrong and Duke Ellington on to the emergence of Charlie Parker's Bop or revisionist jazz.

A literary theme, however authentic, would come to nothing without rhetorical eloquence or mastery of metaphor. But to experience the study of the common places of invention is an apt training in the apprehension of aesthetic value in poetry and in prose.

Volume Introduction by Harold Bloom

Defining dark humor is virtually impossible because its manifestation in great literature necessarily involves irony, the trope in which you say one thing and mean another, sometimes the opposite of what is said. The great specialist in literary irony was the Anglo-Irish clergyman Jonathan Swift, who digresses endlessly into acidic ironies in *A Tale of a Tub* and *Gulliver's Travels*. G. K. Chesterton liked to assert that sometimes Chaucer's ironies are too large to be seen. That is even truer of Shakespeare, the master of dark humor as he is of every other literary mode.

Shakespeare's geniuses of dark humor include Falstaff, Hamlet, Iago, and the Fool in *King Lear*, though they abound elsewhere in virtually all the plays. Since Falstaff is the grandest comic creation in all of literature, his variety of dark humor proves very much his own. His mode of wit has no precursors, while Hamlet owes something to Montaigne. Iago is again a true Original, in dark humor as in onto-logical malice, while Lear's Fool has a touch in him of Biblical irony, of Ecclesiastes and of the Wisdom of Solomon in the Apocrypha.

The most loyal of Falstaffians, I will devote myself to him here, though he is boundless and my compass must be brief. Falstaff's central target is power, and he is audacious enough to satirize King Henry IV as well as Hal and Hotspur. So subtle is the Socrates of Eastcheap, Falstaff, that he ironizes even Hal's murderous ambiva-lence which primarily is directed against the fat knight himself.

Falstaff will die the poignant death of the rejected teacher, and Shakespeare astonishingly transmutes even that into dark humor. I brood much on that transformation and come to the insight that Falstaff, more even than Hamlet let alone Hal/Henry V, represents the charismatic in Shakespeare. Charisma emanates neither from society nor history: it emanates out from a major personality who manifestly bears the blessing of more life:

> Embowelled? If thou embowl me today, I'll give you leave to powder me and eat me too tomorrow. 'Sblood, 'twas time to counterfeit, or that hot termgant Scot had paid me, scot and lot too. Counterfeit? I lie, I am no counterfeit: to die is to be a counterfeit, for he is but the counterfeit of a man, who hath not the life of a man: but to counterfeit dying, when a man thereby liveth, is to be no counterfeit , but the true and perfect image of life indeed.

That is Falstaff's transmemberment of dark humor into his own ecstasy of sheer being. Call it the Sublime of dark humor and go on from there.

THE PLAYS OF ARISTOPHANES

"Aristophanes' Comic Apocalypse"
by Louise Cowan,
in *The Terrain of Comedy* (1984)

INTRODUCTION

Louise Cowan argues that one ethical question drives the work of Aristophanes: "The question of how a person can achieve blessedness in the midst of war, avarice, contention, and falsehood." For Cowan, Aristophanes employs dark humor as an apocalyptic writer with "double vision." This duality, according to Cowan, "allows the writer to be possessed by a spirit of nonsense, absurdity, and contradiction, so that he may undertake his supremely difficult task of raising earthly existence to a new plane of being." Aristophanes, dreaming of a better world, exposes Athens's moral decline while saving with his plays "a permanent part of the *mundus imaginalis* available to all citizens everywhere through the comic imagination—an image of that one city we keep dreaming of building."

Cowan, Louise. "Aristophanes' Comic Apocalypse." *The Terrain of Comedy*. Ed. Louise Cowan. Dallas, Texas: Dallas Institute of Humanities, 1984, 61–88.

Ordinarily overlooked as one of the paradigms of comedy in its full scope is the canon of Aristophanes, whose plays are considered by common consent brilliant though limited examples of satire and farce—uninhibited but conservative, naughty but nice. Taken in its entirety, however, Aristophanic comedy is much more comprehensive than this initial judgment would indicate, much more pregnant with things to come. It is, in fact, religious drama, in the same sense that medieval drama is religious. Both Old Attic Comedy and the liturgical comedy of the Middle Ages were essentially popular theatrical productions dramatizing a divine story, with such certainty of its sacrality that they could submit its holiest mysteries to burlesque.

Drama, as Muriel Bradbrook suggests, is "the cooperative, creation of author, actors, and audience."[1] At its highest realization it exists in a kind of communion among these three, "an intercourse from which it issues and on which it depends." The Greek and medieval English theaters were such cooperative creations, "Acts of Faith," she would have it, "directed to a God who might be both subject and audience of the play."

For the Greeks, the god who is "both subject and audience of the play" was, of course, Dionysus, the divinity of wine and harvest, whose presence is marked by pain and ecstasy and who testifies to both incarnation and transcendence. Walter Otto's extensive study reveals him to be "the god who comes," and emphasizes his distinction from the Olympians.[2] The Greeks knew the sudden appearance of a god, according to Carl Kerenyi, not only as *epiphaneia* but also as *epidemia*, a "divine 'epidemic'—whose kinship with 'visitation by a disease' is undeniable at least insofar as it was always the incursion of something overpowering. . . . "[3] As the god who comes, the epiphanic and epidemic god, Dionysus is experienced not as a governing and sustaining deity, timeless, beyond change, but as one who in time suffers, reveals, destroys, and fulfills. "The evidence is clear," Kerenyi maintains, "that the core of the Dionysian religion, the essence that endured for thousands of years and formed the very basis of its existence" was the coming of the god, his "cruel death," and, as "indestructible *zoe*," his resurrection.[4]

In his humanity as the son of a mortal mother, Dionysus traces throughout his earthly career the course of human life and hence provides for drama its subliminal subject. In his divinity, as the offspring of Zeus, he is the hidden but all-seeing audience of a theater in which a people come to self-knowledge. But it is not simply that Dionysus expresses a duality inherent in existence. More importantly, he brings about a new order. As Otto comments, "he symbolizes an entire world whose spirit reappears in ever new forms and unites in an eternal unity the sublime with the simple, the human with the animal, the vegetative and the elemental."[5] He is the "archetypal image of indestructible life," according to Kerenyi,[6] opening for man what James Hillman calls "a new psychic geography."[7]

Athenian tragedy and comedy both grew out of ceremonies dedicated to Dionysus, and in both genres, as subject and audience, he has the effect of being "the god who comes." In tragedy he appears to the proud and self-righteous ruler and to the rigidly structured city, manifesting himself to rend and destroy. Whenever men set themselves up as gods, Dionysus comes—bringing ecstasy and terror, vision and death. In comedy, by contrast, his purpose is to bring life back to a degraded and disintegrating city. In this undertaking he works by uniting a community of people in a collective exuberance, sweeping aside the barriers that divide human beings from animals, from gods, from themselves. Intoxication and festivity give rise to inspiration and fantasy, driving out the darkness of oppression, pain, and death. Dionysus comes, bringing revelry and joy, resurrection and life.

What is traditionally called "Old Comedy" is thought to have had its origin in phallic ceremonies at the festival of Dionysus, in the carnival revelry in his honor (the *komos*, or processional). Although it flourished in Athens for several centuries as popular entertainment as well as religious and mythic liturgy, comedy was not officially recognized as part of the two Athenian Dionysian celebrations until the early fifth century B.C. The names of nearly 200 authors of Greek comedy have survived, dating from the sixth century B.C. to the second century A.D. But the work of only one of them has been preserved, copied, and annotated by the Byzantine scholars, admired by the Church Fathers, his texts brought into Italy after the Fall of Constantinople and rendered into Latin long before the translation of the great tragedians. It is Aristophanes of whom I speak, of course, the comic genius who has shocked the Western world ever since his translation but who is universally regarded, in Moses Hadas's words, as "the most brilliant and artistic and thoughtful wit our world has known."[8]

Nothing remains of Old Comedy except Aristophanes' extant eleven plays (out of some forty-odd he is known to have written).

Hence, when we speak firsthand of this entire mode of comic drama, we address ourselves to one author whose work was considered significant enough to be kept alive, translated, and constantly read. For all practical purposes Aristophanes stands alone, with his "terrible graces" (*phoberai charites*).[9] And yet to make this admission is not necessarily to hold, with the general opinion, his utter separation from tradition. A recent director of Aristophanic comedy, Alexis Solomos, is an extreme spokesman for this position. He maintains that Old Comedy (by which he means Aristophanic comedy) had no ancestors and no progeny—that, in fact, the Western comic tradition stems solely from Greek middle and new comedy, the style and form of which were adopted by the Roman and European playwrights in an unbroken tradition of "comedy of manners":

> The Old Attic Comedy, on the contrary, does not belong to that millennial tradition; it stands apart; its style cannot be adjusted to the normal orbit of theatre history; it is a mythological monster without parents and without seed; it resembles the satyrs and the Centaurs, the Sphinx and the Gorgons, in being half human and half supernatural.[10]

Solomos's basic insight is of course true: the comedies of Aristophanes have something fantastic, weird, and supernatural about them. Still, it seems unjustified to set them aside from the major comic tradition and to consider them a kind of monstrous, even if magnificent, eruption.

What Mikhail Bakhtin has to say about medieval carnival[11] provides some understanding of the kind of "tradition" within which Aristophanes worked and which continued on after his time, even surviving the defeat of Greece. Old Comedy was shaped, as we have said, by festivals celebrating the rites of Dionysus, a pattern of communal imagination much like, and no doubt one might even say a forerunner of, the kind that gave rise to the wild and festive carnivals of the Middle Ages. Like carnival, the Greek rituals emphasized food, drink, sexuality, and an overturning of official order while at the same time celebrating and deepening an awareness of cultic mysteries. According to Bakhtin, we find in Aristophanes a veritable "heroics of the comic." All the things and events of ordinary life are transformed in his plays to become "cultic acts reinterpreted on the literary plane":

... they lose their private-everyday character, they become significant in human terms in all their comic aspect, their dimensions are fantastically exaggerated; we get a peculiar heroics of the comic, or, more precisely, a *comic myth*.... In Aristophanes we can still see the cultic foundation of the comic image, and we can see how everyday nuances have been layered over it, still sufficiently transparent for the foundation to shine through them and transfigure them.[12]

Bakhtin's is an illuminating comment; there can be no doubt that it is something like a comic myth that Aristophanes presents or that much of the strength of his comedy derives from its being a poetic reenactment of a cultic image or, as Bradbrook has said in a more general context, an act of faith. Both of these comments imply the action of *memoria*, as indeed in part drama must be said to be. In Aristophanic comedy, a deeply pious and conservative strain goes back to ancient fertility rites and the cultivation of the earth. But what seems fully as distinctive in these plays is the reach of their aspiration toward futurity, the projection of their spiritual and phenomenal being away from the earth into poetic space. For, unlike Homer and the author of Genesis, Aristophanes does not reveal the world and history to be comic in themselves; they are only implicitly so until seen in the light of the Dionysian imagination, which in touching and altering things, brings them to a new creation.

C. G. Jung has described what he calls "primordial experiences" that are to be found in the work of some writers, experiences that characterize a "visionary mode" of artistic creation:

The expression that furnishes the material for artistic expression is no longer familiar. It is a strange something that derives its existence from the hinterland of man's mind—that suggests the abyss of time separating us from pre-human ages.... It arises from timeless depths; it is foreign and cold, many-sided, demonic and grotesque.... the primordial experiences rend from top to bottom the curtain upon which is painted the picture of an ordered world.... [13]

Jung has here described the literature that in effect tears apart the veil of the cosmos, as opposed to that which, as he says earlier

in the same passage, deals with the foreground of life. His emphasis
is on a primordial experience which arises, as he says, "from timeless
depths. There is another kind of visionary literature, however, which
emerges from somewhere other than the abyss; it finds its material in
transcendence—in the circles of light surrounding the heavenly city.
It too is grotesque and strange, though fantastic and bizarre rather
than monstrous, and its evocation is more of rapture and terror than
of dread and horror. This is the apocalyptic, which erupts into human
consciousness from above rather than below, from the future rather
than the past. An apocalypse, in its root sense, is an uncovering, a
disclosure, a revelation of final things, not so much at the end of time
as outside time.[14] The images that rise from that realm bespeak spiritual
realities through grotesque patterns loosely associated with the vivid
sense experiences that arise from ecstasy and terror. Northrop Frye
contrasts apocalyptic with demonic, one a desirable world, the other
undesirable: "The apocalyptic world," he writes, "the heaven of religion, presents, in the first place, the categories of reality in the forms of
human desire, as indicated by the forms they assume under the work
of human civilization."[15] His comment is apt, though for my purposes
it needs some slight amendment. For, one must object, apocalyptic
seems to speak less of the "heaven of religion" than to provide strange
and marvelous images of the threshold surrounding that realm. It is
in the nature of apocalyptic poetic revelation for fantasy to seize upon
an intuition of something incomprehensible and to shape its patterns
into allegory, out of which emerges the sweet dream of peace, a vision
of the new city *coming to be* where tears are wiped away and lions and
lambs lie down together.

Both archetype and apocalypse manifest themselves through
images; both are collective and not private. It is as though the first
emerges out of the primordial past and testifies to those aspects of
the soul which were imprinted with the *imago dei*, though marred and
distorted by a warp of darkness. The second appears as if refracted into
the present from an unseen future and thus carries the force of revelation. Its images are of the never-experienced and hence imperfectly
comprehended fields of light, a realm which when its face is turned
toward time can appear as an avenging angel of destruction and judge-
ment, but which in itself is the still point, the kingdom of peace.

The Aristophanic vision, without doubt, is apocalyptic.[16] It is
concerned with images and signs of what Rudolf Otto, speaking of

apocalypse, calls "the atmospheric pressure of that which is ready to break in with mysterious dynamic."[17] An apocalypse is inherently uncanny and marvelous, as Saint John the Divine shows, with his "new heaven and new earth" and his opulent imagery of renewal and re-making: two-edged swords, golden candles, beasts with eyes in their wings, trumpets, a woman clothed in the sun, and a beast with seven heads, bear-like feet, and the mouth of a lion. And the general movement of apocalyptic is comic. For, though it announces an unsparing final judgment, its tone is one of comfort and reassurance. Despite its terror, what it symbolizes is the value of the individual soul, able to find within itself, even though confronted by principalities and powers, the strength and grace to resist evil.

Far from being monstrous, then, as Solomos would have it, the comedy of Aristophanes is apocalyptic. It reveals a total pattern of imagination, apprehended in the cult and celebration of the community. For, as Kerenyi has said, "in myth and image, in visionary experience and ritual representation [the Greeks] ... possessed a *complete expression* of the essence of Dionysus."[18] Aristophanes was thus provided by his culture with a mythic structure embracing both origins and ends; and as comic genius, his focus was upon an ultimate order manifesting itself through and in mortal life. Because of this double vision, it is in his work that comedy can first be known for what it is. Hence his plays stand at the head of, not apart from, the development of comedy. Like Homeric epic or Aeschylean tragedy, Aristophanic comedy contains within itself the lineaments of an entire genre. Nothing in the long comic tradition introduces elements not at least intimated in Aristophanes. Admittedly, in later works emphases are altered, further dimensions of meaning added; but it is not too much to say that the entire reach of the comic universe, as a possibility in itself, was first apprehended by Aristophanes.

This imaginary universe lying behind and sustaining each of Aristophanes' comedies is one that supposes and responds to the absolute audacity of the human person. It is shown to be available by aspiration and boldness, whatever one's situation. In it, comic heroes are able to outwit their opponents, to reign supreme by simple absence of malice and love of pleasure, and to conquer enemies without becoming bellicose or ill-humored. The revealed kingdom of peace is startlingly vital, manifesting the essential harmony of body and mind, flesh and spirit, age and youth, femininity and masculinity, word and deed. Laws of logic and of probability hold no sway over it; free of the limitations of time and space, improbability and contradiction are its structural modes. It contains the entire universe of comic paraphernalia: carnival, saturnalia, festivity, farce, buffoonery, satire, romance, allegory, fantasy, nonsense, absurdity, and all manner of modes and styles. It is a vision of human possibility that is at one and the same time strange and familiar, both like and unalterably unlike it.

To ignore the apocalyptic element in Aristophanes' dramas is to miss their deepest significance; although it is certainly true that even when his plays are judged by ordinary standards for comedy they show themselves to be masterpieces of comic technique. His plots are skillfully wrought; his language is shot through with wit. His characters, if one goes by what Aristotle maintained comic characters ought to be, are far "worse" than people actually are, much engaged in vices that provoke ridicule without causing pain. But from the very start, the plays imply more than Aristotle's sketch of comedy as social corrective can account for. Underneath their surface of naturalistic detail is hidden a strange pattern which is almost, but not quite, recognizable. As it takes over, everything becomes exaggerated and distorted. The language of wit turns into a pyrotechnic of creation: the mechanics of farce are blown up into absurdly stylized fantasy; personal abuse and satire take on the lineaments of grotesque allegorical caricature; bodily appetites develop an inordinate zest. Aristophanes' "maculate muse"[19] renders his obscenity absolute: the bawdiness and outright indecency of excremental and sexual details, in language as in image and act, elevate them to a level of abstraction where they are all but stripped of realistic reference. It is as though the plays move from a commonplace situation into a kind of electric field, where events and words are charged with energy and leap the barriers separating human action from the irrational and preposterous, upsetting and exploding the order of probability.

But, as we have already indicated, there is more even than this outrageous genius in the comedies of Aristophanes. His thought is at one and the same time as visionary and as astutely political as Plato's. His concern is the actual, his remedy the imagined, city. Over and over he castigates Athens for its venality and stupidity, defending the old ways in politics, education, and morals. Along with this scolding goes a defense of comic poetry, which, as he constantly teaches, has a privileged if largely unappreciated social importance. This critical and political wisdom, expressed all through the plays, is, to be sure, worthy of being taken seriously; and admittedly a great portion of Aristophanes' genius is to be found in his social satire. But even his invective is touched with irony and the grotesque. Cedric Whitman has suggested a scale of comic techniques, all essential to the uniqueness of the Aristophanic method—satire, wit, humor, and nonsense. "Satire, denounces the world," he maintains, "wit penetrates it, humor accepts it, but nonsense transforms it."[20] There can be no doubt that Aristophanes is a master of all four modes. But very often it is the nonsensical in his work that is least valued by his readers. Whitman makes a brilliant defense of nonsense, citing Baudelaire's important distinction between the "significant comic and the absolute comic," in the latter of which a nonsensical invention or creation evokes a larger sphere of meaning. But the visionary quality that I have mentioned in Aristophanes goes even further; in his comic extravaganzas fantasy becomes much more than satire, absurdity, or nonsense, more even than absolute comedy. In almost all his plays fantasy, the establishment of an imaginary realm, is a means toward transcendence and transformation. Within Aristophanes' polis of the imagination, sublime and impossible action can take place—the battle between truth and falsity can be fought out on different grounds, desire can be fulfilled, the joys and pleasures of life celebrated, language enhanced, fertility ensured, the city renewed.

Thus the Aristophanic vision consists of two worlds: one is debased and dangerously declining; the other, bright with possibility. The first is, or pretends to be, Athens—at war, taught by sophists, vitiated by pretense, racked by vanity and the love of money, rent by constant recourse to courts of law. The other is a possibility—a realm of peace instead of war, with the lowly raised high and the self-important brought low. It posits fullness instead of parsimony, fertility and potency rather than barrenness and impotence. In this vision of human fulfillment the "good things" of life, the appetites, are truly good, and the body is worthy of respect. Sex, wine, food are endowments that are meant to be enjoyed. Agrarian rather than urban life is the model, even within the polis, since city ways render people selfish, avaricious, litigious, and dishonest. Tradition and common sense are the standard for right behavior rather than any new kind of abstract and vain learning. Blessedness and celebration are the proper state of humanity, a condition to be achieved only by audacity, by what Whitman considers the chief characteristic of the Aristophanic comic hero, *poneria*, a certain good-hearted rascality and cheerful resource-fulness that ensure survival.[21] In this fantastic world that Aristophanes creates before us, one in which the invisible city, as an object of desire, has begun to assume more importance than the visible city, everything is topsy-turvy: women are put in charge of things, old men become young again, slaves outsmart masters, the lowly little Chaplinesque figures become important and powerful, and the simple become wise. It is a vision, in its own way, of the new Jerusalem.

The question of how a person can achieve blessedness in the midst of war, avarice, contention, and falsehood is the burden of Aristophanes' comedies. His three "peace" plays—*Acharnians*, *Peace*, and *Lysistrata*—are indispensable guides to his answer to this question, for they focus on the overt contrast between harmony and strife. Peace in these plays is indicative not simply of the literal peace that Athens so sorely needs but of an intuitive and revelatory vision of the ends of human life—an apocalyptic image. The state of peace is thus for Aristophanes a massive symbol of the right order of things in the cosmos, *physis*, or the great flow of nature; in the city, harmony and freedom; in the soul joy and delight, and overall, *zoe*, everlasting life. The dominant metaphor for this ecstasy of blessedness is different in each of the three plays concerned with peace.

In the *Acharnians*, Aristophanes' earliest preserved play, it is wine that not only brings about peace, but in a daring merging of meta-phor and reality, is peace itself. The peace treaties brought back to the lonely little farmer Dikaiopolis (Just City or Just Citizen) are three wineskins filled with five-, ten-, and thirty-year wines. He has sent his own messenger to Sparta to make a private peace for himself, his wife, and children. The messenger shortly comes running back with his "samples" of peace, pursued by the Acharnians, old warriors who fought at Marathon and now misguidedly resent any attempt at reconciliation with the other city-states. When Dikaiopolis tastes the samples, he spews out the five- and ten-year "treaties," since one smells of tar and warships and the other of military negotiations. But when he rolls the thirty-year treaties on his tongue, he exclaims:

> O Festival of Dionysus!
> These have a fragrance of ambrosia and nectar
> And suggest nothing, about a three-day ration,
> But on my tongue proclaim, Go where you like.[22]

The message of the well-aged wine, the thirty-year treaties, is peace and freedom: "Go where you like." This permission is like Virgil's to Dante when, at the peak of Mount Purgatory, after the pilgrim has been cleansed, he advises: "Take pleasure as your guide"—and the implication, in both instances, is that the person so liberated will do no evil. What is suggested here is the boundless state of the soul when it is in harmony with the good and realizes its own authority. After a taste of this heady wine, Dikaiopolis feels himself released from war and war's alarms and, since the city will not celebrate its traditional festival in honor of Dionysus, he sets out on this own to celebrate the rural Dionysia.

The theme of regeneration runs through all Aristophanes' comedies, and true to that movement, this play has not only Dikaiopolis but the chorus of Acharnians as well begin as old men, impotent, ignored, unsuccessful. They have been forgotten by the people whom they have guarded. In their place, hired soldiers and ambassadors perform their duties only perfunctorily; nobody respects the men who have served the state with patriotic devotion. Citizens are vain and gullible; prominent men are notorious homosexuals and cowards; even poetry is debased, with Euripides much preferred to Sophocles or Aeschylus. Everything is for sale. In the midst of the general corruption, citizens have succumbed to venality and, under the pressures of a war with neighbors, allowed themselves to be deprived of trade with their friends. It is out of love for the delicious Beoetian eels, the pungent Megarian garlic, the delectable Prasiaian leeks that Dikaiopolis begins again the exchange of goods by trading illicitly with inhabitants of other city-states. And it is from his rejection of war as the opposite of festivity that he and the Acharnians are, in the end, rejuvenated and potent. When the old men, won over to the side of peace, make love to Reconciliation (the first of Aristophanes' lovely allegorized maidens) they declare that as good husbandmen they will plant first a row of vines next to the little green figs and then finally the domestic olive where, despite their age, they will pursue lovemaking with the proper unction (991–99). Their festivity blends with Dikaiopolis's celebration, expressing an unaging vitality and abundance. They have learned the secret of the comic hero's inclusive attitude toward life and will no longer suffer from penury and fanaticism. Various citizens come to Dikaiopolis to obtain a few drops of his precious peace-wine, but he will yield none—except to a bride, so that she may keep her husband home from war. Even in this early play there is the implication of the *hieros gamos*, the sacred marriage which is the source of all peace.

However, though it is joyous and transformative, the revelry of Dikaiopolis and his friends stops short of changing the entire city and must exist within an alien regime, like a current flowing within a stagnant lake. In this, the first comic drama that we possess, what is remarkable is Aristophanes' recognition that the "green world," as it has been called, the kingdom of peace, is within the soul, available when all else fails.

Dikaiopolis invites everyone to a feast in honor of Dionysus; Lamachos, a blustering braggart soldier, calls everyone to war. Both leave the stage; but Lamachos soon reappears in disarray, pierced by a vinestake while leaping over a trench. In triumphant contrast, Dikaiopolis reappears with a pretty girl on each arm (1190–1203). Thus the fertility spirit itself, the peace and plenty of wine and festivity, has the last say. The groin of war, the allegorical figure destructive of wine and the blessings of peace, is wounded by the very emblem of what it has flouted—a vinestake. The little peaceable Dikaiopolis moves on, with a growing number of cohorts, from the Rural Dionysia to the festival of wine, the Anthesteria, where he wins the drinking contest, and the blessedness of the god is copiously manifested.

If in *Acharnians* the central symbol for reconciliation, the peace that passes understanding, is wine, in *Peace* the focus for that blessedness is food. In this, Aristophanes' fifth surviving play, it is not a thirty-year-old wine, gentle on the tongue, that possesses such magical and spiritual powers, but the harvest and fertility promised by a beautiful maiden Opora (Harvest, Bounty, Fruitfulness), along with her twin sister Theoria (Mayfair, Festivity, Ceremony). By the end of the play Opora is to wed Trygaios, a little old rustic (whose name means "crop"); and her sister is to wed the President of the Athenian Council. One young woman therefore represents rural fertility, the other urban festivity—nature and art. These two maidens have been brought to earth from the divine realm, along with the goddess Peace, who has been exhumed from a cave in which she was buried when the Olympian gods departed, leaving the dread Polemos (War) in control.

That food, as a cluster of images, is in this play the key to the way in which one reaches love and joy may be discerned in the dialogue that takes place when Hermes gives Opora to Trygaios, telling him that she is to be his bride and partner in his fields. "Marry her," he says, "and generate new vines." Trygaios asks whether after his long absti-nence it won't hurt him if he partakes too copiously of her abundance. Hermes replies, "Not if you take a dose of pennyroyal" (710–15). (The scholiast noted pennyroyal as a remedy for eating too much fruit.)

Food and its accompanying festivity and lovemaking embody peace in this fantasy of paradise regained, with the bountiful harvest of autumn replacing the spring Rural Dionysia of the earlier play. Hence imagery of the entire process of consuming—eating and defeca-tion—runs throughout the play. The opening act begins, in fact, with the servants of Trygaios complaining about the dung beetle that their master is coddling; they have to pat excrement into delicate cakes for this great beast of an insect's finicky appetite. Apparently, they conjec-ture, their master is mad; he gazes all day long at the sky, begging Zeus not to destroy Greece. He has been muttering, "If only I could somehow get to Zeus!" (69–70) and has tried unsuccessfully scaling heaven by means of ladders. He has recently acquired a huge Aetnaean beetle, calls it "little Pegasus, my flying champion" (76)—and now, just as we're watching, begins his ascent to heaven astride his mount. His daughter vainly attempts to call him back, doubting the dignity of a flight upon so lowly a creature. Should he not harness the actual Pegasus and so in tragic rather than comic style approach the gods? "No," Trygaios answers her, "for then I would have need of double supplies" (136–39). As it is, he tells her, there is a certain excremental economy in the arrangement with the beetle.

The food imagery continues throughout the play. In heaven, for instance, Trygaios finds War (Polemos) getting ready to make a salad of the Greek city-states, to grind them in his gigantic mortar. He throws in leeks for Prasiai, garlic for Megara, cheese for Sicily, and honey for Attica. But just when he is ready to toss his salad, he finds he must leave the scene to obtain a pestle; and it is while he is away that the chorus of farmers, suddenly appearing from nowhere, "pull for peace" and extricate the goddess from the cave, along with the two accompanying maidens. When Trygaios, returning to earth, seeks for the beetle, he finds that it has been transmogrified: as part of Zeus's entourage, serving with his horses, it is now fed on ambrosia. The transformation of dung to ambrosia could be taken as a governing image of metamorphosis for the entire drama, which has begun with unsavory images and ends with delectable ones. When Trygaios pulls the goddess Peace and the two lovely girls out of the earth and kisses them, exclaiming lyrically over their delicious scent, Hermes remarks: "They don't smell much like a knapsack, do they?" to which Trygaios replies:

> Ugh! that filthy bag of filthy men,
> It stinks of rank and putrid onion breath;
> But SHE of feasts and harvests, banquets, plays,
> Thrushes, festivals, flutes, the songs of Sophocles.... (525–31)

Peace is everything delightful, beautiful, sweet-smelling, delicious; whereas War has been shown to be everything filthy, ugly, fetid, foul-tasting.

After Peace has been brought back to earth, Opora given to Trygaios, and Mayfair to the Council, the action consists largely of a pageantry of rejoicing, preparations for the bridal, cooking, and feasting. The last part of the play, celebrating peace and fecundity, focuses chiefly on foods. Figs, olives, wine and myrtles, barley, flowers, fruit, herbs, and spices—all are told over lovingly as coming from the goddess's blessings. At the wedding supper, everyone is exhorted to eat and chomp away with gusto: guests are admonished to use their teeth on the festive meal and to take their fill of food and drink (1306–10). In the well-wishing for the bride and groom, they are told to dwell in peace, see their figs grow ripe, and reap their yield (1339–46).

The festive imagery of *Peace* includes in its encompassing benevolence drinking and lovemaking, as well as feasting. It is, of course, an ancient combination. Eating has traditionally been considered a communal act, binding people together by nourishment, from its most basic aspects to its most refined. Archetypally, both eating and sex are acts of union hedged about with mystery, their implications spanning the distance from humanity's dark communion with matter to its spiritual capacity for delight. Linked with two of the most fundamental motives of a society, both represent powerful communal drives toward survival. In Aristophanes' comedy they emerge as poetic symbols not only of physiological goods but of spiritual grace. The return of Peace to earth, the marriage of the old farmer to fertility, and the harvest festivals bringing together song, dance, ritual, poetry, feasting, and drinking become an image of the new creation, made all the more tender by its embodiment in old and familiar things.

If, as we have seen, *Acharnians* portrays a separate small communal peace within a warring city and *Peace* a general return among the farmers to tranquil and fruitful agrarianism, *Lysistrata* shows how peace may be restored to the political life of an entire city and, in fact, all of Greece. And the way is not through wine or food (though both are present in abundance in the feast of amity and friendship at the end of the play), but through sex—lovemaking between husband and wife, within the family, in a harmonious and ordered city. And just as wine and food are complex images in the preceding plays, taking on increasingly expanded meaning (the dung becomes ambrosia, plenteous crops from the fruitful earth, an entire nonpredatory way of life, and—to go on—a spiritual blessedness), so the grossly exaggerated sexual language and sexual gesture in *Lysistrata* become the carrier for love between husband and wife, the inner life of desire, the sacredness of the home, the harmony and order of the city, and finally even the outreaching *agape* by which one loves one's enemies.

This play is the most realistic of Aristophanes' dramas, requiring no supernatural machinery to carry out the happy idea. Its plot is more clearly structured than those of the other comedies, its characters more lifelike. It may be true that within it at times, as Douglass Parker points out, Aristophanes' "linguistic exuberance deserts him"[23] but it is nonetheless a brilliant play exhibiting unmistakable marks of its author's genius. Its comic hero is a woman, less a *poneros* than a *spoudaios* (Aristotle's virtuous person who, in comedy, is a serious character around whom comedy occurs). Lysistrata, whose name means Disbander, or Ender, of the Army, is a noble and intelligent woman, much akin to an Athena. Yet she is realistic enough to be credible as a woman, undergoing the same deprivation she demands from others. When, at the beginning of the play, she summons all the women of the Hellenic city-states to hear her "happy idea," they find it, to be sure, difficult to believe—Greece saved by women! One of her friends asks in wonderment, "How could we do / Such a wonder? We women who sit / Adorning ourselves in our saffron silks?" "These are the very weapons of the contest" (36–46), Lysistrata assures her and goes on to reveal her demanding scheme: "We must give up all love-making" (124). The women immediately turn to go home: she calls them back and shames them into acquiescence. If they will deliberately increase their attractiveness and yet refuse to yield to their husbands unless all fighting is ended, she tells them, they can strike a blow for peace that no man has yet been able to deliver.

Lysistrata's plan initiates a general war between the sexes. The old women of the city assemble against the old men and take over the Acropolis. When the men attempt to regain it, they fight with fire in the agon that ensues, while the women fight with water, the element that frustrates fire—something the younger women must do in quite a different theater. They join the older women in the Acropolis, where they occupy the very heart of the city and hold out until finally the men surrender. Lysistrata lectures Athenian and Spartan warriors on the virtues of peace while they gaze longingly at the pretty girl, Reconciliation, and are vanquished finally by her attraction. There is a force in the ongoing of life, the drama announces, toward which even the act of generation must bow—for a time. The most demanding of desires in the domestic realm must be thrust aside if the political realm is so awry that this life-force is threatened: indeed, these very desires can be used to rectify the political order, Aristophanes reminds us in *Lysistrata*. Authority lies finally in the will, a spiritual, not an animal quality. At the end of the play a great feast unites all of Greece, with each man promised that he may take his wife home after the celebration. In their revelry, the Athenians call upon Artemis, Apollo, Dionysus, Zeus, and Hera as holy witnesses to the noble peace they have made with the aid of Aphrodite; and the Spartans call upon Athena by her Spartan cult name, goddess of the Brazen temple, and invite Helen, a Spartan, to lead the dance.

The state of peace, as Aristophanes presents it in the plays just discussed, is not at all a humanistic compromise in which people of good will learn to tolerate one another. It is not, in actuality, a literal peace at all. These are not plays about pacifism. They depict, instead, a transformed spiritual condition, requiring for its attainment an assumption, a lifting up out of oneself. Being drunk with wine, filled with good things, caught up in the delight of lovemaking—these are both metaphors and models for such a metamorphosis. Peace in Aristophanic comedy is therefore a supra-rational condition, inaccessible to wise and sober planning and available, rather, to folly, to audacity, to a loss of self in the bounty of the divine. Its reference, therefore, as I have argued earlier, is not to a primitive garden state but to a new creation, the transformed actual city. Hence, peace, as Aristophanes depicts it, is an apocalyptic image, an image from an intuited future. It is this permanent and unchanging city, as an entire guiding presence in men's minds, that is shown to be the only trustworthy model for right action in the temporal order.

In both the *Acharnians* and *Lysistrata* this city of peace and love is possible in the midst of things, by an act of imagination, courage, and bold enterprise. In *Peace*, however, with customary methods failing, what is required is an outrageous leap into the unknown. The comic hero must seek somewhere other than in ordinary life the blessedness ardently desired and even expected by the heart. Similarly, in two other comedies—*Frogs* and *Birds*—the protagonists leave the realm of history to seek elsewhere a better destiny. In this searching for the heavenly city, Aristophanes is engaging directly in the supreme act of the comic imagination, an act that governs the entire terrain of comedy. Some seventeen centuries later, Dante, a greater poet, was able, with the aid of a coherent theology, to develop a spiritual universe in consistent detail and to display the paradigmatic modes of comic existence. His *Inferno, Purgatorio*, and *Paradiso* are metaphors depicting possible states of souls after death—that is, possible spiritual conditions encountered in human life, seen, however, under the aspect of eternity. These realms are defined by characters who are in one of three basic relationships to the good. They are those who in the most profound depths of their wills have chosen self at the cost of all else; or the good without being able to achieve it; or the good at the expense of self. These three states represent, in a sense, the entire range of choices possible to individual persons and to human communities, and in their full scope, with all their variation, make up the comic universe. Most writers of comedy, knowingly or not, show their characters as recognizably falling somewhere in their scheme, though they most often depict them realistically, in their daily habitat, amidst familiar things. Dante was able to turn comedy inside out, so to speak, and to place his literal action within a fantastic cosmos, with a clear notion of how it related to mundane reality. In taking his actual steps in the other world, Dante's pilgrim would have behind him an entire culture that could accept the literal sense of his action without scandal. Aristophanes, however, in ascertaining these spiritual conditions, had to rely solely on fantasy, nonsense, and an intuitive vision. Nevertheless, his work displays the same governing design. The plays *Frogs, Peace*, and *Birds* may be regarded as the most evident examples of his infernal, purgatorial, and paradisal realms, though these states of soul may be found in his other comedies as well. These are clearly apocalyptic dramas, since in each it is necessary for the protagonist to leave the earthly city in search of another; and, further, in each of the plays the other realm, either below or above ordinary space and time, is related to human action and even follows from it as a spiritual outcome and judgment rather than being entirely separate and independent of human history.

In *Frogs* the *poneros* is Dionysus himself, desirous of a poet to save Athens and aware that all the good poets have long since departed this life. His yearning takes him on an arduous and hilarious journey to the underworld, in search, as he thinks, of Euripides, whom he longs for as one might crave pea soup, or strawberries. On his journey across the river Styx, a chorus of frogs engages him in a singing contest. These creatures, for whom the play is named, are appropriate to the region of the dead, the chthonic world of darkness, containing the past and human history. Beings of earth and water, the heaviest and most base elements in the cosmos, the amphibian frogs are fitting conductors to a realm totally lacking in inspiration or grace. In it the order of the day is every man for himself; the accustomed course of action is based on trickery, lying, deception, rivalry, envy—all the devices of the ego to preserve itself. Even Aeschylus and Euripides are quarreling, in competition with each other over the place of honor at Pluto's table, which Aeschylus had held in uncontested splendor before Euripides' arrival. Pluto has decided to settle the issue with a contest: lines from the plays of each dramatist are to be weighed, with Dionysus serving as judge, and the tragedian he chooses will be taken back with him to earth. From here on, the action serves to reverse Dionysus's opinion of Euripides: he begins to reevaluate what this latter-day playwright has done to the art of tragedy and to the city. According to every literary criterion, Aeschylus is the superior poet; but Dionysus is still undecided. "I must not lose the love of either," he declares: "One I think wise [*sophos*], the other delights me" (1411–13). He recalls that he came after a poet so that the city could keep its choral festivals and thus be saved; hence he changes his standards of judgment from purely aesthetic criteria to ethical ones: "Whichever has the best advice for the city is the one / I mean to take back" (1420–21).

There follows a rigorous examination in which a remarkable thing occurs: whereas Euripides' answers are all extreme, sophistical, and ingenious, Aeschylus answers with the moderation and even compromise that seems characteristic of a *comic*, not a tragic outlook. When asked for his advice concerning the problem of Alcibiades, Aeschylus replies that it would be best not to raise up a lion in the city but that once one has been raised up, it is best to yield to its ways. This is the answer comedy gives: life itself is worth something; in charting the course of an entire city, one should not take an extreme stand which might possibly endanger the whole populace. To endure is to hope that somehow conditions may change of their own accord and that time can remedy a predicament seemingly beyond help. In a longer questioning, Aeschylus manages to make Dionysus see that things are not simplistically black and white: the city does not hate the good, nor does it love the bad; it simply uses those whom it must. When pressed for a remedy, Aeschylus first demurs, saying that he will speak when he is there, not here. But he is finally forced to prescribe. The city and its citizens will be saved, he says,

> When they think of their land as enemy territory
> And the enemy's possessions as their own; their ships as real
>   wealth,
> Their only resource hardship and poverty.... (1460–65)

Dionysus has made his decision: "I'll choose him for whom my soul yearns" (1468). And when reproached by Euripides for not selecting the poet he had sworn to reclaim from Hades, Dionysus replies that it was only his tongue that so swore, vanquishing Euripides with a line from his own *Hippolytus*. In an atmosphere of rejoicing, Aeschylus and Dionysus begin their journey home, blessed by Pluto and the holy torches of the initiates, taking with them wisdom and poetry, as well as a more sinister gift—a rope for the necks of Kleophon, Nikomakos, and others, along with an invitation to join the troops in Hades with no delay. These concerns seem more the domain of the comic than the tragic poet. Perhaps Aristophanes is indicating that to rescue someone from the other world is to come back with a changed person, one who has learned the value of life and who is less likely to be concerned with absolute principles than with a genial acceptance of everything human except those forces that, destroying life and goodness, belong in the infernal realm. The underworld is shown to be a place of absence of life—darkness, selfishness, and ignorance. For Aeschylus to be delivered from that region is a kind of harrowing of hell.

In *Peace*, as we have seen, yearning and anguish over the fate of the declining city arise in a heroic bosom much like Dionysus's, not, however, out of desire for a vanished mortal or any hope of retrieving the city's noble past. Instead, Trygaios recognizes that divine aid must be obtained if the city of man is to endure; the heavenly image of Peace herself must be retrieved for a city that has forgotten her visage. He therefore leaves the earthly realm, storming heaven by the strength of his desire. He brings back to earth the goddess's statue, the idea of Peace, accompanied by her counterpart, a flesh and blood young woman who is the embodiment of fruitfulness. The point to be emphasized is that peace and fertility must be brought to earth from the abode of the gods; they are not a product of earth, but a gift to earth. The vision is purgatorial, with people represented less as vicious than as helpless. The chief structuralizing virtue of this middle stage of comedy is hope, just as its highest reach of attainment is the earthly paradise, an image of which is presented to us in the festivals celebrating the marriage of the old farmer with Opora.

Birds, however, is paradisal comedy, bizarre, strange, and other-worldly. It is generally considered Aristophanes' most puzzling play, though much admired for its exquisite lyricism and gorgeous spectacle. It has been interpreted as pure fantasy (that is, as having no meaning except wish-fulfillment), as a drama of escape, as a kind of Nietzschean act of impiety, a satire on a Utopian scheme, and even as the description of a plan for the military expansion of Athens.[24] To see it as apocalyptic, as a fantastic dramatization of man's assumption into a spiritual kingdom, is to resolve many of its difficulties.

Like the other two plays, *Birds* begins with a disenchantment with Athens. It is not a desire to save the city, however, that moves the two comrades to set out on their journey to the birds; rather, it is a longing to get away from the tedium and unpleasantness of a community that has lost its life-spirit. Like Dionysus and Xanthias in *Frogs*, Peisthetairos (Plausible) and Euelpides (Helpful) are a pair of good-natured rogues setting out on an ostensibly impossible and, in their case, utterly selfish mission. Guided by a jackdaw and a crow, they wander into wild and desolate country, seeking Tereus, the Hoopoe, who was once the unhappy Thracian king. When he does appear, in his terrifying bird regalia, they manage, despite their fear, to inquire of him where they might find a pleasant city—one where good will and pleasure prevail. Then, on sudden inspiration, they question the Hoopoe about what it's like to live among the birds. "Not much amiss," he tells them. "You don't need a purse here at all" (154–55).

This is of course an appealing thought for the two Athenians. Peisthetairos suddenly comes up with the "happy idea"; "join together and build a bird city" (170). The hoopoe is dubious about the birds' ability to rule a town, but Peisthetairos reminds him that the feathery creatures are accustomed to power: the whole air is their domain, the realm between the gods and men. The hoopoe calls to his wife, the nightingale; great crowds of birds come in response, and, regarding human beings as their worst enemies, fall upon the two travelers with savagery. They are turned back, however, by the hoopoe's advice: You should listen even to your enemies. The two men, quaking with terror, begin to outline their plan. Peisthetairos, taking the lead, reminds the birds of their ancient royalty.

By reference to Aesop's fables and other myths, legends, and proverbs, he engenders in them some pride in their ancestry. The primitive birds, he tells them preceded the deities, the earth, the heavens (475–85). Later, in the lovely lyric choral parabasis, the birds sing of their own origins: In the beginning, a mystical egg was formed out of darkness; out of the egg flew Love, the golden and glorious Eros. This mighty force brought about the engendering that took place between Tartarus and Chaos, the parents of the birds, before the gods had come into being. The birds, then, are more ancient than the gods and have Love alone as their author (689–722). Thus their ancient rights are based on love, not law. The birds are finally convinced that they must have their rightful kingship. Peisthetairos and Euelpides are given an herb that enables them to grow wings and so themselves become, in a sense, birds. They build a huge fortified city, Cloud-cuckooland, cutting the gods off from earth, so that the smoke of the offerings made to them is intercepted. The fame of the city spreads on earth, and anything having to do with birds or flying has become highly modish. Mortals seek to reap the benefits of citizenship in the new metropolis. A poet, a prophet, a surveyor, an inspector, a statute salesman, and other opportunists beg with persuasive words to be part of the new city, only to be rejected; they have come after the fact, without sharing in the absurd daring of the mighty deed. Prometheus, still the enemy of Zeus, arrives as a spy to tell the birds that the gods are sending an envoy in an attempt to make peace. He advises Peisthetairos not to accept their terms unless the gods restore the scepter to the birds and offer as wife Basileia (Royalty),[25] the maiden who keeps Zeus's thunderbolts in order. When the embassy arrives, made up of Poseidon, Herakles, and Triballus (one of the primitive gods), Peisthetairos states his terms: the birds will be agents for the gods and will cooperate with them, but only if he is given the maiden Royalty to be his wife. Poseidon objects but is finally overruled. Peisthetairos sends for his wedding garment, and the play ends with the dazzling brilliance of the nuptial celebrations and his general acclamation as lord of all things.

The vision of the mistress of Zeus, Basileia, coming down from Olympus to wed the *poneros* Peisthetairos is deeply shocking. It is like the dream of Bottom, in which he is "translated"—lifted up in the arms of the Fairy Queen. But it is more like the vision in Revelation of the heavens opening and the bride, the heavenly city, the New Jerusalem coming down to wed her beloved. Before one can understand the implications of the Aristophanic apocalypse, however, one needs to look closely at the character of Peisthetairos. Like Dikaiopolis (*Acharnians*), Trygaios (*Peace*), and to some extent Strepsiades (*Clouds*), Philokleon (*Wasps*), and the sausage-seller (*Knights*)—and certainly like the character Dionysus (*Frogs*)—Peisthetairos is an image of the god Dionysus. He loves revelry and pleasure; he is quick-thinking and spirited, outrageous and creative; he hates pretentiousness and pomposity. Though he is childlike and open, his advice is always wise; he is a skillful practitioner of the divine art of persuasion. Words themselves, as he tells one of the suppliants, are winged, a kind of bird. He is, in short, a comic figure of divinity. The crowning of Peisthetairos lord of the cosmos and the celebration of the *hieros gamos* that takes place represent the apotheosis of Dionysus, and along with him, the human race.[26] The gods will be closer to man because of the agency of the birds, ancient remnants of divinity, abiding with human beings as visible symbols of transcendence.

The kingdom of the birds thus represents a liminal region of the soul, wherein resides an intuition of human destiny, the apocalyptic images. The birds themselves are creatures of a universe that can only be imagined, one to which the poet has primary access, a comic terrain concerned less with good and evil than with the qualities of things in themselves and with an overriding *eros* that embraces them. To build a city with the birds is to build an imaginary city, full of lyrical forms and garish, unearthly beauty. Something innate in man is divine, the play tells us, deserving to have its royalty recognized and to be wed to the godhead. *The Birds* is a triumphal vision of things to come and a vindication of the true order that exists unacknowledged and unseen in the present. It is one of the world's few examples of true paradisal comedy.

The kind of transformation Aristophanes accomplishes in his plays is always the result of fantasy: it can be exercised as we have seen, through language, through sexual ecstasy, drinking and feasting, through daring to fly to heaven, setting out to invade the bowels of the underworld, or constructing a city in the sky. But nearly always the basic pattern is the same: the comic hero, the *poneros*, is willing to climb, drag, or hoist himself into this other world by the strength of his hope and his yearning. Whitman says of Aristophanic fantasy that it is "a structure, an elaborate and powerful one"; and he continues, "as such it evokes response from the mind's most basic function, which is to transform the chaotic spate of sense experience into an order of intelligible classes."[27] A fantasy, then, he believes, is an imaginatively constructed reality similar to the mind's creation of intelligible order. In Aristophanes, I maintain, this fantastic structure is not only a way of coping with or evading the intractability of the world but of projecting on the plane of the imagination archetypal and apocalyptic images. These figures allow hidden realities to manifest themselves and so enable the soul to attain the freedom for which it is destined and the city to renew its life-spirit.

For the task undertaken by Aristophanes is nothing short of the regeneration of the earthly city. Several of his parabases—choral odes at midpoint in the plays—indicate overt moral concern for the city; and though these addresses to the audience cannot be taken as literal statements of the poet's aims, they nonetheless serve as a kind of fictional interpretation of the dramas of which they are a part. As breaks in the narrative flow of the plot they serve as openings into the encompassing cosmos in which the plays exist—the world of the comic imagination, which possesses its own intrinsic structures. In his *Commedia* Dante verified the authenticity of his imagined world by having speakers come forward to instruct the two pilgrims and thus become part of the action. But the Aristophanic parabasis reveals the comic terrain in itself, existing independently of the comic plot, as though the characters in the *Inferno* joined hands and came forward to comment on life in general, totally apart from the goings-on around them. Later on, Rabelais, Cervantes, Sterne, Gogol, and others would use this device of apparent address to the reader and for the same effect: not so much to reveal the authors' thoughts on a subject as to open a larger universe in which their comic vision could operate.

In several of the early plays the choral parabases not only praise Aristophanes himself and attack his enemies but go on to a defense of the comic poet in general. The writer of comedies is declared one of the best benefactors of the city, blessing it with his "righteous and true" art that offers protection from flattery and lies (*Acharnians*). In *Wasps*, the parabasis adds a further dimension to the poet's benefits: it is not mere men that he attacks, but a fierce monster. The beast he challenges is "jagged-fanged, red-eyed, dirty, malodorous as a seal, his head covered with hundreds of slavering flattering tongues" (1030–36). The chorus speaks in the same way of the fearsome monster in *Peace* and makes clear that Aristophanes' comic art is a war against this beast, one in which he engages for the good of the people, even if they are unappreciative. These passages establish that it is not individuals against whom the comic writer does battle, but spiritual powers, like Dante's Geryon; Spenser's dragon of Error; Ivan Karamazov's tawdry devil; Faulkner's Flem Snopes—all images of the beast of the Apocalypse, the ultimate source and target of dark comedy. This is the falsehood that can enslave a people, debasing their taste and judgment, devouring their purpose and strength, flattering them into complacency. This monster symbolizes all that is wrong with the earthly city—the powers of darkness which must be overcome if the human enterprise is to prevail. Only in comedy can the beast be seen for what he is, his hollowness revealed by the cathartic principle of laughter.

Hence the comic writer's work is to reveal this essential "banality of evil," to borrow Hannah Arendt's phrase.[28] And the way he performs this task is not only by ridiculing falsehood and vice, but by positing another world over and beyond this one, where the right order of things prevails and harmony and love are dominant. This invisible reality—the comic universe—may exist only as memory or hope for some writers of comedy; or it may lie in the standard domestic happy ending of romance. For the apocalyptic writer, such as Aristophanes, Dante, Dostoevsky, and Flannery O'Connor, this realm is gained by a fantasy, by scaling heaven, so to say, and then, through superimposing one image on another, seeing the ordinary world with a double vision. This duality allows the writer to be possessed by a spirit of nonsense, absurdity, and contradiction, so that he may undertake his supremely difficult task of raising earthly existence to a new plane of being.

Athens failed to heed Aristophanes' warnings, continued its moral decline and its war with Sparta, moving inexorably to its defeat in a parallel course with Aristophanes' comic writings. Did the poet fail? Was the city not aided by his writings? How do we go about answering these questions? We must first admit, I think, that the poet is never concerned primarily with restoring a particular political regime (one thinks of Shakespeare's England, Dostoevsky's Russia, Faulkner's South, Joyce's Dublin) but with giving form to—realizing—the city hidden within the earthly community where the right order of being resides. The city Aristophanes "saved" in these and his other plays makes up a permanent part of the *mundus imaginalis* available to all citizens everywhere through the comic imagination—an image of that one city we keep dreaming of building.

NOTES

1. M. C. Bradbrook, *The Growth and Structure of Elizabethan Comedy* (Baltimore, 1963), 21.
2. Walter F. Otto, *Dionysus: Myth and Cult* (Bloomington, Ind., 1965), 79.
3. C. Kerenyi, *Dionysus: Archetypal Image of Indestructible Life* (Princeton, N.J.), 139.
4. Ibid., 179.
5. Otto, 202.
6. Kerenyi, p. 179. Kerenyi makes a distinction between *bios* and *zoe*, the two Greek words for life, the first meaning "characterized life" (xxxiii) and the second, "non-death" (xxxiv). The difference, he feels, is clear: *zoe* presupposes "the experience of *infinite life*" (xxxvi).
7. James Hillman, *The Myth of Analysis* (Evanston, Ill., 1972), 269.
8. Moses Hadas, Introduction, *The Complete Plays of Aristophanes*, ed. Moses Hadas (New York, Toronto, London, 1962), 11.
9. *Anthologia Graeca* IX 1863–4 (Paton, ed., III, 96), as cited in Kerenyi, 333.
10. Alexis Solomos, *The Living Aristophanes* (Ann Arbor, Mich., 1974), 43.

11. Mikhail Bakhtin develops the idea of carnival as a popular festive medieval form in *Rabelais and His World*, trans. Helene Iswolsky (Cambridge, Mass., 1968) and *Problems of Dostoevsky's Poetics*, trans. R. W. Rotsel (Ann Arbor, Mich., 1973).

12. Mikhail Bakhtin, *The Dialogic Imagination*, trans. Michael Holquist (Austin, Tex., 1981), 219.

13. C. G. Jung, *Modern Man in Search of a Soul* (New York, 1959), 156–57.

14. For a discussion of the apocalyptic tradition, see Christopher Rowland, *The Open Heaven: A Study of Apocalyptic in Judaism and Early Christianity* (London, 1982); Klaus Koch, *The Rediscovery of Apocalyptic*, trans. Margaret Kohl (Naperville, Ill., 1972); H. H. Rowley, *The Relevance of Apocalyptic*, rev. ed. (New York, 1963); Rudolf Otto, *The Kingdom of God and the Son of Man*, trans. Floyd V. Filson and Bertram Lee-Wolf (London, 1943). The apocalyptic mode, according to Otto and others, was not "purely" Jewish, but eclectic, partaking of Oriental and Hellenistic elements as well. I mean to be treating it as a mode of vision universally available to the poetic imagination, totally apart from its special revelation in the Judaeo-Christian tradition.

15. Northrop Frye, *Anatomy of Criticism* (Princeton, N.J., 1957), 141.

16. It is no longer agreed among scholars, as it was until fairly recently, that a secret cult of "Orphism" existed among the Greeks, that it was from fragments of an Orphic apocalypse that Plato took his details of the Other World, or that Aristophanes' *Birds* is a parody of an Orphic "Theogony." See E. E. Dodds, *The Greeks and the Irrational* (Berkeley, Los Angeles, 1951), 147–56.

17. Rudolf Otto, *The Kingdom of God and the Son of Man*, 57.

18. Kerenyi, xxviii–xxix.

19. This is Jeffrey Henderson's phrase: *The Maculate Muse: Obscene Language in Attic Comedy* (New Haven, 1975).

20. Cedric Whitman, *Aristophanes and the Comic Hero* (Cambridge, Mass., 1964), 269.

21. See Whitman's brilliant analysis of this quality in the Aristophanic comic hero, 29–58.

22. Aristophanes, *Acharnians*, 195–98. The line numbers cited for all the plays refer to the Greek text of Aristophanes edited by F. W. Hall and W. M. Geldart (Clarendon: Oxford Press, 1906–07). I have consulted and compared the following translations: *Acharnians*, Patric Dickinson, vol. 1 (Oxford Univ. Press, 1970); Douglass Parker, The Mentor Greek Comedy Series (New American Library, 1961); B. B. Rogers, vol. 1 (William Heinemann Ltd., G. P. Putnam's Sons, 1927); Alan H. Sommerstein, *The Comedies of Aristophanes*, vol. 1 (Aris and Philips, Ltd.: Biddles Ltd., 1980); *Birds*, William Arrowsmith (Ann Arbor: Univ. of Michigan Press, 1961); Dickinson, vol. 2; Dudley Fitts, *Four Comedies* (Harcourt Brace, 1954); Gilbert Murray (London, 1908); Rogers, vol. 2; R. H. Webb, in Hades; *Lysistrata*, Dickinson, vol. 2; Fitts; Douglass Parker, in *Four Comedies by Aristophanes*, ed. William Arrowsmith (Univ. of Michigan Press, 1961); Rogers; R. H. Webb (Univ. of Virginia Press, 1963); *Peace*, Dickinson, vol. 1; Rogers, vol. 2.
23. Douglass Parker, Introduction, *Lysistrata*, in *Four Comedies by Aristophanes*.
24. For a comprehensive survey of critical opinion concerning Birds, see Arrowsmith's introduction to his brilliant translation.
25. K. J. Dover, in *Aristophanic Comedy* (Berkeley and Los Angeles, 1972), argues convincingly from the scansion of the lines that the Greek word is *basileia*, queen, a title of goddesses, not *basileia*, monarchy (p. 31).
26. Gilbert Murray, in the introduction to his translation (London, 1966), refutes the apparent "impiety" of the ending of the play by referring to the familiarity of the Greeks with the vegetation cults, in which an old king is overthrown by a new. He cites a passage from the *Orphica*: "His father seats him on the royal throne, puts the sceptre in his hand, and makes him king of the Cosmic gods" (p. 7).
27. Whitman, p. 260.
28. Hannah Arendt, *Eichmann in Jerusalem: A Report on the Banality of Evil* (New York, 1963).

THE PLAYS OF SAMUEL BECKETT AND THE THEATRE OF THE ABSURD

"The Theatre of the Absurd"
by Martin Esslin, in *Theatre in the Twentieth Century* (1956)

INTRODUCTION

Informed both by knowledge of absurdist philosophy and by his friendship with Samuel Beckett, Martin Esslin provides a critical definition of absurd drama. For Esslin, the Theatre of the Absurd is a darkly comic form that places great demands upon audiences, asking them to juxtapose incongruencies and to make sense out of often horrific laughter. Thus, as a form of dark humor, it "may be riotously funny, wildly exaggerated and oversimplified, vulgar and garish, but it will always confront the spectator with a genuine intellectual problem, a philosophical paradox, which he will have to try to solve even if he knows that it is most probably insoluble."

The plays of Samuel Beckett, Arthur Adamov, and Eugene Ionesco have been performed with astonishing success in France, Germany, Scandinavia, and the English-speaking countries. This reception

Esslin, Martin. "The Theatre of the Absurd." *Theatre in the Twentieth Century.* Ed. Robert W. Corrigan. New York: Grove Press, 1956. 229–244.

is all the more puzzling when one considers that the audiences concerned were amused by and applauded these plays fully aware that they could not understand what they meant or what their authors were driving at.

At first sight these plays do, indeed, confront their public with a bewildering experience, a veritable barrage of wildly irrational, often nonsensical goings-on that seem to go counter to all accepted standards of stage convention. In these plays, some of which are labeled "anti-plays," neither the time nor the place of the action are ever clearly stated. (At the beginning of Ionesco's *The Bald Soprano* the clock strikes seventeen.) The characters hardly have any individuality and often even lack a name; moreover, halfway through the action they tend to change their nature completely. Pozzo and Lucky in Beckett's *Waiting for Godot*, for example, appear as master and slave at one moment only to return after a while with their respective positions mysteriously reversed. The laws of probability as well as those of physics are suspended when we meet young ladies with two or even three noses (Ionesco's *Jack or the Submission*), or a corpse that has been hidden in the next room that suddenly begins to grow to monstrous size until a giant foot crashes through the door onto the stage (Ionesco's *Amédée*). As a result, it is often unclear whether the action is meant to represent a dream world of nightmares or real happenings. Within the same scene the action may switch from the nightmarish poetry of high emotions to pure knock-about farce or cabaret, and above all, the dialogue tends to get out of hand so that at times the words seem to go counter to the actions of the characters on the stage, to degenerate into lists of words and phrases from a dictionary or traveler's conversation book, or to get bogged down in endless repetitions like a phonograph record stuck in one groove. Only in this kind of demented world can strangers meet and discover, after a long polite conversation and close cross-questioning, that, to their immense surprise, they must be man and wife as they are living on the same street, in the same house, apartment, room, and bed (Ionesco's *The Bald Soprano*). Only here can the whole life of a group of characters revolve around the passionate discussion of the aesthetics and economics of pinball machines (Adamov's *Ping-Pong*). Above all, everything that happens seems to be beyond rational motivation, happening at random or through the demented caprice of an unaccountable idiot fate. Yet, these wildly extravagant tragic farces and farcical tragedies, although they have suffered their share of protests and scandals, do arouse interest and are received with laughter and thoughtful respect. What is the explanation for this curious phenomenon?

The most obvious, but perhaps too facile answer that suggests itself is that these plays are prime examples of "pure theatre." They are living proof that the magic of the stage can persist even outside, and divorced from, any framework of conceptual rationality. They prove that exits and entrances, light and shadow, contrasts in costume, voice, gait and behavior, pratfalls and embraces, all the manifold mechanical interactions of human puppets in groupings that suggest tension, conflict, or the relaxation of tensions, can arouse laughter or gloom and conjure up an atmosphere of poetry even if devoid of logical motivation and unrelated to recognizable human characters, emotions, and objectives.

But this is only a partial explanation. While the element of "pure theatre" and abstract stagecraft is certainly at work in the plays concerned, they also have a much more substantial content and meaning. Not only *do* all these plays make sense, though perhaps not obvious or conventional sense, they also give expression to some of the basic issues and problems of our age, in a uniquely efficient and meaningful manner, so that they meet some of the deepest needs and unexpressed yearnings of their audience.

The three dramatists that have been grouped together here would probably most energetically deny that they form anything like a school or movement. Each of them, in fact, has his own roots and sources, his own very personal approach to both form and subject matter. Yet they also clearly have a good deal in common. This common denominator that characterizes their works might well be described as the element of *the absurd.* "Est absurde ce qui n'a pas de but . . ." ("Absurd is that which has no purpose, or goal, or objective"), the definition given by Ionesco in a note on Kafka,[1] certainly applies to the plays of Beckett and Ionesco as well as those of Arthur Adamov up to his latest play, *Paolo Paoli,* when he returned to a more traditional form of social drama.

Each of these writers, however, has his own special type of absurdity: in Beckett it is melancholic, colored by a feeling of futility born from the disillusionment of old age and chronic hopelessness; Adamov's is more active, aggressive, earthy, and tinged with social and political overtones; while Ionesco's absurdity has its own fantastic knock-about flavor of tragical clowning. But they all share the same deep sense of human isolation and of the irremediable character of the human condition.

As Arthur Adamov put it in describing how he came to write his first play *La Parodie* (1947):

> I began to discover stage scenes in the most commonplace everyday events. [One day I saw] a blind man begging; two girls went by without seeing him, singing: "I closed my eyes; it was marvelous!" This gave me the idea of showing on stage, as crudely and as visibly as possible, the loneliness of man, the absence of communication among human beings.[2]

Looking back at his earliest effort (which he now regards as unsuccessful) Adamov defines his basic idea in it, and a number of subsequent plays, as the idea "that the destinies of all human beings are of equal futility, that the refusal to live (of the character called N.) and the joyful acceptance of life (by the employee) both lead, by the same path, to inevitable failure, total destruction."[3] It is the same futility and pointlessness of human effort, the same impossibility of human communication which Ionesco expresses in ever new and ingenious variations. The two old people making conversation with the empty air and living in the expectation of an orator who is to pronounce profound truths about life, but turns out to be deaf and dumb (*The Chairs*), are as sardonically cruel a symbol of this fundamentally tragic view of human existence as Jack (*Jack or the Submission*), who stubbornly resists the concerted urgings of his entire family to subscribe to the most sacred principle of his clan—which, when his resistance finally yields to their entreaties, turns out to be the profound truth: "I love potatoes with bacon" ("J'adore les pommes de terre au lard").

The Theatre of the Absurd shows the world as an incomprehensible place. The spectators see the happenings on the stage entirely from the outside, without ever understanding the full meaning of these strange patterns of events, as newly arrived visitors might watch life in a country of which they have not yet mastered the language.[4] The confrontation of the audience with characters and happenings which they are not quite able to comprehend makes it impossible for them to share the aspirations and emotions depicted in the play. Brecht's famous "Verfremdungseffekt" (alienation effect), the inhibition of any identification between spectator and actor, which Brecht could never successfully achieve in his own highly rational theatre, really comes into its own in the Theatre of the Absurd. It is impossible to identify oneself with characters one does not understand or whose motives remain a closed book, and so the distance between the public and the happenings on the stage can be maintained. Emotional identification with the characters is replaced by a puzzled, critical attention. For while the happenings on the stage are absurd, they yet remain recognizable as somehow related to real life with its absurdity, so that eventually the spectators are brought face to face with the irrational side of their existence. Thus, the absurd and fantastic goings-on of the Theatre of the Absurd will, in the end, be found to reveal the irrationality of the human condition and the illusion of what we thought was its apparent logical structure.

If the dialogue in these plays consists of meaningless clichés and the mechanical, circular repetition of stereotyped phrases—how many meaningless clichés and stereotyped phrases do we use in our day-to-day conversation? If the characters change their personality halfway through the action, how consistent and truly integrated are the people we meet in our real life? And if people in these plays appear as mere marionettes, helpless puppets without any will of their own, passively at the mercy of blind fate and meaningless circumstance, do we, in fact, in our over-organized world, still possess any genuine initiative or power to decide our own destiny? The spectators of the Theatre of the Absurd are thus confronted with a grotesquely heightened picture of their own world: a world without faith; meaning, and genuine freedom of will. In this sense, the Theatre of the Absurd is the true theatre of our time.

The theatre of most previous epochs reflected an accepted moral order, a world whose aims and objectives were clearly present to the minds of all its public, whether it was the audience of the medieval mystery plays with their solidly accepted faith in the Christian world order or the audience of the drama of Ibsen, Shaw, or Hauptmann with their unquestioned belief in evolution and progress. To such audiences, right and wrong were never in doubt, nor did they question the then accepted goals of human endeavor. Our own time, at least in the Western world, wholly lacks such a generally accepted and completely integrated world picture. The decline of religious faith, the destruction of the belief in automatic social and biological progress, the discovery of vast areas of irrational and unconscious forces within the human psyche, the loss of a sense of control over rational human development in an age of totalitarianism and weapons of mass destruction, have all contributed to the erosion of the basis for a dramatic convention in which the action proceeds within a fixed and self-evident frame-work of generally accepted values. Faced with the vacuum left by the destruction of a universally accepted and unified set of beliefs, most serious playwrights have felt the need to fit their work into the frame of values and objectives expressed in one of the contemporary ideolo-gies: Marxism, psychoanalysis, aestheticism, or nature worship. But these, in the eyes of a writer like Adamov, are nothing but superficial rationalizations which try to hide the depth of man's predicament, his loneliness and his anxiety. Or, as Ionesco puts it:

> As far as I am concerned, I believe sincerely in the poverty of the poor, I deplore it; it is real; it can become a subject for the theatre; I also believe in the anxieties and serious troubles the rich may suffer from; but it is neither in the misery of the former nor in the melancholia of the latter, that I, for one, find my dramatic subject matter. Theatre is for me the outward projection onto the stage of an inner world; it is in my dreams, in my anxieties, in my obscure desires, in my internal contradictions that I, for one, reserve for myself the right of finding my dramatic subject matter. As I am not alone in the world, as each of us, in the depth of his being, is at the same time part and parcel of all others, my dreams, my desires, my anxieties, my obsessions do not belong to me alone. They form part of an ancestral heritage, a very ancient storehouse which is a portion of the common property of all mankind. It is this, which, transcending their outward diversity, reunites all human beings and constitutes our profound common patrimony, the universal language. . . . [5]

In other words, the commonly acceptable framework of beliefs and values of former epochs which has now been shattered is to be replaced by the community of dreams and desires of a collective unconscious. And, to quote Ionesco again:

> . . . the new dramatist is one . . . who tries to link up with what is most ancient: new language and subject matter in a

dramatic structure which aims at being clearer, more stripped of non-essentials and more purely theatrical; the rejection of traditionalism to rediscover tradition; a synthesis of knowledge and invention, of the real and imaginary, of the particular and the universal, or as they say now, of the individual and the collective ... By expressing my deepest obsessions, I express my deepest humanity. I become one with all others, spontaneously, over and above all the barriers of caste and different psychologies. I express my solitude and become one with all other solitudes.... [6]

What is the tradition with which the Theatre of the Absurd—at first sight the most revolutionary and radically new movement—is trying to link itself? It is in fact a very ancient and a very rich tradition, nourished from many and varied sources: the verbal exuberance and extravagant inventions of Rabelais, the age-old clowning of the Roman mimes and the Italian *Commedia dell'Arte*, the knock-about humor of circus clowns like Grock; the wild, archetypal symbolism of English nonsense verse, the baroque horror of Jacobean dramatists like Webster or Tourneur, the harsh, incisive and often brutal tones of the German drama of Grabbe, Büchner, Kleist, and Wedekind with its delirious language and grotesque inventiveness; and the Nordic paranoia of the dreams and persecution fantasies of Strindberg.

All these streams, however, first came together and crystallized in the more direct ancestors of the present Theatre of the Absurd. Of these, undoubtedly the first and foremost is Alfred Jarry (1873–1907), the creator of *Ubu Roi*, the first play which clearly belongs in the category of the Theatre of the Absurd. *Ubu Roi*, first performed in Paris on December 10, 1896, is a Rabelaisian nonsense drama about the fantastic adventures of a fat, cowardly, and brutal figure, *le père* Ubu, who makes himself King of Poland, fights a series of Falstaffian battles, and is finally routed. As if to challenge all accepted codes of propriety and thus to open a new era of irreverence, the play opens with the defiant expletive, "*Merde!*" which immediately provoked a scandal. This, of course, was what Jarry had intended. *Ubu*, in its rollicking Rabelaisian parody of a Shakespearean history play, was meant to confront the Parisian bourgeois with a monstrous portrait of his own greed, selfishness, and philistinism: "As the curtain went up I wanted to confront the public with a theatre in which, as in the magic mirror . . . of the fairy tales . . . the vicious man sees his reflection with bulls' horns and the body of a dragon, the projections of his vicious-ness. . . ."[7] But Ubu is more than a mere monstrous exaggeration of the selfishness and crude sensuality of the French bourgeois. He is at the same time the personification of the grossness of human nature, an enormous belly walking on two legs. That is why Jarry put him on the stage as a monstrous pot-bellied figure in a highly stylized costume and mask—a mythical, archetypal externalization of human instincts of the lowest kind. Thus, Ubu, the false king of Poland, pretended doctor of the pseudoscience of Pataphysics, clearly anticipates one of the main characteristics of the Theatre of the Absurd, its tendency to externalize and project outwards what is happening in the deeper recesses of the mind. Examples of this tendency are: the disembodied voices of "monitors" shouting commands at the hero of Adamov's *La Grande et la Petite Manoeuvre* which concretizes his neurotic compulsions; the mutilated trunks of the parents in Beckett's *Endgame* emerging from ashcans—the ashcans of the main character's subconscious to which he has banished his past and his conscience; or the proliferations of fungi that invade the married couple's apartment in Ionesco's *Amédée* and express the rottenness and decay of their relationship. All these psychological factors are not only projected outwards, they are also, as in Jarry's *Ubu Roi*, grotesquely magnified and exaggerated. This scornful rejection of all subtleties is a reaction against the supposed *finesse* of the psychology of the naturalistic theatre in which everything was to be inferred between the lines. The Theatre of the Absurd, from Jarry onwards, stands for explicitness as against implicit psychology, and in this resembles the highly explicit theatre of the Expressionists or the political theatre of Piscator or Brecht.

To be larger and more real than life was also the aim of Guillaume Apollinaire (1880–1918), the great poet who was one of the seminal forces in the rise of Cubism and who had close personal artistic links with Jarry. If Apollinaire labeled his play *Les Mamelles de Tirésias* a "*drame surrealiste*," he did not intend that term, of which he was one of the earliest users, in the sense in which it later became famous. He wanted it to describe a play in which everything was *larger than life*, for he believed in an art which was to be "modern, simple, rapid, with the shortcuts and enlargements that are needed to shock the spectator."[8] In the prologue to *Les Mamelles de Tirésias*, a grotesque pamphlet purportedly advocating an immense rise in the French birthrate, Apollinaire makes the Director of the Company of Actors who perform the play, define his ideas:

> For the theatre should not be an imitation of reality
> It is right that the dramatist should use
> All the illusions at his disposal ...
> It is right that he should let crowds speak, or inanimate
>   objects
> If he so pleases
> And that he no longer has to reckon
> With time and space
> His universe is the play
> Within which he is God the Creator
> Who disposes at will
> Of sounds gestures movements masses colors
> Not merely in order
> To photograph what is called a slice of life
> But to bring forth life itself and all its truth ...

Accordingly, in *Les Mamelles de Tirésias* the whole population of Zanzibar, where the scene is laid, is represented by a single actor; and the heroine, Thérèse, changes herself into a man by letting her breasts float upwards like a pair of toy balloons. Although *Les Mamelles de Tirésias* was not a surrealist work in the strictest sense of the term, it clearly foreshadowed the ideas of the movement led by André Breton. Surrealism in that narrower, technical sense found little expression in the theatre. But Antonin Artaud (1896–1948), another major influence in the development of the Theatre of the Absurd, did at one time belong to the Surrealist group, although his main activity in the theatre took place after he had broken with Breton. Artaud was one of the most unhappy men of genius of his age, an artist consumed by the most intense passions; poet, actor, director, designer, immensely fertile and original in his inventions and ideas, yet always living on the borders of sanity and never able to realize his ambitions, plans, and projects.

Artaud, who had been an actor in Charles Dullin's company at the Atelier, began his venture into the realm of experimental theatre in a series of productions characteristically sailing under the label *Théâtre Alfred Jarry* (1927–29). But his theories of a new and revolutionary theatre only crystallized after he had been deeply stirred by a performance of Balinese dancers at the Colonial Exhibition of 1931. He formulated his ideas in a series of impassioned manifestos later collected in the volume *The Theatre and Its Double* (1938), which continues to exercise an important influence on the contemporary French theatre. Artaud named the theatre of his dreams *Théâtre de la Cruauté*, a theatre of cruelty, which, he said, "means a theatre diffi-cult and cruel above all for myself." "Everything that is really active is cruelty. It is around this idea of action carried to the extreme that the theatre must renew itself." Here too the idea of action larger and more real than life is the dominant theme. "Every performance will contain a physical and objective element that will be felt by all. Cries, Wails, Apparitions, Surprises, *Coups de Théâtre* of all kinds, the magical beauty of costumes inspired by the model of certain rituals. . . . " The language of the drama must also undergo a change: "It is not a matter of suppressing articulate speech but of giving to the words something like the importance they have in dreams." In Artaud's new theatre "not only the obverse side of man will appear but also the reverse side of the coin: the reality of imagination and of dreams will here be seen on an equal footing with everyday life."

Artaud's only attempt at putting these theories to the test on the stage took place on May 6, 1935 at the Folies-Wagram. Artaud had made his own adaptation ("after Shelley and Stendhal") of the story of the Cenci, that sombre Renaissance story of incest and patricide. It was in many ways a beautiful and memorable performance, but full of imperfections and a financial disaster which marked the beginning of Artaud's eventual descent into despair, insanity, and abject poverty. Jean-Louis Barrault had some small part in this venture and Roger Blin, the actor and director who later played an important part in bringing Adamov, Beckett, and Ionesco to the stage, appeared in the small role of one of the hired assassins.

Jean-Louis Barrault, one of the most creative figures in the theatre of our time, was in turn, responsible for another venture which played an important part in the development of the Theatre of the Absurd. He staged André Gide's adaptation of Franz Kafka's novel, *The Trial*, in 1947 and played the part of the hero K. himself. Undoubtedly this performance which brought the dreamworld of Kafka to a trium-phant unfolding on the stage and demonstrated the effectiveness of this particular brand of fantasy in practical theatrical terms exercised a profound influence on the practitioners of the new movement. For here, too, they saw the externalization of mental processes, the acting out of nightmarish dreams by schematized figures in a world of torment and absurdity.

The dream element in the Theatre of the Absurd can also be traced, in the case of Adamov, to Strindberg, acknowledged by him as his inspiration at the time when he began to think of writing for the theatre. This is the Strindberg of *The Ghost Sonata*, *The Dream Play* and of *To Damascus*. (Adamov is the author of an excellent brief monograph on Strindberg.)

But if Jarry, Artaud, Kafka, and Strindberg can be regarded as the decisive influences in the development of the Theatre of the Absurd, there is another giant of European literature that must not be omitted from the list—James Joyce, for whom Beckett at one time is supposed to have acted as helper and secretary. Not only is the Nighttown episode of *Ulysses* one of the earliest examples of the Theatre of the Absurd—with its exuberant mingling of the real and the nightmarish, its wild fantasies and externalizations of subconscious yearnings and fears—but Joyce's experimentation with language, his attempt to smash the limitations of conventional vocabulary and syntax has probably exercised an even more powerful impact on all the writers concerned.

It is in its attitude to language that the Theatre of the Absurd is most revolutionary. It deliberately attempts to renew the language of drama and to expose the barrenness of conventional stage dialogue. Ionesco once described how he came to write his first play. (Cf. his "The Tragedy of Language," *Tulane Drama Review*, Spring, 1960.) He had decided to take English lessons and began to study at the Berlitz school. When he read and repeated the sentences in his phrase book, those petrified corpses of once living speech, he was suddenly overcome by their tragic quality. From them he composed his first play, *The Bald Soprano*. The absurdity of its dialogue and its fantastic quality springs directly from its basic ordinariness. It exposes the emptiness of stereotyped language; "what is sometimes labeled the absurd," Ionesco says, "is only the denunciation of the ridiculous nature of a language which is empty of substance, made up of clichés and slogans...."[9] Such a language has atrophied; it has ceased to be the expression of anything alive or vital and has been degraded into a mere conventional token of human intercourse, a mask for genuine meaning and emotion. That is why so often in the Theatre of the Absurd the dialogue becomes divorced from the real happenings in the play and is even put into direct contradiction with the action. The Professor and the Pupil in Ionesco's *The Lesson* "seem" to be going through a repetition of conventional school book phrases, but behind this smoke screen of language the *real* action of the play pursues an entirely different course with the Professor, vampire-like, draining the vitality from the young girl up to the final moment when he plunges his knife into her body. In Beckett's *Waiting for Godot* Lucky's much vaunted philosophical wisdom is revealed to be a flood of completely meaningless gibberish that vaguely resembles the language of philosophical argument. And in Adamov's remarkable play, *Ping-Pong*, a good deal of the dramatic power lies in the contrapuntal contrast between the triviality of the theme—the improvement of pinball machines—and the almost religious fervor with which it is discussed. Here, in order to bring out the full meaning of the play, the actors have to act *against* the dialogue rather than with it, the fervor of the delivery must stand in a dialectical contrast to the pointlessness of the meaning of the lines. In the same way, the author implies that most of the fervent and passionate discussion of real life (of political controversy, to give but one example) also turns around empty and meaningless clichés. Or, as Ionesco says in an essay on Antonin Artaud:

> As our knowledge becomes increasingly divorced from real life, our culture no longer contains ourselves (or only contains an insignificant part of ourselves) and forms a "social" context in which we are not integrated. The problem thus becomes that of again reconciling our culture with our life by making our culture a living culture once more. But to achieve this end we shall first have to kill the "respect for that which is written" ... it becomes necessary to break up our language so that it may become possible to put it together again and to re-establish contact with the absolute, or as I should prefer to call it, with multiple reality.[10]

This quest for the multiple reality of the world which is real *because* it exists on many planes simultaneously and is more than a mere unidirectional abstraction is not only in itself a search for a re-established *poetical* reality (poetry in its essence expressing reality in its ambiguity and multidimensional depth); it is also in close accord with important movements of our age in what appear to be entirely different fields: psychology and philosophy. The dissolution, devaluation, and relativization of language is, after all, also the theme of much of present-day depth psychology, which has shown what in former times was regarded as a rational expression of logically arrived at conclusions to be the mere rationalization of subconscious emotional impulses. Not everything we say means what we intend it to mean. And likewise, in present-day Logical Positivism a large proportion of all statements is regarded as devoid of conceptual meaning and merely emotive. A philosopher like Ludwig Wittgenstein, in his later phases, even tried to break through what he regarded as the opacity, the misleading nature of language and grammar; for if all our thinking is in terms of language, and language obeys what after all are the arbitrary conventions of grammar, we must strive to penetrate to the real content of thought that is masked by grammatical rules and conventions. Here, too, then is a matter of getting behind the surface of linguistic clichés and of finding reality through the break-up of language.

In the Theatre of the Absurd, therefore, the real content of the play lies in the action. Language may be discarded altogether, as in Beckett's *Act Without Words* or in Ionesco's *The New Tenant*, in which the whole sense of the play is contained in the incessant arrival of more and more furniture so that the occupant of the room is, in the end, literally drowned in it. Here the movement of objects alone carries the dramatic action, the language has become purely incidental, less important than the contribution of the property department. In this, the Theatre of the Absurd also reveals its anti-literary character, its endeavor to link up with the pre-literary strata of stage history: the circus, the performances of itinerant jugglers and mountebanks, the music hall, fairground barkers, acrobats, and also the robust world of the silent film. Ionesco, in particular, clearly owes a great deal to Chaplin, Buster Keaton, the Keystone Cops, Laurel and Hardy, and the Marx Brothers. And it is surely significant that so much of successful popular entertainment in our age shows affinities with the subject matter and preoccupation of the avant-garde Theatre of the Absurd. A sophisticated, but nevertheless highly popular, film comedian like Jacques Tati uses dialogue merely as a barely comprehensible babble of noises, and also dwells on the loneliness of man in our age, the horror of overmechanization and overorganization gone mad.

Danny Kaye excels in streams of gibberish closely akin to Lucky's oration in *Waiting for Godot*. The brilliant and greatly liked team of British radio (and occasionally television) comedians, the Goons, have a sense of the absurd that resembles Kafka's or Ionesco's and a team of grotesque singers like "Les Frères Jacques" seems more closely in line with the Theatre of the Absurd than with the conventional cabaret.

Yet the defiant rejection of language as the main vehicle of the dramatic action, the onslaught on conventional logic and unilinear conceptual thinking in the Theatre of the Absurd is by no means equivalent to a total rejection of all meaning. On the contrary, it constitutes an earnest endeavor to penetrate to deeper layers of meaning and to give a truer, because more complex, picture of reality in avoiding the simplification which results from leaving out all the undertones, overtones, and inherent absurdities and contradictions of any human situation. In the conventional drama every word means what it says, the situations are clear-cut, and at the end all conflicts are tidily resolved. But reality, as Ionesco points out in the passage we have quoted, is never like that; it is multiple, complex, many-dimensional and exists on a number of different levels at one and the same time. Language is far too straightforward an instrument to express all this by itself. Reality can only be conveyed by being *acted out* in all its complexity. Hence, it is the theatre, which is multidimensional and more than merely language or literature, which is the only instrument to express the bewildering complexity of the human condition. The human condition being what it is, with man small, helpless, insecure, and unable ever to fathom the world in all its hopelessness, death, and absurdity, the theatre has to confront him with the bitter truth that most human endeavor is irrational and senseless, that communication between human beings is well-nigh impossible, and that the world will forever remain an impenetrable mystery. At the same time, the recognition of all these bitter truths will have a liberating effect: if we realize the basic absurdity of most of our objectives we are freed from being obsessed with them and this release expresses itself in laughter.

Moreover, while the world is being shown as complex, harsh, and absurd and as difficult to interpret as reality itself, the audience is yet spurred on to attempt their own interpretation, to wonder what it is all about. In that sense they are being invited to school their critical faculties, to train themselves in adjusting to reality. As the world is being represented as highly complex and devoid of a clear-cut purpose or design, there will always be an infinite number of possible interpretations. As Apollinaire points out in his preface to *Les Mamelles de Tirésias*: "None of the symbols in my play is very clear, but one is at liberty to see in it all the symbols one desires and to find in it a thousand senses—as in the Sybilline oracles." Thus, it may be that the pinball machines in Adamov's *Ping-Pong* and the ideology which is developed around them stand for the futility of political or religious ideologies that are pursued with equal fervor and equal futility in the final result. Others have interpreted the play as a parable on the greed and sordidness of the profit motive. Others again may give it quite different meanings. The mysterious transformation of human beings into rhinos in Ionesco's latest play, *Rhinoceros*, was felt by the audience of its world premiere at Duesseldorf (November 6, 1959) to depict the transformation of human beings into Nazis. It is known that Ionesco himself intended the play to express his feelings at the time when more and more of his friends in Rumania joined the Fascist Iron Guard and, in effect, left the ranks of thin-skinned humans to turn themselves into moral pachyderms. But to spectators less intimately aware of the moral climate of such a situation than the German audience, other interpretations might impose themselves: if the hero, Bérenger, is at the end left alone as the only human being in his native town, now entirely inhabited by rhinos, they might regard this as a poetic symbol of the gradual isolation of man growing old and imprisoned in the strait jacket of his own habits and memories. Does Godot, so fervently and vainly awaited by Vladimir and Estragon, stand for God? Or does he merely represent the ever-elusive tomorrow, man's hope that one day something will happen that will render his existence meaningful? The force and poetic power of the play lie precisely in the impossibility of ever reaching a conclusive answer to this question.

Here we touch the essential point of difference between the conventional theatre and the Theatre of the Absurd. The former, based as it is on a known framework of accepted values and a rational view of life, always starts out by indicating a fixed objective towards which the action will be moving or by posing a definite problem to which it will supply an answer. Will Hamlet revenge the murder of his father? Will Iago succeed in destroying Othello? Will Nora leave her husband? In the conventional theatre the action always proceeds toward a definable end. The spectators do not know whether that end will be reached and how it will be reached. Hence, they are in suspense, eager to find out *what* will happen. In the Theatre of the Absurd, on the other hand, the action does not proceed in the manner of a logical syllogism. It does not go from A to B but travels from an unknown premise X toward an unknowable conclusion Y. The spectators, not knowing what their author is driving at, cannot be in suspense as to how or whether an expected objective is going to be reached. They are not, therefore, so much in suspense as to *what* is going to happen next (although the most unexpected and unpredictable things do happen) as they are in suspense about what the next event to take place will add to their understanding of *what is happening*. The action supplies an increasing number of contradictory and bewildering clues on a number of different levels, but the final question is never wholly answered. Thus, instead of being in suspense as to what will happen next, the spectators are, in the Theatre of the Absurd, put into suspense as to *what* the play *may mean*. This suspense continues even after the curtain has come down. Here again the Theatre of the Absurd fulfills Brecht's postulate of a critical, detached audience, who will have to sharpen their wits on the play and be stimulated by it to think for themselves, far more effectively than Brecht's own theatre. Not only are the members of the audience unable to identify with the characters, they are compelled to puzzle out the meaning of what they have seen. Each of them will probably find his own, personal meaning, which will differ from the solution found by most others. But he will have been forced to make a mental effort and to evaluate an experience he has undergone. In this sense, the Theatre of the Absurd is the most demanding, the most intellectual theatre. It may be riotously funny, wildly exaggerated and oversimplified, vulgar and garish, but it will always confront the spectator with a genuine intellectual problem, a philosophical paradox, which he will have to try to solve even if he knows that it is most probably insoluble.

In this respect, the Theatre of the Absurd links up with an older tradition which has almost completely disappeared from Western culture: the tradition of allegory and the symbolical representation of abstract concepts personified by characters whose costumes and accoutrements subtly suggested whether they represented Time, Chastity, Winter, Fortune, the World, etc. This is the tradition which stretches from the Italian *Trionfo* of the Renaissance to the English Masque, the elaborate allegorical constructions of the Spanish *Auto sacramental* down to Goethe's allegorical processions and masques written for the court of Weimar at the turn of the eighteenth century. Although the living riddles the characters represented in these entertainments were by no means difficult to solve, as everyone knew that a character with a scythe and an hourglass represented Time, and although the characters soon revealed their identity and explained their attributes, there was an element of intellectual challenge which stimulated the audience in the moments between the appearance of the riddle and its solution and which provided them with the pleasure of having solved a puzzle. And what is more, in the elaborate allegorical dramas like Calderón's *El Gran Teatro del Mundo* the subtle interplay of allegorical characters itself presented the audience with a great deal to think out for themselves. They had, as it were, to translate the abstractly presented action into terms of their everyday experience; they could ponder on the deeper meaning of such facts as death having taken the characters representing Riches or Poverty in a Dance of Death equally quickly and equally harshly, or that Mammon had deserted his master Everyman in the hour of death. The dramatic riddles of our time present no such clear-cut solutions. All they can show is that while the solutions have evaporated the riddle of our existence remains—complex, unfathomable, and paradoxical.

NOTES

1. Ionesco, "Dans les Armes de la Ville," *Cahiers de la Compagnie Madeleine Renaud-Jean-Louis Barrault*, No. 20 (October, 1957).
2. Adamov, "Note Préliminaire," *Théâtre II*, Paris, 1955.
3. *Ibid.*
4. It may be significant that the three writers concerned, although they now all live in France and write in French have all come to live there from outside and must have experienced a period of adjustment to the country and its language. Samuel Beckett (b. 1906) came from Ireland; Arthur Adamov (b. 1908) from Russia, and Eugène Ionesco (b. 1912) from Rumania.
5. Ionesco, "L'Impromptu de l'Alma," *Théâtre II*, Paris, 1958.
6. Ionesco, "The Avant-Garde Theatre," *World Theatre*, VIII, No. 3 (Autumn, 1959).
7. Jarry, "Questions de Théâtre," in *Ubu Roi, Ubu Enchaîné*, and other Ubuesque writings. Ed. René Massat, Lausanne, 1948.

8. Apollinaire, *Les Mamelles de Tirésias*, Preface.

9. Ionesco, "The Avant-Garde Theatre."

10. Ionesco, "Ni un Dieu, ni un Demon," *Cahiers de la Compagnie Madeleine Renaud-Jean-Louis Barrault*, No. 22–23 (May, 1958).

CATCH-22
(JOSEPH HELLER)

"Catch-22 and Angry Humor: A Study of the Normative Values of Satire"
by James Nagel, in *Studies in American Humor* (1974)

INTRODUCTION

James Nagel argues that Joseph Heller's darkly humorous war novel *Catch-22* is a modern-day Juvenalian satire, one whose "angry" humor, rather than affirming conservative norms that its audience can agree on, questions and undermines many values at the heart of American life. "[A]ggressive capitalism, bureaucracy, and certain 'insane' and destructive elements of modern civilization which endure at the expense of humanity and compassion" are caricatured in Heller's novel. According to Nagel, Heller's caricatures are often made grotesque by "the psychological equivalent of character reduction": monomania. Thus, Milo Minderbender and his capitalism-run-amok empire are made to stand for corporate greed and amorality by Heller's hyperbolic portrayal of his single-mindedness. Such satire, for Nagel, betrays a new twist on the Juvenalian satire: Rather than affirming commonly held beliefs in his

---

Nagel, James. "*Catch-22* and Angry Humor: A Study of the Normative Values of Satire." *Studies in American Humor* 1.2 (1974): 99–106.

caricatures, Heller and other dark humorists of the postwar
period are informed by a radical agenda. Nagel identifies this
sensibility as "essentially opposed to war, capitalism, bureaucracy, and traditional religion, and in favor of freedom, peace,
agnosticism, sex, and life."

☙❧

In one of the earliest reviews of Joseph Heller's *Catch-22*, Whitney
Balliett, writing in the *New Yorker*, charges that

> Heller uses nonsense, satire, non-sequiturs, slap-stick, and
> farce. He wallows in his own laughter, and finally drowns in it.
> What remains is a debris of sour jokes, stage anger, dirty words,
> synthetic looniness, and the sort of antic behavior the children
> fall into when they know they are losing our attention.[1]

It seems somewhat strange now to remember such initial misgivings
about the humor of *Catch-22*, particularly in view of the fact that
Heller's novel has become increasingly conspicuous among those
discussed in studies of the comedy of horror, black humor, or, indeed,
"angry" humor. The paradox inherent in each of these phrases indicates
something of the complexity of any attempt to codify the humor of
the novel, as does Balliett's variety of terms for it. There has not yet
been published a single substantial article which specifies precisely
what is funny about it, what the implications of such humor are, and
what generic associations are implicit in its form.

The importance of genre classification for a study of the novel is, of
course, a matter of attempting to come to it on its own terms, without
imposing irrelevant standards and obscuring fundamental themes.
This is a problem which many reviewers encountered when they
judged *Catch-22* as a realistic "Novel" and found it wanting in verisimilitude, depth of characterization, and plot. However, a few recent
critical studies attempt some classification of genre. In the best of
these, Constance Denniston develops an interpretation of the book as
a "romance-parody."[2] In other articles, Eric Solomon argues that it is a
parody of serious war fiction,[3] and Victor Milne calls it a mock-epic.[4]
These discussions, although they make some important contributions,
do not satisfactorily describe the generic properties of *Catch-22*, for it
is demonstrably a satire, essentially a Juvenalian satire which functions

within the historical patterns of that form. What pure "comedy" exists is patently superficial, if enjoyable, and serves only as a surface for the underlying thematic foundation of the novel.

The humor of *Catch-22* is not the gentle entertainment of comedy but the harsh derision and directed social attack of satire. Unlike comedy, which depicts failures or excesses of basic human nature, the satire of Heller's novel is selective, hitting out against definable groups within American society and creating a unified front against a corrupt and ridiculous enemy. In effect, as David Worcester theorizes, "Satire enters when the few convict the many of stupidity."[5] In the case of *Catch-22*, one might say "stupidity and wickedness," for its objects of satire are portrayed as being both fools and knaves, and a sympathetic reader, laughing at the satirized subjects, feels himself to be a member of a select aristocracy based on virtue and intelligence. As Northrop Frye has indicated, satire requires at least two elements: humor resulting from the portrayal of fantasy, the grotesque, or the absurd; and a definable object of attack.[6] *Catch-22* easily meets these requirements: Milo's bombing of his own squadron on Pianosa is fantasy; the old man of the whore house, to mention just one character, is grotesque; and the continuing logic and inexorability of the regulation Catch-22 lapses into absurdity. The attack seems to center upon aggressive capitalism, bureaucracy, and certain "insane" and destructive elements of modern civilization which endure at the expense of humanity and compassion.

As an art form, *Catch-22* uses the standard devices of satire to enforce its traditional thesis that "vice is both ugly and rampant"[7] and that the solution of the problem is to "live with fortitude, reason, . . . honor, justice, simplicity, the virtues which make for the good life and the good society."[8] To make these points, the method of characterization becomes caricature: Heller's military officers, like Swift's Yahoos and Pope's Dunces, are reductive and distorted projections of human personality types. In this matter, Heller's novel is not so purely Juvenalian as Philip Roth's *Our Gang*, which launches a vituperative assault on thinly disguised individual human beings. Rather, in *Catch-22* each character becomes associated with an "aspect of the civilization under attack, the whole range embracing a wide variety of social levels and attitudes."[9] The psychological equivalent of character reduction is monomania, and Heller is a master at portraying this condition: Milo Minderbinder, a modern reincarnation of Defoe's economic man, is a myopic encapsulation of the Madison Avenue mentality. He can make a profit on anything from making chocolate-covered cotton to selling supplies to the Germans, an enterprise he justifies in classical business terms. At one point he even has a Piltdown Man for sale.[10]

Lieutenant Scheisskopf, who becomes a General before the novel is over, is perfectly willing to nail men together in formation, or to wire their hands to their sides, it if will result in more orderly parades. His decision not to do so is not the result of compassion but of the inaccessibility of nickel-alloy swivels and good copper wire. In addition to Milo and Scheisskopf, Captain Black (with his Loyalty Oath Crusade), General P. P. Peckham (who wants all the tents to face Washington and thinks the USO should take over military operations—which it finally does), and Colonel Cathcart (who wants desperately to be featured in the *Saturday Evening Post*), are caricatures who cannot be evaluated by realistic standards. If they are to develop any functional thematic depth at all, they must be seen in their satiric roles as symbols of social attitudes, traditions, and patterns of behavior.

Just as the characterizations of *Catch-22* are within the framework of satire, so are other elements of the novel. For example, a traditional satiric plot tends to be both episodic and cyclical,[11] as are the rapid, almost jarring, shifts of scene in *Catch-22*. Also conventional in satire is the pattern of action which intensifies, rather than resolves, the central conflict. In addition, the setting of satire is often chaotic, crowded, and filled with images of corruption and decay. Alvin Kernan says that the satiric scene is one where "the deformed faces of depravity, stupidity, greed, venality, ignorance, and maliciousness group closely together for a moment, . . . break up, and another tight knot of figures collects. . . ."[12] Kernan cites as examples Juvenal's Rome, Pope's land of Dunces, and Don Juan's London, but he could easily have used Heller's setting: Aarfy for depravity, Cathcart for stupidity, Milo for greed, the old man for venality, and almost any of Yossarian's superiors for maliciousness.

Yet another characteristic of satire, the ubiquitous image, has several expressions in Heller's novel: images of a soldier covered entirely in white, of Yossarian naked in a tree at Snowden's funeral, of the trunk of Kid Sampson tottering momentarily on a raft, and of the horrible moment when Yossarian opens Snowden's flight jacket. These brutal and shocking images underscore the serious threats to human life which are behind Yossarian's dilemma.

Perhaps the most significant dimension in which it is important to distinguish the humor of *Catch-22* from simple comedy is that of the normative values which are essential to satire. As Northrop Frye points out, unlike a comedy, a satire's "moral norms are relatively clear, and it assumes standards against which the grotesque and absurd are measured."[13] From this point of view, a critical reading of the novel as a satire, indeed *any* reading of the novel, must formulate and describe those norms which are the basis of ethical conflict and which make the satire operative.

In his essay "Notes on the Comic," W. H. Auden says that "satire flourishes in a homogeneous society with a common conception of the moral law, for satirist and audience must agree as to how normal people can be expected to behave, and in times of relative stability and contentment, for satire cannot deal with serious evil and suffering."[14]

Auden's premises would seem to be viable in dealing with traditional satire but wholly inadequate in describing the mode of *Catch-22*. America is not a homogeneous society; it has no unifying moral law; these are not times of stability; and Heller's satire *does* deal with serious problems. What has happened to the satire of modern America is that the traditional conservative norm has been abandoned in favor of a "radical" one, one not endorsed by the majority of the population.

One of the effects of this fundamental alteration is to create an uneasy humor resulting from the singularity of the normative base. Such humor, often employing scenes of violence or even horror, has been variously described in criticism as "angry" or "black" comedy. The social implication of this device is to call into question the prevailing ethical structure of the society, rather than to use its norms as a point of reference. Heller's method is the inversion of the satirical mode employed by Aristophanes in *Lysistrata*, in which war and society are satirized from the perspective of conservative norms. *Lysistrata* emphasizes that a return to the style of life of the recent past, a style clearly defined historically, would be a solution to the problems, whereas in *Catch-22* what seems to be advocated is a movement forward toward some ill-defined yet positive and brave new world. In intellectual terms, such a stance is tenuous at best, and yet even this amorphous norm is effective in the satire. At this time of social misgiving and disenchantment, *Catch-22* allows its readers to celebrate their ethical superiority over, and distance from, the military machine and bureaucratic structure, which are made to look ridiculous and insane in the novel but seem unassailable and incorrigible in reality.

Modern angry humor, which has its historical foundation in Juvenalian satire, is an attack on the basic principles and fundamental order of society. Such an attack is not far beneath the surface of Heller's novel. The knaves and fools of *Catch-22* are all embodiments of the weaknesses in American middle-class morality. There is a Texan who believes that "people of means—decent folk—should be given more votes than drifters, whores, criminals, degenerates, atheists and indecent folk—people without means" (p. 9). Appleby, whom Yossarian hates and whom Orr smashes in the head with a Ping-Pong paddle, is "a fair-haired boy from Iowa who believed in God, Motherhood and the American Way of Life, without ever thinking about any of them . . ." (p. 18). Major Major's father is described as a "long-limbed farmer, a God-fearing, freedom-loving, law-abiding rugged individualist who held that federal aid to anyone but farmers was creeping socialism" (p. 82). The humor here results, at least in part, from the revelation of the corruption within the middle-class ethic itself, a theme made even more clear in the description of Major Major, who always did exactly what his elders told him: "He never once took the name of the Lord his God in vain, committed adultery or coveted his neighbor's ass. In fact, he loved his neighbor and never even bore false witness against him. Major Major's elders disliked him because he was such a flagrant nonconformist" (p. 84).

Nearly every facet of American life is made laughable through either diminution or hyperbole, from Milo's incredible capitalism to the Anabaptist chaplain's Christianity, which is expected to assist in getting tighter bomb patterns. The American economic classes are well represented in Nately, a wealthy but somewhat simple romantic, Aarfy, an economic striver who is the most blind and corrupt character of all, and Dunbar, the son of a poor man who worked himself to death trying to compete within the system. Perhaps this economic theme is most clear in the chapter "Nately's Old Man," in which Nately's father, who never wears anything but Brooks Brothers shirts and knows all the answers, is contrasted with the lecherous old man of the whore house who has no answers at all but professes the life ethic that Yossarian finally adopts: "anything worth dying for . . . is certainly worth living for" (p. 242). The old man is pragmatic and unpatriotic, but he convinces Nately that his father is a "Son of a Bitch" (p. 243).

Nately thus moves toward the radical norm, as indeed do Dunbar, Orr, and Yossarian. Even the chaplain, who had always believed in an "immortal, anthropomorphic, English-speaking, Anglo-Saxon, pro-American God" (p. 279), wavers in the faith, develops lust for his wife, comes to sympathize with Yossarian, and finally *lies* to get himself into the hospital (p. 356). It would seem clear that the normative values of Heller's satire are essentially opposed to war, capitalism, bureaucracy, and traditional religion, and in favor of freedom, peace, agnosticism, sex, and life.

The conflict between these two sets of values is related to the most pervasive theme of the novel, that of insanity. Madness is, of course, a consistent motif in satire: as Kernan says, the satirist "typically believes that there is no pattern of reason left in the world."[15] The logical order of daily existence has somehow gone awry, leaving the satirist "alone in the lunatic world to stay its progressive degeneration. . . . He becomes the only champion of virtue who dares to speak the truth in a world where the false insolently maintains itself as the real."[16] This assessment of traditional satire goes a long way toward defining the operative norms of modern angry humor—especially in Ken Kesey's *One Flew Over the Cuckoo's Nest* and *Catch-22*. From the beginning it is clear that Yossarian's mind is not in harmony with the established thinking around him. Either he is maladjusted to a logical world, or the world is itself insane. The structure of the novel moves systematically to a demonstration that the latter is the case. In the first chapter Yossarian reveals his position when he says to the chaplain, "insanity is contagious. . . . Everybody is crazy but us. This is probably the only sane ward in the whole world, for that matter" (p. 14). What is sane about them is, of course, that they have opted out of the war by going to the hospital. The Narrator's judgments, which intrude frequently, support Yossarian's perspective: "Men went mad and were rewarded with medals. . . . The only thing going on was the war, and no one seemed to notice but Yossarian and Dunbar. And when Yossarian tried to remind people, they drew away from him and thought he was crazy" (p. 16). But Yossarian is "mad" only in terms of his inability to accept the absurdity of war and in his compulsive desire to remain alive.

Many of the other characters are "deranged" in more destructive ways. In addition to the obvious monomaniacs, Milo and Scheisskopf, McWatt is crazy in that he does not mind the war (p. 59) and flies straight in over a target, and because he risks lives unnecessarily by flying low over Yossarian's tent. The dangerous potential of his acrobatics is realized when he zooms over the raft and slices Kid Sampson in half (p. 331). In *Catch-22*, insanity becomes definable as an inability to recognize the reality of danger. Clevinger is insane because he doesn't believe Yossarian's conviction that "the enemy . . . is anybody who's going to get you killed" (p. 122). Aarfy is also insane in his complacent indifference to danger (p. 147). The resolution of this theme comes when Yossarian is analyzed by a psychiatrist, Major Sanderson, who pronounces him mad. Sanderson says,

> "The trouble with you is that you think you're too good for all the conventions of society. . . . You have a morbid aversion to dying. . . . You have deep-seated survival anxieties. And you don't like bigots, bullies, snobs or hypocrites. . . . You're antagonistic to the idea of being robbed, exploited, degraded, humiliated or deceived. Misery depresses you. Ignorance depresses you. Persecution depresses you. Violence depresses you. Slums depress you. Greed depresses you. Crime depresses you. Corruption depresses you. You know, it wouldn't surprise me if you're a manic-depressive!" (pp. 297–98)

A moment later, when Yossarian seeks assurance from Doc Daneeka that "they're not going to send a crazy man out to be killed, are they?" Daneeka responds, "Who else will go?" (p. 299).

It is clear that the military, with its form letter of condolence, its power struggles, its bureaucracy, its bombing of villages to block roads, is the insane factor in the novel and that Yossarian, who really does feel himself "too good for all the conventions of society," endorses a much more humane standard for sanity. By the end of the novel, Kraft, Mudd, Snowden, Clevinger, Dunbar, the soldier in white, Hungry Joe, McWatt, Kid Sampson, the old man, Michaela, and Nately are all dead. In such a world, standing naked in formation, walking backward with a gun, and taking off for Sweden may well be the actions of a sane man.

In Yossarian's desertion at the conclusion of the novel, there seems to be little humor. Such a development is within the tradition of Juvenal, whose works move from comic to tragic satire when the protagonist is left alone as the enemy becomes increasingly more powerful.[17] Yossarian's rejection of Cathcart's deal is not only a moral act in itself, but is consistent with the traditional response of the reader to Juvenalian satire. As Ronald Paulson explains, "with Horace the reader's experience is to feel complicity in the guilt; with Juvenal it is to feel repugnance at the evil."[18] Yossarian's rejection of Cathcart and his world allows him to escape the role of tragic victim and to become an agent in his own destiny. He declares himself apart from and above the military world, and as he does, the poles of values become distinct and stable. *Catch-22* conforms to Maynard Mack's description of traditional satire: "madness and blindness are … the emblems of vice and folly, evil and good are clearly distinguishable, criminals and fools are invariably responsible (therefore censurable), and standards of judgment are indubitable."[19] As a result, the basic assumptions and organization of American society are effectively satirized and, through juxtaposition with idealistic norms, are shown to be wanting in fundamental humanity. It is in this dimension, as social commentary, that Heller's satire develops its most profound themes, themes which emerge with clarity and force from the depth of its angry humor.

NOTES

1. Whitney Balliett, *New Yorker*, 37 (Dec. 9, 1961), 248.
2. Constance Denniston, "The American Romance-Parody: A Study of Purdy's *Malcolm* and Heller's *Catch-22*," *ESRS*, 14, No. 2 (1965), 42–59, 63–64.
3. Eric Solomon, "From *Christ in Flanders* to *Catch-22*: An Approach to War Fiction," *Texas Studies in Literature and Language*, 11 (1969), 851–66.
4. Victor J. Milne, "Heller's 'Bologniad': A Theological Perspective on Catch-22," *Critique*, 12, No. 2 (1970), 50–69.
5. David Worcester, *The Art of Satire* (Cambridge: Harvard Univ. Press, 1940), p. 77.
6. Northrop Frye, *Anatomy of Criticism* (Princeton: Princeton Univ. Press, 1957), p. 244.
7. Alvin Kernan, *The Cankered Muse: Satire of the English Renaissance* (New Haven: Yale Univ. Press, 1959), p. 23.
8. Kernan, p. 18.
9. G. B. Mck. Henry, "Significant Corn: *Catch-22*." *Melbourne Critical Review*, 9 (1966), 138.

10. Joseph Heller, *Catch-22* (New York: Simon and Schuster, 1961), p. 365. All subsequent references will be made in the text.

11. Kernan, pp. 30–34.

12. Kernan, pp. 7–8.

13. Frye, p. 223.

14. W. H. Auden, "Notes on the Comic," *Thought*, 27 (1952), 68–69.

15. Kernan, p. 20.

16. Kernan, p. 21.

17. Ronald Paulson, *The Fictions of Satire* (Baltimore: Johns Hopkins, 1967), p. 31.

18. Paulson, p. 30.

19. Maynard Mack, "The Muse of Satire," *New Yorker*, 41 (1951), 85.

CAT'S CRADLE
(KURT VONNEGUT)

"Dark Humor in *Cat's Cradle*"
by Blake Hobby, University of North Carolina at Asheville

"In humour we orbit eccentrically around a black sun."
(Simon Critchley, On Humor)

"'What Can a Thoughtful Man Hope for Mankind on Earth, Given the Experience of the Past Million Years?'—'Nothing.'"
(Kurt Vonnegut, Cat's Cradle)

"The exploration of meaninglessness is a grim and hilarious game: the explorer wins when he can laugh and loses when he cannot."
(Richard Hauck, A Cheerful Nihilism)

For Simon Critchley, the darkness of comedy commingles with its lightness; comedy captures the "sublimity and suffering of the human situation" (111). All humor involves negations, absurdities, and dark truths about our lives, including our inability to defeat death and the conflicted way we cope with this darkest of all dark realities. In the wildly farcical novel *Cat's Cradle*, Kurt Vonnegut responds to the frailty of our lives, the futility of our utopian dreams, and the absurdities of science and religion with his classic hope and dark humor.

With his wit, dark humor, and humanitarian vision, Kurt Vonnegut Jr. became an icon for the baby boom generation. Idolized by the American counterculture of the 1960s and 1970s, Vonnegut spoke to people disillusioned by ineffective institutions, the nuclear arms race, and the Vietnam War. Often labeled a science-fiction writer (a designation that Vonnegut abhorred), he addressed contemporary socio-political concerns by creating experimental, fantastical worlds populated with grotesque characters. As Vonnegut said, "I have been a soreheaded occupant of a file drawer labeled 'science fiction' . . . and I would like out, particularly since so many serious critics regularly mistake the drawer for a urinal" (*Wampeters* 1). Questioning who we are, why we are here, and what it is that we as social beings should be doing, Vonnegut's often scathing and bitterly satirical works depict a world in which God is strangely absent, a place where stock characters and fantastical creations negotiate a world of chance. There Vonnegut's creations bear witness to the various shortcomings that make us fallible, comic creatures. Thus Vonnegut often touches upon the limits of reason, the illusion of progress, the horrors of war, the absurdity of nuclear proliferation, the reality of class differences, the construct of race, and the need for human beings to erect meaning-making systems, such as the facetious religion of Bokonon in *Cat's Cradle*. Combining high hilarity with rather pessimistic depictions of humanity's frailty and self-centered tendencies, Vonnegut comments upon the delusions that round our lives and often distract us from real, pressing social concerns. He shows us who we are through a distorted, funhouse mirror lauding the power of fiction to re-envision our place in the world, and challenging us to create a better, more humane society.

It was with *Cat's Cradle* that Vonnegut first received a wide readership. An apocalyptic novel about an island society, *Cat's Cradle* is an absurdist retelling of the Genesis creation story. As Vonnegut's cult following grew, *Cat's Cradle* was propelled into the mainstream, eventually becoming required reading in many high schools and colleges. The novel's dark satire spoke to a generation disillusioned with war, institutions, and religious dogma. In this way, *Cat's Cradle* helped foster the counterculture of the 1960s. At stake in the novel is the increasing paranoia over the Cold War and the very real threat of nuclear annihilation. Ice-Nine—the substance that ends the world in *Cat's Cradle*—can be understood as an example of the technology that, in attempting to better the world, actually has the power to end all life on the planet.

The novel's title is taken from a child's game called "Cat's Cradle," a game well-known for its series of string figures. While the game may explain the book's strung-together, mini-chapter form, we learn of the game's symbolic significance when the narrator/protagonist discusses it with Newt, Felix's diminutive son, who recounts how his father (a fictional co-inventor of the atom bomb) enjoyed playing the game and then taunting him, making him a disillusioned "little person" at odds with the world. *Cat's Cradle* has a simple plot. It is set in the United States and in a mythical Caribbean republic called "San Lorenzo," where the military dictator, Papa Monzano, conspires with Bokonon, the inventor of the island's religion (which is called Bokononism). A writer researching a book on the bombing of Hiroshima contacts the three children of atomic bomb scientist Dr. Felix Hoenikker, and journeys to San Lorenzo to speak with the middle child, Frank, who is minister of science and progress on San Lorenzo. The writer (Jonah/John) ends up running into all three Hoenikker children, falling in love with the island's object of beauty, Mona, converting to Bokononism, and witnessing the end of the world brought about by one of Dr. Hoenikker's inventions: Ice-Nine.

We arrive at the island of San Lorenzo and at an understanding of the Hoenikker family, the religion of Bokonon, and the inhumanity of science, through the eyes of John. John calls himself Jonah, a name with tragicomic biblical overtones, for the Book of Jonah in the Bible is both dark and humorous. In the biblical story, God sends Jonah to the sinful city of Ninevah to prophesy its destruction. Rather than make this trip, Jonah immediately boards a ship to another city (Tarshish). When God sees this, he creates a mighty storm. The other sailors on the ship realize that Jonah has incurred the wrath of God and throw him overboard, where a whale swallows him. Jonah remains inside the whale for three days and three nights. God then sends Jonah on this mission again; this time Jonah prophesies gloom and doom, the end of the world. Ironically, God saves Ninevah, making Jonah a failed, dejected prophet. The narrator and protagonist of *Cat's Cradle*, Jonah/John is obsessed with a single cataclysmic moment in human history: August 6, 1945, the day the U.S. dropped the atomic bomb "Little Boy" on Hiroshima, Japan, killing more than 140,000 people. There are many interesting comparisons that come about from Vonnegut's use of the Jonah allusion. One lies in Vonnegut's "outsider" status as a social critic; he is a kind of gloom-and-doom prophet whose warnings go unheeded. But the story of Jonah also reveals the mystery of God: the strange way that justice, which is not absolute, lies beyond human understanding. In this way, Jonah in the Bible, John/Jonah in his novel about the end of the world, Bokonon in his sacred books, and Vonnegut in *Cat's Cradle* perform prophetic roles for lost worlds. Places where human beings, with their inward-focused vision and with their desire to control, lose sight of moral concerns. At the center of Vonnegut's world and perhaps of Jonah/John's "karass"—one of Bokonon's terms, referring in this case to a group of people who, without knowing one an other, are fated to complete or take part in historical event—are the Hoenikker children. Abandoned by their often nihilistic father, who invests himself fully only in science, the Hoenikker children live in a world without morals, a world where God is absent.

The Hoenikker children are obsessed with the doomsday substance their father has made, each covertly carrying pieces of it wherever he or she goes. Angela, the eldest child, who is taken out of high school in her sophomore year to be a housekeeper and stand-in wife for her father, marries Harrison C. Connors, a man who desperately wants Ice-Nine. Her younger brother, Frank, who, like his father, has strong ideas but can't face the public, becomes the minister of science and progress of San Lorenzo after bribing the dictator with Ice-Nine. Lastly, there is Newt, the youngest Hoenikker child, who is psychically wounded by his Cat's Cradle playtime with his father, is sent to a school for grotesque children (Newt is a "little person"), and creates paintings that cynically depict the meaninglessness of life. While these characters are over-the-top creations, they collectively suggest how modern society worships technology and science, how we all desire power and control, and how easily power and knowledge can corrupt and deform.

Vonnegut often draws upon his own experiences in his novels. Significantly, Vonnegut's idea for *Cat's Cradle* came from his time working for General Electric and a particular scientist that Vonnegut satirized in the character of Felix Hoenikker. In a *Paris Review* interview, Vonnegut explains the genesis of the Felix Hoenikker character and Ice-Nine:

> Dr. Felix Hoenikker, the absentminded scientist, was a caricature
> of Dr. Irving Langmuir, the star of the GE research laboratory.
> I knew him some. My brother worked with him. Langmuir

was wonderfully absentminded. He wondered out loud one time whether, when turtles pulled in their heads, their spines buckled or contracted. I put that in the book. One time he left a tip under his plate after his wife served him breakfast at home. I put that in. His most important contribution, though, was the idea for what I called "Ice-9," a form of frozen water that was stable at room temperature. He didn't tell it directly to me. It was a legend around the laboratory—about the time H.G. Wells came to Schenectady. That was long before my time. I was just a little boy when it happened—listening to the radio, building model airplanes. . . . Anyway—Wells came to Schenectady, and Langmuir was told to be his host. Langmuir thought he might entertain Wells with an idea for a science-fiction story—about a form of ice that was stable at room temperature. Wells was uninterested, or at least never used the idea. And then Wells died, and then, finally, Langmuir died. I thought to myself: finders, keepers—the idea is mine. Langmuir, incidentally, was the first scientist in private industry to win a Nobel Prize.

To grasp the significance of *Cat's Cradle*'s dark humor, we should think about the tradition of realism usually associated with the novel form. Especially in the late nineteenth century, American authors were concerned with "verisimilitude," the appearance of reality in fiction, and the long tradition of representation that Aristotle refers to in his *Poetics* as "mimesis." Thus, Melville, for example, provides pages and pages of taxonomical descriptions of whales—a sort of scientific grounding for his novel—throughout *Moby-Dick*. With *Cat's Cradle*, however, Vonnegut breaks from this tradition and creates an "anti-novel," an experimental form with no pretensions of verisimilitude. For Samuel Beckett, Michel Butor, and Alain Robbe-Grillet, significant experimental novelists that prefigure Vonnegut's work, the novel is an elastic form. The anti-novel is often bizarre and absurd and relies on the reader to provide both concrete references and to supply meaning. Characteristics of the anti-novel include experiments with vocabulary, punctuation, syntax, variations of time sequence, alternate endings and beginnings, and collage—a form that allows authors to piece together discontinuous fragments. The anti-novel can also lack plot, character development, and many other traditional elements we associate with literature.

With its opening epigraph, "Nothing in this book is true"—both Vonnegut's chosen line and an excerpt from the book embedded in the novel called "The Books of Bokonon"—the author breaks with the tradition of representing reality in fiction. *Cat's Cradle*, as well as the non-existent religious text it frequently describes, announces its own status as artifice even before the narrative starts. This self-referential quality, where fiction calls attention to its own status as art, is a hallmark of what is often referred to as "metafiction." Though many novels throughout the literary tradition exhibit some metafictional qualities, they predominate in contemporary fiction, especially in the works of authors such as Italo Calvino, Gabriel García Márquez, and others who are known for breaking with the conventions of realism. Vonnegut's novel about the end of the world contains a mixture of forms in its 127 short chapters, including parables and poetry. It is a kind of Bible. We can note the close proximity of *The Books of Bokonon*, Bokonon's (given-name Lionel Boyd Johnson) bogus religious text in Vonnegut's work, with *The Book of Mormon*, the sacred text purportedly dictated to Joseph Smith that forms the basis for the Church of Jesus Christ of Latter-day Saints. Not only does Vonnegut poke fun at Mormonism but at organized religion as a whole in this book in which religious followers know they believe in lies. Thus, throughout the novel, Vonnegut satirizes everything from religion to law to science to technology to nuclear proliferation to the Cold War. Though Vonnegut's works depart from the tradition of realism we associate with the conventional novel, his use of satire attempts to amend vices Vonnegut sees in our world, vices especially relevant to the period during which he was writing, when the U.S. and the Soviet Union were engaged in a heated arms race and many Americans were beginning to protest the Vietnam War.

According to Jonathan Swift, one of the finest satirists in the English language, "Satire is a sort of glass wherein beholders do generally discover everybody's face but their own, which is the chief reason for the kind of reception it meets in the world, and that so very few are offended with it" ("The Preface of the Author," *The Battle of the Book*). Of course, as George Meredith tells us, "the satirist is a moral agent, often a social scavenger, working on a storage of bile"

(44). Such subversive moral agency may account for Vonnegut's outsider status and his appeal to disgruntled youth, especially when one considers that Vonnegut, like Swift, is a master satirist who is often misunderstood. Satire is a flexible form that enables Vonnegut to replace the conventions of realism with grotesque characters, an unbelievable plot, and an apocalyptic setting. In the end, *Cat's Cradle* is a work that can be described by the last lines of *The Books of Bokonon*, which are both chilling and hilarious. As Bokonon does, Vonnegut creates a history of human stupidity, one that challenges, horrifies, and finally brings us to reimagine our place in the world. Although there may be "No damn cat. No damn cradle," we must create ways of living that are more humane and come to grips with the paradox central to Bokononist thought: ". . . the heartbreaking necessity of lying about reality, and the heartbreaking impossibility of lying about it" (*Cat's Cradle* 284).

WORKS CITED AND CONSULTED

Allen, William Rodney, ed. *Conversations with Kurt Vonnegut.* Jackson, Miss.: U of Mississippi P, 1988.

———. *Understanding Kurt Vonnegut.* Columbia, S.C.: U of South Carolina P, 1991.

Boon, Kevin A., ed. *At Millennium's End: New Essays on the Work of Kurt Vonnegut.* Albany, N.Y.: State U of New York P, 2001.

———. *Chaos Theory and the Interpretation of Literary Texts: The Case of Kurt Vonnegut.* Lewiston, N.Y.: Edwin Mellen Press, 1997.

Broer, Lawrence R. *Sanity Plea: Schizophrenia in the Novels of Kurt Vonnegut.* Second edition. Tuscaloosa, Ala.: U of Alabama P, 1994.

Chernuchin, Michael, ed. *Vonnegut Talks!* Forest Hills, N.Y.: Pylon Press, 1977.

Critchley, Simon. *On Humour.* London; New York: Routledge, 2002.

Giannone, Richard. *Vonnegut: A Preface to His Novels.* Port Washington, N.Y.: Kennikat P, 1977.

Goldsmith, David H. *Kurt Vonnegut: Fantasist of Fire and Ice.* Bowling Green, Ohio: Bowling Green University Popular Press, 1972.

Hauck, Richard. *A Cheerful Nihilism: Confidence and "the Absurd" in American Humorous Fiction.* Bloomington: Indiana UP, 1971.

Klinkowitz, Jerome. *Slaughterhouse-Five: Reforming the Novel and the World.* Boston: Twayne, 1990.

————. *Kurt Vonnegut*. London: Methuen, 1982.

————. *Papers Relating to Kurt Vonnegut: 1969–1978*. University of Delaware
    Special Collections Department. URL: http://www.lib.udel.edu/ud/spec/
    findaids/klinkvon.htm

————. *The Vonnegut Effect*. Columbia, S.C.: U of South Carolina P, 2004.

————. *Vonnegut in Fact: The Public Spokesmanship of Personal Fiction*.
    Columbia, S.C.: U of South Carolina P, 1998.

Leeds, Marc. *The Vonnegut Encyclopedia: An Authorized Compendium*. Westport,
    Conn.: Greenwood Publishing Group, 1995.

Leeds, Marc and Peter J. Reed. *Kurt Vonnegut: Images and Representations*.
    Westport, Conn.: Greenwood Publishing Group, 2000.

Lundquist, James. *Kurt Vonnegut*. New York: Ungar, 1977.

Marvin, Thomas F. *Kurt Vonnegut: A Critical Companion*. Westport, Conn.:
    Greenwood Publishing Group, 2002.

Mayo, Clark. *Kurt Vonnegut: The Gospel from Outer Space*. San Bernardino, Calif:
    Borgo Press, 1977.

Meredith, George. "An Essay on Comedy." *Comedy*. New York: Doubleday and
    Company, 1956.

Merrill, Robert, ed. *Critical Essays on Kurt Vonnegut*. Boston: G. K. Hall, 1990.

Morse, Donald E. *Novels of Kurt Vonnegut: Imagining Being an American*.
    Westport, Conn.: Praeger Publishers, 2003.

————. *Kurt Vonnegut*. San Bernardino, Calif.: Borgo Press, 1992.

Mustazza, Leonard, ed. *Critical Response to Kurt Vonnegut*. Westport, Conn.:
    Greenwood Publishing Group, 1994.

————. *Forever Pursuing Genesis: The Myth of Eden in the Novels of Kurt
    Vonnegut*. Lewisburg, Pa.: Bucknell UP, 1990.

Pieratt, Asa B., Julie Huffman-Klinkowitz and Jerome Klinkowitz. *Kurt
    Vonnegut: A Comprehensive Bibliography*. North Haven, Conn.: Archon
    Books, 1987.

Rackstraw, Loree, ed. *Draftings in Vonnegut: The Paradox of Hope*. Cedar Falls,
    Iowa: U of Northern Iowa P, 1988.

Reed, Peter J. *Short FiConn.ion of Kurt Vonnegut*. Westport, Conn.: Greenwood
    Publishing Group, 1997.

Reed, Peter J. and Marc Leeds, eds. *Vonnegut Chronicles: Interviews and Essays*.
    Westport, Conn.: Greenwood Publishing Group, 1996.

Schatt, Stanley. *Kurt Vonnegut, Jr*. Boston: Twayne, 1976.

Vonnegut, Kurt. *Bagombo Snuff Box: UncolleConn.ed Short FiConn.ion*. New
    York: G. P. Putnam's Sons, 1999. 9–10.

————. *Cat's Cradle*. New York: Dell, 1963.

———. Interview by David Hayman, David Michaelis, Richard Rhodes. The Art of Fiction 64. *The Paris Review* 64 (Spring 1977). URL: http://www. theparisreview.com/viewinterview.php/prmMID/3605

———. *Wampters, Foma, and Granfalloons*. Dell: 1974.

Yarmolinsky, Jane Vonnegut. *Angels Without Wings: A Courageous Family's Triumph over Tragedy*. Boston: Houghton Mifflin, 1987.

A CLOCKWORK ORANGE
(ANTHONY BURGESS)

"*A Clockwork Orange* and the Metaphysics of Slapstick"
by Matthew J. Bolton,
Loyola School, New York City

A man jabs his thumb into his companion's eye. The victim retaliates not by striking back at his attacker, but by punching the man next to him in the nose. That man scowls in pain, then claws at the first man, grabbing him by the ear and shaking him until he writhes and wiggles. Anyone who witnesses such a cycle of violence ought to be appalled. Yet if the three men in question are Larry, Mo, and Curly, and the witness is an appreciative audience, these acts of random and meaningless violence are met with laughter. Why should a Three Stooges film—or any work of slapstick, for that matter—strike us as comic rather than as tragic? What does the mode of slapstick "do" to violence to render it not merely palatable, but *funny*, and funny on the most primal of levels?

Understanding the metaphysical underpinnings of slapstick sheds light on the complex reactions that most readers have to Anthony Burgess's 1962 novel *A Clockwork Orange*. The book's violence, like its violent narrator himself, is both appalling and appealing. We are horrified by the beatings, murders, rapes, and other crimes that Alex and his gang of *droogs* commit, and we find that we have much more in common with the victims of these crimes than with the aggressors. Yet because Alex's account of his activities is entirely devoid of sentiment or morality, these acts of violence are tinged with the comic sensibility of the Three Stooges rather than with the tragic one of, say, the bloody final act of *Hamlet*. We laugh despite ourselves, and our laughter complicates and qualifies our moral disapproval of Alex. Somehow, the reader sympathizes with Alex—a young man who is himself without sympathy. This complex and layered response suggests that comedy, and slapstick in particular, reveals some of the basic contradictions of human nature and of social relations. *A Clockwork Orange* is not merely a portrayal of inhuman violence but a philosophical investigation of what makes us human in the first place.

In the opening chapter of *A Clockwork Orange*, Alex and his three friends kick off a night on the town by beating, stripping, and robbing an elderly man. It is a deplorable act. Yet Alex finds it a source of comedy:

> We began to filly about with him. Pete held his rookers and Georgie sort of hooked his rot wide open for him and Dim yanked out his false zoobies, upper and lower ... The old veck began to make sort of chumbling shooms—'wuf waf wof'—so Georgie let go of holding his goobers apart and just let him have one in the toothless rot with his ringy fist, and that made the old veck start moaning a lot then, then out comes the blood my brothers, real beautiful. (14)

They strip the old man, sending him staggering off in his long underpants while they "had a snigger at him and riffled through his pockets" (14). The crime seems to have been entirely pointless, for the old man has so little money that the teenagers "gave all his messy little coin the scatter treatment, it being hen-korm to the amount of pretty polly we had on us already" (15). Not only did they not need his money, but in fact they will set out next to "unload" more of their own money so that "we'd have more of an incentive like for some shop-crasting" (15). Beating the old man was not a means to an end but an end in and of itself; Alex and his droogs profit only in their laughter.

The reader's response to the scene ought to be simple: He or she should find the crime reprehensible. Yet while most readers will feel an element of such disapproval, it is most likely not the sum total of their response. Tugging against one's moral outrage is an involuntary recognition that something about this beating is, in fact, funny. Reading the scene, one may break out in a grin or a laugh, those primal reactions that so often are at odds with our more elevated theories and opinions. Much of it comes down to diction. A line such as "The old veck began to make sort of chumbling shooms—'wuf waf wof'" is funny in a way that "The old man began to make indecipherable noises" would not be. Burgess, an aficionado of James Joyce, has created a wild new language for Alex. The youth plays with words—his own and others—and his fulgent slang, his dead-on mimicry, and his mock-sentimentality are utterly beguiling. Another source of comedy lies in the wide gap between the old man's words and Alex's. A moment before the beating starts, the man protests against Alex and his friends snatching his library books: "The starry prof type began to creech 'But those are not mine, those are the property of the municipality, this is sheer wantonness and vandal work,' or some such slovos" (13). We agree with the old man, of course: The teenagers should not have taken his books, and this is indeed sheer wantonness. Yet they do not argue the point with him; instead, they snatch out his false teeth, so that his well-formed sentences give way to a "wuf waf wof." When they send him off with a kick, we see, at least for a moment, why the teenagers find his condition to be so funny. Pantless, toothless, wordless, staggering down the street—the image is at once terrible and ridiculous.

It is easy to say why we disapprove of the gang's treatment of the old man, but it's rather more difficult to explain why we find some aspects of that treatment funny. The late nineteenth- and early twentieth- century French philosopher Henri Bergson explores the nature of physical comedy in his essay "Laughter: An Essay on the Meaning of the Comic." Bergson sees a certain kind of humor as being bound up and produced by the dialectic between mind and body. He writes, "The attitudes, gestures and movements of the human body are laughable in exact proportion as that body reminds us of a mere machine" (79). As an illustration of this principle, Bergson cites the following example:

> A man, running along the street, stumbles and falls; the passersby burst out laughing. They would not laugh at him, I imagine, could they suppose that the whim had suddenly seized him to sit down on the ground. They laugh because his sitting down is involuntary. Consequently, it is not his sudden change of attitude that raises a laugh, but rather the involuntary element in this change ... (66).

This is the principle behind the oldest slapstick gag in the book: slipping on a banana peel. The pratfalls of Buster Keaton, Jerry Lewis, or Chevy Chase—not to mention those of President Gerald Ford—likewise fit into this category of the body going through an involuntary change. So, too, does the gross-out humor of films like *There's Something About Mary* or *The 40-Year-Old Virgin*, in which gag after gag revolves around involuntary bodily functions. Farting, hiccupping, belching, vomiting, defecating, ejaculating: All of these acts can be funny, since all remind us that a person's body can act of its own accord. Bergson goes on to draw a general principle of this kind of bodily humor:

> We have one and the same effect, which assumes ever subtler forms as it passes from the idea of an artificial MECHANISATION of the human body, if such an expression is permissible, to that of any substitution whatsoever of the artificial for the natural. . . . But that is only a matter of degree, and the general law of these phenomena may be formulated as follows: ANY INCIDENT IS COMIC THAT CALLS OUR ATTENTION TO THE PHYSICAL IN A PERSON WHEN IT IS THE MORAL SIDE THAT IS CONCERNED" (91–3).

Such a "general law" certainly applies to the encounter with the old man, whose moral argument is countered with a physical retaliation. Rather than responding to his words, the teenagers yank out and stomp on his dentures. The speed of the youths' response, and the unexpected switch from the moral plane to the physical one, surprises and amuses us the way a good punch line would.

Bergson's formulation speaks to the themes of the novel as a whole, for the title *A Clockwork Orange* itself illustrates the "substitution . . . of the artificial for the natural." The title is taken from a book within the book, an overblown manifesto on free will and the oppression of the state. In the suburban home that Alex and his friends invade, a writer named F. Alexander is working on a manuscript by this name. Alex seizes it and says, "That's a fair gloopy title. Who ever heard of a clockwork orange?" He then reads aloud:

> The attempt to impose upon man, a creature of growth and capable of sweetness, to ooze juicily at the last round the

bearded lips of God, to attempt to impose, I say, laws and conditions appropriate to a mechanical creation, against this I raise my sword-pen. (27)

Ironically, it is out of the very free will the writer champions that Alex and his friends have broken into the man's home. In reading the manuscript, Alex undercuts its thesis, for here is a free-willed creature that does not seem to be "capable of sweetness." The treatment that Alex will eventually undergo at the hands of the state aims to replace his free will—a capacity, admittedly, that he turns to no good use and that eventually lands him in prison serving a sentence for murder—with a series of mechanized, preprogrammed, socially-acceptable responses. A prison chaplain who has befriended Alex urges him to serve out his time rather than to participate in the experimental treatment that will lead to his speedy reformation and release. He says, after Alex has elected to undergo the treatment: "You are passing now to a region where you will be beyond the reach of the power of prayer. A terrible thing to consider" (96). In subjecting himself to the reprogramming experiment, Alex will become as mechanized as a clockwork orange.

Alex's treatment and his subsequent "ethical" behavior are therefore inherently comic, according to Bergson's definition, for they involve his physical body rather than his moral character. Alex is made to watch films of violent acts, and as he does so, a drug in his system induces nausea. His normal response to these crimes—beatings, gang rapes, and robberies like the ones in which he has participated, as well as archival footage of Nazi and Imperial Japanese war crimes—would be to laugh. But by producing in his body the physical responses associated with disgust and horror, the scientists teach Alex the proper moral response to violence. This might be thought of as slapstick therapy. Up until now, Alex has reacted to all violence as if it were a comedy routine: Doling out savage beatings, sexual violence, and torture is no different from watching a Three Stooges routine. If most of us know slapstick through the medium of film, Alex knows it through his own activities. Now cinema, or "sinnys" as Alex tellingly calls films, will teach him about sinfulness. The state's film-and-drug regimen systematically breaks down Alex's association of violence with comedy. In this sense, then, he is being weaned away from a slapstick mentality.

Yet on a second level, the treatment itself is an exercise in slapstick, for it operates on a wholly physical plane. After his course of treatment, Alex will act ethically not out of his own free will but rather because he doubles up in pain or vomits whenever he contemplates violence. The effect, of course, is broadly comic. When the scientists show him a film of a beautiful girl, for example, Alex first thinks, "I would like to have her right down there on the floor with the old in-out real savage" and immediately becomes violently ill (127). To make the wave of nausea pass, he shouts out, "O most beautiful and beauteous of devotchkas, I throw like my heart at your feet for you to trample all over. If I had a rose I would give it to you" (127). Alex's words are ridiculous, for they are entirely at odds with his true feelings. In the outside world, he will likewise find himself in one ridiculous situation after another in which his aversion to violence plays itself out through his own body. He is set upon by a pack of old men in the library, beaten by his former droogs, and eventually must throw himself out of an upper-story window in order to escape from the classical music that he once loved but now associates with his film treatment. In short, Alex's course of treatment simply reverses his position in a hierarchy of slapstick violence: Where once he doled out violence, now he suffers it.

It would be a mistake, however, to oversimplify Burgess's treatment of slapstick or his conception of free will. *A Clockwork Orange* may be intensely violent, but it does not necessarily condone violence, nor does it posit violence to be some sort of radical expression of individuality and free will. Rather, Burgess explores and exploits the reader's pre-existing capacity to see violence as a source of humor. It is Alex's narrative that first draws us in. Were we to read a newspaper account of Alex's beating of the old man, we would find nothing amusing in it. There the incident would be stated baldly: Four youths set upon an elderly man, destroying his property, hurting him, and taking his money. But when Alex tells it, with the old man "creeching" and the boys stomping on his "zoombies," the very same incident is rendered comic. This ought to send us back to re-examine Bergson's argument that comedy arises from unintended actions. The philosopher had given this example: "A man, running along the street, stumbles and falls; the passers-by burst out laughing." But will the crowd always burst out laughing? What if the man is running from a burning building? Or what if he is a fireman, running to save someone in a burning building? His stumbling and falling are no less unintentional in this context, but the response of the passers-by might be quite different. Then again, a staple routine in the circus involves clowns running out of a burning building while a clown fire brigade ineptly tries to put out the fire—and here the audience does, in fact, burst out laughing. So there is something beyond intention and beyond even context that determines whether the effect of any action is comic or dramatic. What Bergson has failed to address in his example is the element of appearance or presentation. Comedy is located not simply in the act of unintentionally falling but in how that fall appears to an audience. When the Three Stooges go into one of their routines of punching and tweaking one another, it is not merely those actions but the stylized appearance of those actions—the mugging of the face, the contortions of the body, the high-pitched squeals, the timing of the attack, and the position and speed of the camera— that makes us laugh. Just as not everyone can tell a joke, not everyone can take a pratfall.

Alex himself is a great clown, and he knows how to present himself and his actions to the reader in a way that elicits our sympathy and laughter. His language is the textual equivalent of the Three Stooges's facial mugging or of the speedy camerawork and frenetic music of a slapstick short film. His narrative is an art that conceals: He knows how to describe a scene in a way that strikes us as funny. We see the comedy in the encounter with the old man, for Alex's lack of anger or of any other sentiment licenses us to laugh at the old man rather than to feel bad for him. Yet Alex—and Burgess, somewhere behind him—is gulling us. The subsequent chapters follow Alex and his friends through an increasingly violent series of crimes as if asking the reader, *Do you still find this funny?* It is a confidence game, in which Alex gets readers on his side and then exploits their sympathies. The narrative arc of this night of crime culminates with the gang invading, at random, the suburban home of F. Alexander, the writer of *A Clockwork Orange*. After thoroughly beating the writer, the teenagers pinion him and force him to watch while the four gang-rape his wife. Later, when he meets a "reformed" Alex, F. Alexander will reveal that his wife has died from the trauma of the attack. Alex's narrative voice changes little from one scene to the next, and his representation of the home invasion is as bemused and as lacking in sentiment as the rest of his account. Yet the reader is no longer laughing, for the crime in this case is entirely abhorrent. We are, at last, disgusted by Alex.

This brutal crime writes large the gap between Alex's sardonic, witty narrative and the trauma that he inflicts on his victims.

The rape scene with which the night ends ought to make us reconsider everything that has come before and to recognize that Alex has cast his crimes into the language of slapstick in order to make us sympathize with him rather than with his victims. To borrow the title and thesis of Stanley Fish's seminal book on Milton's *Paradise Lost*, we are "surprised by sin." Fish argues that Milton portrays Satan as a tragic figure in order to lull the reader into sympathizing with him instead of with God; as a result, *Paradise Lost* produces in its reader the same sort of temptation and fall from grace that Adam and Eve suffered. Burgess employs a similar strategy, tapping into our willingness to laugh at violence and calling on us to sympathize with the aggressors rather than the victims. If we have grinned or chuckled at any of the earlier scenes of violence, the rape scene causes us to pass judgment not only on Alex and his droogs but on ourselves. We are surprised by our own inherent capacity to accept violence when it is presented to us in an unsentimental way.

Yet Alex and his friends, too, have stopped laughing by the end of the home invasion. Alex generally presents himself as inhabiting a world without consequences—one like that of the Three Stooges, where violence can be bandied about the way normal people toss off jokes and one-liners. Yet if Alex fully possesses such an unsentimental slapstick mentality, he ought not feel any pity or regret for what he has done. After the rape, however, the teenagers are disquieted: "Then there was like quiet and we were full of like hate, so we smashed what was left to be smashed—typewriter, lamp, chairs" (29). It is a telling line, one of the very rare instances in which Alex speaks of his own emotional state and that of his friends. The modifier "like," which appears before the words "quiet" and "hate," gives the impression that Alex is struggling to find words that will adequately describe his mood. Alex's "like" is a verbal tic, a stalling for time on the part of someone who is supremely confident in all matters except for those relating to his own inner life. The line is reminiscent of a phrase that William Faulkner's villainous Jason Compson uses several times in *The Sound and the Fury*. Faced with any situation that should elicit a sympathetic response, Jason reports that he feels "funny" (203). Talking to his sister Caddy at their father's funeral, for example, he thinks, "then I got to thinking about when we were little and one thing and another and I got to feeling funny again, kind of mad or something" (203). The man simply does not recognize in himself emotions other than amusement or anger. He is not "kind of mad" but rather full of grief and sadness and regret. Jason's fumbling for words shows how alien these emotions are to him. Like Jason, Alex's language becomes imprecise as he tries to describe inner rather than outer realities. At the end of the harrowing scene in the suburban home, Alex acknowledges—however obliquely—his own rage and regret. But he also acknowledges the destruction that he has brought to his victims. As he and his gang leave the house, Alex observes: "The writer veck and his zheena were not really there, bloody and torn and making noises. But they'd live" (29). This final line is a bare consolation and is not even true: F. Alexander later reveals that his wife died soon after the attack. In describing the couple as "not really there," Alex shows that he does still have some capacity to empathize with others. The image of the writer and his wife "bloody and torn and making noises" is one of a world of consequences, where violence takes a lasting toll on its victims.

Alex's slapstick treatment represents a great reversal of fortunes for the youth, for he spends the last third of the novel suffering at the hands of his former victims. When F. Alexander and his subversive friends discover Alex, for example, they recognize him as "a superb device . . . for the cause" (160). Alex will be a tool with which they can reveal the inhumanity of the totalitarian state. Ironically, these freedom fighters have no more regard for the youth's individuality and welfare than did the scientists who reprogrammed him. Taking him to a grim high-rise apartment block, they lock Alex into an apartment and blare classical music—the third symphony of Otto Skadelig—through the walls. The scientists who reprogrammed Alex took advantage of the youth's love of classical music, setting their violent films to classical accompaniment and hence rendering music itself a source of terrible pain for Alex. Locked in an upper-story apartment with classical music "blasting away" (165), Alex has little choice but to take the only exit available: He throws himself out the window. The novel therefore reaches its climax with a staple of slapstick: the pratfall. At the start of the twentieth century, when film was in its infancy, directors and cameramen realized that this new medium could be used not only to faithfully record the real world but to create illusions and tricks that seemed to break the rules governing the real world. A camera crew could throw a dummy from an upper-story window, for example, filming its long fall to the ground. They could then stop the camera and have an actor assume the position of the dummy. When the film is played back, a man seems to fall four or five stories, get to his feet, and dust himself off. Film gave us a world of violent actions without violent consequences, and the pratfall was one of many illusions that this new world offered.

The pratfall that Alex takes, on the other hand, does carry lasting consequences. He is laid up in the hospital, injured and no longer able to form words beyond a helpless "er er er" (167). Like the old man who was once his victim, Alex tries to make a series of elevated and indignant speeches but can only produce a comic babble. When he eventually recovers his speech, Alex finds that his appetite for violence has returned as well. Somehow, the great fall and the concomitant injuries have undone Alex's reprogramming. Agents of the state show him a series of pictures, and Alex gleefully recounts the violent thoughts with which each one fills him. As Alex puts it in the last line of the American edition, "I was cured all right" (175). *A Clockwork Orange* actually has two endings: The British edition carries a final, twenty-first chapter that Burgess's American publishers dropped. In this closing chapter, which Burgess insisted was central to an under-standing of the novel, Alex shows signs of making a conversion that is natural rather than forced. Disenchanted with gang life, he daydreams about being married and carries in his pocket a picture of a baby cut from a magazine. Reflecting on his violent past, Alex describes a child's windup toy and concludes, "Being young is like being one of these malenky machines" (190). Not only is Alex ready to put away the things of a child, but he is ready to admit that as a child he was a kind of thing. Whereas once his behavior was as automatic as that of a machine, now Alex has begun to make deliberate and individual choices about how best to live his life.

In choosing which of these two endings to consider definitive, one is really choosing between two definitions of comedy. Is the purpose of comedy simply to divert its audience by pointing out the inconsisten-cies of the world and of the audience's own response to the world? Or does comedy point these things out with an eye toward transforming them? The American version, in which Alex simply reverts to his old ways, suggests the former. But the underlying structure and method of Burgess's novel, as well as the more-hopeful ending included in the British version, insist that comedy is meant to be transformative. Throughout *A Clockwork Orange*, Burgess invokes the conventions of slapstick in order to challenge the reader's conditioned response to violence. Alex's narrative causes one first to laugh and then to inquire into the dark sources of that laughter. The final chapter extends this self-reflexive comic mode to Alex himself, so that it is not only the audience, but the clown, who will laugh his way back to humanity.

WORKS CITED

Bergson, Henri. "Laughter: An Essay on the Meaning of the Comic." *Comedy*. Ed. Wylie Sypher. Baltimore: Johns Hopkins University Press, 1956.

Burgess, Anthony. *A Clockwork Orange*. New York: Norton, 1962.

Fish, Stanley. *Surprised by Sin*. Cambridge: Harvard University Press, 1967.

ON DARK HUMOR IN LITERATURE

"The Comedy of Entropy:
The Contexts of Black Humour"
by Patrick O'Neill, in *Canadian Review of Comparative Literature* (1983)

INTRODUCTION

In his study of dark humor in literature, Patrick O'Neill defines the genre, covering a host of writers who employ what O'Neill refers to as "entropic" or "black" humor. While the term "black humor" is now seen by some to be a pejorative, O'Neill, writing in the early 1980s, uses the term to describe dark or "gallows" humor, citing key studies on the subject and arguing that dark humor "allows us to envisage the faceless-ness of the void and yet be able to laugh rather than despair. Entropic humour, which in the end is seen to be simply an intensification of the disturbing dynamics common to all humour, comes in many shapes and forms, and our laughter may contain many degrees of bitterness and hollowness, mirthlessness and parody and pain, but in the end—we do laugh, and while we laugh there's hope."

O'Neill, Patrick. "The Comedy of Entropy: The Contexts of Black Humour." *Canadian Review of Comparative Literature* 10.2 (June 1983): 145–166.

Though 'black humour' is a phrase which nowadays crops up fairly frequently in casual conversation as well as in literary criticism, there is no general agreement as to what exactly black humour is. This is, of course, hardly surprising, since there is no general agreement either as to what humour is, though most people are convinced that they know it when they meet with it. Since Plato's day, and doubtless before, there have been theories of humour, laughter, and the comic at first from the poets and philosophers, then, from the beginning of this century, from the sociologists and psychologists, neurophysiologists and semioticians. A recent international conference on humour—held in Wales in 1976—drew almost one hundred separate papers, mostly from psychologists; a bibliography printed with the proceedings, covering only selected material in English, ran to 1,500 items, and all concerned were agreed that research into the nature of humour, after a full two millennia, was still in its infancy.[1] Perhaps the most striking symptom of this infancy is the continued lack of any generally accepted taxonomy of humour though there are those psychologists and literary critics, of course, who argue that the whole area is essentially unclassifiable.

The concept of 'black' humour is an area in which there has been an upsurge of interest, especially in North America, in the last two decades or so, and here too the lack of an agreed terminology has been apparent. Different writers use the term to mean humour which is variously grotesque, gallows, macabre, sick, pornographic, scatological, cosmic, ironic, satirical, absurd, or any combination of these. There are those who would limit its application as a literary term to a particular decade in a particular country; there are those who would use it typologically as an inherent trait of human nature; there are those who claim that in its highest form it is not a species of humour at all; and there are those who would suggest that all humour is at bottom black. Standard dictionaries and encyclopedias offer little help: most of them simply do not include the term 'black humour.' The 1975 edition of the *New Columbia Encyclopedia*, one of the very few exceptions, defines it as 'grotesque or morbid humour used to express the absurdity, insensitivity, paradox, and cruelty of the modern world' and refers the reader for examples to the work of Stanley Kubrick and Jules Feiffer, Kurt Vonnegut, Thomas Pynchon, John Barth, Joseph Heller, and Philip Roth—all of them, we notice, writing in the sixties, and all Americans, as if the phenomenon were of local and recent vintage. Ungar's *Encyclopedia of World Literature in the 20th Century*, in the same year, confirms this impression by using the term exclusively as a label for the work of certain American writers of fiction during the sixties.

Turning to French, where the phrase 'humour noir,' as we shall see, has a longer ancestry than its English equivalent, we find in the *Grand Larousse de la langue française* that 'humour noir' is that form of humour which, using cruelty, bitterness, and sometimes despair, underlines the absurdity of the world—neither necessarily modern nor American, we notice. The 1972 edition of Harrap's *New Standard French and English Dictionary*, incidentally, translates 'humour noir' more laconically, giving the primary meaning as 'sick humour' and only a secondary meaning as 'bitter, sardonic humour.' None of the standard Spanish, Italian, or German works consulted yielded anything at all, with the one exception of the 1969 edition of Gero von Wilpert's *Sachwörterbuch der Literatur,* which explains 'schwarzer Humor' as a new name for what it calls a completely traditional form of 'humorloser Scherz,' a joke without humour, characterized by 'absurd terror, horrible comicry, macabre ridiculousness, dark grotesquerie, and crass cynicism, achieving its comic (but not humorous) effect primarily through exaggeration.'

Of our four definitions, then, the American is specific as to time and place. The French and German on the other hand regard the phenomenon as typological, although the German definition differs in denying the humour-content of the concept and in a definitely censorious approach, which is perhaps echoed in the British Harrap's definition of 'humour noir' as 'sick,' an equivalence which seems to correspond to the most general usage of the term in the English-speaking world. To add an historical dimension at this point, the *OED* records seventeenth- and eighteenth-century occurrences of the phrase 'black humour' as referring to 'black choler' or melancholy, also known as 'black bile' in the medieval theory of physiological humours. Even ignoring the obvious possibility of linguistic confusion between black humour and 'ethnically' black literature, we thus have a range of meanings from the medical and psychological to the dual application in literary criticism as either a period label or a stylistic device.

* * *

In North America black humour as a literary concept first attracted widespread attention as the result of the publication in

1965 of a mass-market paperback entitled, simply, *Black Humor*. The volume comprised a collection of thirteen heterogeneous pieces of fiction from writers as different as J.P. Donleavy, Edward Albee, Joseph Heller, Thomas Pynchon, John Barth, Vladimir Nabokov, Bruce Jay Friedman, who was also the editor, and—a final odd bedfellow—Céline. Friedman is reluctant to define his conception of black humour, but suggests that what holds the collection together is a feeling of insecurity, of a 'fading line between fantasy and reality,' a sense of 'isolation and loneliness of a strange, frenzied new kind,' and above all the element of social satire in a world gone mad. A new 'chord of absurdity has been struck' in the sixties, wrote Friedman, and a 'new style of mutative behavior afoot, one that can only be dealt with by a new, one-foot-in-the-asylum style of fiction,' since the normal reaction of the satirist had of necessity been preempted by the daily newspapers. These writers of the new sensibility, says Friedman, move in 'darker waters somewhere out beyond satire.'[2]

Friedman, though he obviously sees black humour as a predominantly contemporary North American phenomenon, manages to have his cake and eat it too by including Céline and by suggesting that black humour 'has probably always been around, always will be around, under some name or other, as long as there are disguises to be peeled back, as long as there are thoughts no one else cares to think.'[3] The usefullness of this attitude is contested, however, in what is to date the fullest critical treatment of modern American black humour fiction, Max F. Schulz's *Black Humor Fiction of the Sixties* (1973), which insists that as a literary term 'black humour' should be restricted to a particular body of fiction produced in North America in the 1960's. Schulz, however, is not primarily interested in the concept of black humour; rather he is interested in those American writers of the sixties who for good reasons or bad have at one time or another been dubbed black humorists. He is unhappy with the term, avoids almost entirely the whole question of humour, and seems in fact rather to disapprove of his authors for having a 'somewhat limited vision capable of the specific aberrations of comedy, rather than the universal condition of tragedy.'[4]

The literary black humorist, for Schulz, is a post-existentialist for whom the condition of universal absurdity no longer needs to be demonstrated. All versions of reality are only mental constructs; no principle is necessarily truer than any other, morally or intellectually, and nothing has any intrinsic value. Life is a labyrinth, multiple, meaningless, and endless, and the black humorist reacts variously with such all-embracing encyclopedic endgames as John Barth's *Sot-weed Factor* or *Giles Goat-boy*, with the programmatic skepticism of a Kurt Vonnegut, or with the parody of all systems, as in Thomas Pynchon— or Jorge Luis Borges, who is allowed to join Friedman's resident aliens Nabokov and Céline as honorary members of the club.

But other non-American names immediately suggest themselves on the basis of Schulz's list of characteristics, and quickly explode any American claim to exclusive rights to the territory: what of Gabriel García Márquez and Julio Cortazar in Spanish, Gunter Grass and Thomas Bernhard in German, Italo Calvino in Italian, Raymond Queneau in French, and, above all perhaps, what about Beckett? All share the same detachment, the same irony, the same mocking apocalyptic tone, the same parodic undercutting of all system, the same one-dimensional characters, wasteland settings, disjunctive structure, and self-conscious delight in artistry—and above all they share one central characteristic: a refusal to treat what one might regard as tragic materials tragically, and this not as a cheap method of shocking or evoking irreverent laughter, but because the comic approach is for them clearly the only remaining approach that is artistically acceptable.

Both our American authors, then, regard literary black humour as essentially a post-existentialist, post-modernist, and almost exclusively American phenomenon. A very different approach is adopted by two European anthologists, separated by almost three decades, one French and one German: Andre Breton's *Anthologie de l'humour noir* of 1939 and, almost simultaneously with the Americans, Gerd Henninger's *Brevier des schwarzen Humors* of 1966.[5] In a preface to a new edition (also in 1966) of his 600-page anthology, Breton claims to have been the first to employ the term 'humour noir,' which, he says, did not exist before his coinage. He casts a very wide net over the whole of European literature since 1700 to include forty-five different authors in all, including Swift, the Marquis de Sade, de Quincey, Grabbe, Poe, Baudelaire, Lewis Carroll, Nietzsche, Rimbaud, Gide, Synge, Jarry, Apollinaire, Picasso, Kafka, Hans Arp, and Salvador Dali. The list, he implies, could be very much longer. The phenomenon of black humour, Breton further claims, has been growing in importance since 1800 to such a degree that, given the nature of modern sensibility, it is doubtful whether *any* contemporary work of poetry or art or even scientific, philosophical, or social theory can be completely valid without some hint of it,[6] that is to say, of a humour that is in almost all cases primarily subversive, a 'révolte supérieure de l'esprit,' as he calls it, disruptive of accepted values and systems, an aggressive weapon in most cases, in others more dearly a defensive strategy, in almost all cases containing a strongly satirical element, and in most cases having a subject matter which would normally be considered taboo. In terms of reader response—which, as a result of the nature of humour, is admittedly a highly unreliable guide here—the humour in some cases is of a type which would 'normally' give rise to bitter or ironic or sardonic laughter or amusement, in other cases it is of a more extreme type which produces less amusement than horror or disgust, and which I would like to examine more closely for a few moments.

A good example is Swift's *Modest Proposal* of 1729, which Breton, naming Swift the father of black humour, sets at the beginning of his collection and thus, to some extent, establishes the tone of what follows. The *Proposal* begins as an urbane and enlightened essay on the alleviation of the distress of the Catholic Irish poor, and without change of tone metamorphoses into the appallingly rational suggestion that serving the better nourished of the infants, properly cooked and seasoned, on the tables of the better classes would simultaneously provide an interesting change of fare for the latter and a source of honest income for the over-reproductive and destitute peasantry—many of whom, Swift adds, suddenly abandoning the urbane tone for one of slashing attack, would consider themselves better off if they too had been quickly cannibalized as children rather than slowly throughout their miserable lives. The enormous power of these seven or eight pages, however, does not depend primarily on any didactic satirical moral, but rather on the comic incongruity of blending the rationality of satire and the understatement of irony on the one hand with the irrationality and exaggeration of the grotesque on the other, the reformer's care for suffering humanity on the one hand with the guilty and perverse glee of savagely debasing that same humanity on the other.

Very much the same is true of many of the writings of the Marquis de Sade, which also owe their effect far less to their satire on Enlightenment belief in rationality and the innate goodness of man than they do to the grotesque energy and almost insane exaggeration and cumulation of sexual enormities and perversions. But to what degree, if at all, can this be seen as humorous? Is it not simply horrifying? Breton uses the 'Ogre of the Appenines' sequence from *Juliette* (1796), for example, where the Russian giant Minski eats cooked babies and has them served up to him on hot chafing dishes which burn into the naked haunches of the crouching young women who are constrained to serve as human tables. Distressingly, there is undoubtedly an element of the comic here, though any incipient comic reaction is immediately challenged and cancelled by a simultaneous feeling of revulsion such as is typically evoked by that form of the grotesque which stresses functional perversions of the human body. Such 'humour' as may be present for 'normal' readers is one of horrified incredulity and protest at the cruelty and debasement of the world portrayed, a world which belongs far more to the tragic than the comic realm—and yet has a deeply disturbing suggestion of the comic about it. Many of Kafka's stories too, one may add, such as 'In der Strafkolonie,' belong to this realm.[7]

Misanthropy, contempt, and loathing, perversely yoked with the comic, become the very yardstick of black humour in its highest manifestation for our German anthologist, Gerd Henninger. Developing and systematizing Breton's conception, Henninger claims that in its highest order black humour obliterates laughter altogether, or rather transmutes it into despair, and he cites as examples passages from the works of Swift and de Sade, Buchner and Poe, the *Nachtwachen des Bonaventura* and the visions of Lautréamont. Henninger has a greater theoretical interest in black humour than had Breton. Following the latter's introduction, he too uses the Freudian model of humour, which Freud had developed in 1905 in *Der Witz und seine Beziehung zum Unbewussten*. Freud had suggested that all humour is a defence mechanism against the deficiencies of life, a self-protective rechannelling by the superego of feelings of guilt, anxiety, fear, or terror into pleasure-producing form, analogous to dream-work or indeed artwork. Following Freud, Henninger sees black humour as a defence against horror, 'das Grauen,' and accounts for its psychological causes and effects in terms of the comic simultaneity of continued repression and playful revelation of guilt-producing aggression; this in turn produces feelings both of pleasure and renewed guilt; and this combination, says Henninger, constitutes what we call black humour.[8]

This is certainly plausible as far as it goes, especially for Henninger's archetypal black humorists, de Sade and Lautréamont. However, we

notice that from the thematic point of view Henninger's definition
rests squarely on the element of taboo, and is of extremely limited use,
for example, when we come to those writers of the American sixties
whom Schulz calls black humorists, Barth, Vonnegut, Pynchon, and
so on, or those other writers whom we might add to his grouping:
Beckett, Grass, García Márquez, and so on. Moreover, while these
later writers are universally agreed to be comic writers, funny, mirth-
provoking, those writers whom both Breton and Henninger regard as
classical black humorists tend to evoke horror rather than mirth. Is the
term 'black humour' then, we may ask, simply not elastic enough to
include writers as diverse as Swift and Nabokov, de Sade and Borges,
Lewis Carroll and Kafka? Is it indeed too clumsy to be of any real use
to criticism, as has been variously suggested?[9] Can we even distinguish
when humour is black and when otherwise? Henninger's definition
of black humour, after all, is different from Freud's definition of all
humour only in degree, not in kind. To attempt an answer to these
questions, and to suggest a foundation for our synthetic model of
black humour, let us turn briefly to some of the better-known theories
of humour.[10]

There are some very few theorists who regard humour and laughter
as being a benign instinct of human beings, primarily amiable and
genial in nature. The majority view, however, as is well known, contests
this, and regards laughter as primarily derisive, a vestige of snarling
attack and the whoop of victory—I believe it was Darwin who said
that the smile is simply a socially acceptable way of showing our teeth.
Biblical laughter is predominantly born of scorn and mockery. The
earliest recorded reference to laughter in the Classics appears to be
that of the Olympians mocking the hobbling gait of the lame Hepha-
estus. In early medieval Ireland a good satire could raise blisters on
the face of its victim and shame him into suicide or exile. Plato held
humour to arise from delight in the suffering of others; Aristotle felt
that the humorous is to be found in some defect, deformity, or ugliness in another; Cicero thought mental affliction to be a prime source
of laughter. Sixteen centuries later Hobbes in his *Leviathan* of 1651
still defined laughter as a kind of 'sudden glory' at the misfortune of
another, and even in our own century Bergson's *Le Rire* of 1900 sees
humour essentially as a punishment inflicted on the unsocial or at least
as a castigation of stupidity. Even when laughter is seen to be primarily
a defensive rather than an aggressive attitude its origins are often felt

to lie in suffering and sorrow rather than joy. 'Man alone suffers so excruciatingly in the world that he was compelled to invent laughter,' says Nietzsche; 'And if I laugh at any mortal thing, 'tis that I may not weep,' says Byron; 'The secret source of humour is not joy but sorrow,' says Mark Twain. Not for nothing does Freud, as we have seen, lay primary stress on the deeply disturbing dynamics behind humour.

One might object here that the humour of the English-speaking world, at least, frequently tends rather towards the genial and amiable, gently tolerant of the foibles of others, recognizing ourselves in those we mock, affirming things as they are in spite of everything. But it is easy to forget that this benign type of humour seems by all accounts to be a very modern phenomenon. Some theorists cannot find it before 1789, few can find it before 1700: the dominant mode of the comic until the end of the seventeenth century at least was that of satire and abrasive wit—aggressive, derisive, and frequently savage. Such a lovable fool as Don Quijote, such a lovable rogue as Falstaff appear to have acquired their amiability mainly in the course of the nineteenth century: to seventeenth-century audiences they seem to have been merely a fool and merely a rogue, butts of comic ridicule as were the 'humorists' of Ben Jonson or Molière. Stuart Tave first coined the phrase 'amiable humour' in 1960,[11] demonstrating that the concept of humour underwent a radical revision in England during the eighteenth and early nineteenth centuries: the ridicule, raillery, and punitive satirical wit of the Restoration gradually lost place to good-natured and good-humoured portrayals of amiable 'originals,' whose peculiarities are no longer satirically instructive, but rather the objects of sympathy, delight, and love. The re-evaluation of Falstaff and Don Quijote was part of this general trend; so was the creation of such figures as Fielding's Parson Adams, Sterne's Uncle Toby, Goldsmith's Vicar of Wakefield, and Dickens's Mr. Pickwick.

The battle between the proponents of Hobbesian superiority and aggressive wit on the one hand and those who associated humour with philanthropy, sympathy, and pathos on the other raged throughout the eighteenth century, and by the beginning of the nineteenth century the new amiable, benign humour was regarded as the norm in England—and had spread to Germany too, mainly through Jean Paul Richter, who, as a disciple of Sterne, declared enthusiastically that benign humour was the Romantic form of the comic as opposed to the cold derision of Classical satire. Whether or not we agree with

Tave that humour in this sense was an historical event beginning around 1710 and ending around 1914,[12] there seems little doubt that derisive humour was the original stock, of which benign humour was merely a specialized offshoot, perhaps even a perversion, as argued by Ronald Knox in a classic paper.[13] Modern psychologists would concur here: Freud provided in his system for a rather grey area of benign or genial or 'harmless' humour, but, as a recent survey of humour theories points out, most subsequent psychoanalytic writers have either ignored or renounced a benign type of humour.[14] Is there something 'black' then after all, something darkly equivocal at the very root of all humour, however much we may have overlaid that fact with the patina of modern democratic and enlightened tolerance? Should we simply conclude that all humour is black humour?

As a philosophical and psychological problem such a suggestion is perhaps not without interest. As practical literary critics, however, we shall hardly be much further forward by simply diffusing the concept to its vanishing point. Nor do we achieve too much by taking the more cautious step of deciding with robust common sense that black humour is quite simply that type of humour which laughs at the 'blacker' sides of life only, at grief, despair, evil, or death, or at subjects protected by more specific taboo, such as rape, murder, suicide, mutilation, or insanity. Certainly such humour very frequently *is* 'black,' of course, in its comic treatment of serious or even tragic material, but it does not always strike us as being *equally* black, since the gamut may range from the cheerful mayhem of a television cartoon through the playful and often silly grotesquerie of Monty Python to the nightmare world of Kafka—which Kafka himself reportedly found hilarious[15]—or the appalling but still largely cartoon-like world of de Sade. Black humour in short cannot be defined in terms of its subject matter alone; it must be defined in terms of its mode of being, and here the existence of a gamut of what might popularly be thought of as black humour ranging from the frivolous to the terrifying provides us with a starting point for a contrastive definition, opposing black humour to other modes of humour, be they benignly understanding or derisively aggressive.

Both the benign and the derisive forms of humour are essentially self-congratulatory, self-reassuring, and spring from an ordered world of unimperilled values—the humour of those inside and safe rather than outside and lost. The world may indeed be threatening, but once the threat has been passed through the protective filter of humour we feel capable once again—even if only momentarily—of handling it and soldiering on. Both the benign and the derisive modes of humour essentially see the self optimistically as a controlling agent in an orderly world. They differ in their mode of expression in that benign humour is warm, tolerant, sympathetic, the humour of sensibility and sentiment, the humour, in a word, of unthreatened norms, while derisive humour is cold, intolerant, unsympathetic, the humour of rejection or correction, the humour of defended norms. They are alike however in that they are both expressions of the humour of certainty, the humour of cosmos. Black humour on the other hand contrasts with both of these in that it is the humour of lost norms, lost confidence, the humour of disorientation. Physicists express the tendency of closed systems to move from a state of order into one of total disorder in terms of the system's entropy: black humour, to coin a phrase, is the comedy of entropy.

Both Breton and Henninger, the only critics so far who have looked in any detail at the historical development of black humour as a literary form, see the eighteenth century as marking its emergence as a force in literature. One could quibble about this and set the date back to at least 1554 and the publication of *Lazarillo de Tormes*, which began the long-lasting tradition of the Spanish and then European picaresque novel. Nonetheless, the very fact that Swift and de Sade could write as they did in the age of Enlightenment, rationality, tolerance, and confidence is startling. It has been variously suggested that modern humour derives ultimately from the breakdown of the medieval world-picture and the consequent intensification of the sense of discrepancy between the real and the ideal. The sense of pessimism thus engendered, combined with the contrary thrust of Renaissance optimism, led, the argument runs, to the new psychological phenomenon of a sense of humour which was conceptual rather than physical, and which we find in varying tinctures in Rabelais, Cervantes, and Shakespeare.[16] Only when the gap between the real and the ideal began to be perceived as extreme, Henninger suggests, when humour began to be self-consciously aware of the futility of its own gestures towards the reconciliation of opposites, did black humour emerge, not any longer as a force of reconciliation, but as one of subversion, of defiance. This 'crisis of humour,' according to Henninger, though prefigured throughout literature in the case of individual writers, reached its fullest development during the eighteenth century, and black humour as a distinguishable literary current was born, as a fundamental criticism of human affairs, sprung from the new, exhilarating, and terrifying freedom of rational thought.[17]

The 'crisis of humour' can be seen as one expression of the larger crisis of the European consciousness in the early years of the eighteenth century as documented by Paul Hazard.[18] If Swift is the father of black humour, his contemporary Shaftesbury, by virtue of the seminal reevaluation of humour in his 'Essay on the freedom of wit and humour' of 1709, has claim to being the father of benign humour. That is to say that black humour and benign humour reached the surface of consciousness, so to speak, virtually simultaneously—Shaftesbury, by the way, detested Swift, whom he considered obscene, profane, and a false wit.[19] We can thus incorporate Henninger's theory of the emergence of black humour as a literary form into a more general theory by seeing it as only one aspect of a polarization of humour which was in its final stages by the eighteenth century: the literary emergence of black humour, tending towards the pornographic horrors of a de Sade, is counterbalanced by the emergence of benign humour, tending towards the joyous affirmation of the virtuous way by such bumbling but lovable characters as Uncle Toby or the Vicar of Wakefield. Both the benign and the black were thus latent in the humour whose dominant expression was derisive until the end of the seventeenth century, infrared and ultraviolet regions just beyond the edges of the narrow visible spectrum. Louis Cazamian has argued persuasively that the self-awareness of benign humour in the eighteenth century, and the subsequent flowering of consciousness of humour as a distinct instrument, came only with the finding of an individual name for the 'new' psychological phenomenon.[20] Black humour had to wait another two centuries before Breton, by assigning it an individual name, incorporated it in the known spectrum.

* * *

The next step towards a comprehensive definition of literary black humour, the comedy of entropy, is to attempt a conceptual model in terms of its range of expressive capability, proceeding from the position that entropic humour is based firstly on an essential incongruity—the comic treatment of material which resists comic treatment—and secondly on the evocation of a particular response, namely the reader's perception that this incongruity is the expression of a sense of disorientation rather than a frivolous desire to shock. Both aspects will remain crucial through the various phases of our model, though the response will vary in nature and intensity as the rendering of the central moves from the predominantly thematic towards the predominantly formal. Since humour of any sort is as much a question of perception as it is of expression, the role of the reader here is obviously crucial: the reevaluation of Falstaff and Don Quijote during the eighteenth and nineteenth centuries may serve as illustration.

If the reader will bear for the moment with some apparent mixing on the terminological level, we may say that the basic modes of articulation of entropic or black humour are five in number and we may call them the satiric, the ironic, the grotesque, the absurd, and the parodic. Samuel Beckett's novel *Watt* (1953) contains one strikingly appropriate definition of their interaction, although to my knowledge Beckett has never made use of the phrase 'black humour.' As Watt enters Mr. Knott's house he encounters the departing Arsène, who comments on 'the laughs that strictly speaking are not laughs, but modes of ululation . . . I mean the bitter, the hollow, and the mirthless.' These correspond, Arsène goes on, to

> successive excoriations of the understanding, and the passage from the one to the other is the passage from the lesser to the greater, from the lower to the higher, from the outer to the inner, from the matter to the form. The laugh that now is mirthless once was hollow, the laugh that once was hollow once was bitter. And the laugh that once was bitter? Eyewater, Mr. Watt, eyewater . . . The bitter laugh laughs at that which is not good, it is the ethical laugh. The hollow laugh laughs at that which is not true, it is the intellectual laugh . . . But the mirthless laugh is the dianoetic laugh . . . It is the laugh of laughs, the *risus purus*, the laugh laughing at the laugh, the beholding, the saluting of the highest joke, in a word the laugh that laughs—silence please—at that which is unhappy.[21]

Black humour of varying degrees of intensity may arise, as we have seen, from the employment of the grotesque as a stylistic device or of taboo materials as subject matter, but as a coherent literary form satire is the soil in which black humour takes root. Satire, though primarily an expression of derisive humour, reflects the spectrum of humour in its own spectrum, which extends from what we might call benign satire, firmly and tolerantly anchored in its own value-system, through derisive satire in the narrower sense, where the emphasis begins to shift from the didactic to the punitive, until finally we reach black or entropic satire, where disorder is seen to triumph over order. At the benign end of the spectrum satire is characterized by a firm belief in its own moral efficacy, by a confidence that the real can indeed be brought closer to the distant ideal. At the entropic end of the spectrum, however, we find an emphatic lack of belief in its own efficacy as an agent of moral education, and didactic confidence gives way to a fascinated vision of maximum entropy, total disorder. Here we have the gradations of Beckett's ethical laugh, directed against that which is not good, and at the black end of the scale we find, for example, Swift and de Sade. The submodes of the comic shade indistinguishably into each other, however, and both of these authors of course also employ the next and more intense of Arsène's 'modes of ululations,' the intellectual laugh, aimed at that which is not true, and characterized primarily by an ironic rather than a satiric vision, that is to say by a vision where moral militancy has given way to detached observation. Moreover, and to considerable effect, in both of these modes there is also a substantial interaction of what I am designating as the third mode of entropic comedy, namely the grotesque. While the grotesque and the satiric, however, both aggressive modes, work together compatibly, the unstable compound of the ironic and the grotesque is a modal conjunction whose volatility provides a formal generator of much of the sense of disjunction characteristic of entropic comedy.

Irony is a constant catalyst of black humour in that it regularly functions as a bridge between the comic and the tragic. Irony, like humour, is variously a literary device, a literary mode, and an existential mode, a way of looking at life. Like humour too it focuses on the discrepancy between the real and the ideal, and like humour it has traditionally been one of the chief devices of satire for this reason. Bergson schematically suggested that, while humour emphasizes the real, irony emphasizes the ideal, and satire attempts to bring them together. While humour points to the real, that is, and laughs, benignly or derisively, at its deficiencies, irony points to the gap separating the real from the ideal, and embodies that disjunction in the inauthentic discourse of ambiguity. As the gap widens, to the point where the real is perceived as no longer being true in Beckett's sense, that is to say no longer reconcilable to the ideal, irony responds less and less to the magnetic attraction of satire, more and more to that of the grotesque, and becomes in the process the dominant mode of entropic comedy in its own right—Frye, we remember, character-izes irony as the dominant mode of western literature over the last century.[22] In the process too, irony, so to speak, subverts itself in that it parallels the development of satire already suggested and becomes entropic in its turn, the disjunction of irony proper shading into the disjunction of the grotesque.

Genetically irony is the weapon of the wily underdog, the *eiron* of Greek-comedy who counters the exaggerations of the boastful *alazon* by the inverse strategy of sly understatement. Irony thus tends to be a finely honed instrument, a rapier rather than a bludgeon. The grotesque, on the other hand, operates precisely by exaggeration rather than understatement, by surprise rather than insinuation. Irony is intellectual and rational; the grotesque is emotional and irrational. Irony is genetically self-confident; the grotesque, to quote Wolfgang Kayser, whose book on the grotesque established its status as an aesthetic category in its own right, rather is 'the artistic expression of that estrangement and alienation which grips mankind when belief in a perfect and protective natural order is weakened or destroyed.'[23] Like the ironic, and like humour in general, the grotesque too is based on incongruity, but while the more self-assured forms of irony and humour emphasize the possible resolution of conflict and only gradu-ally become entropic, the grotesque always emphasizes the unresolved clash of incompatibles, and it is this primary incongruity in the very nature of the grotesque compounded by the secondary incongruity of combining the exaggeration of the grotesque and the understatement of irony which causes our simultaneous horror and exhilaration when we read Swift's *Modest Proposal* or Kafka's *Verwandlung* or Beckett's hilarious accounts of human misery.

The grotesque functions as our third mode of entropic comedy rather than as a group of formal devices primarily because it is always associated with some form of threat to the perceived autonomy of the individual self vis-à-vis the world. I believe that Philip Thomson is right when he says that it is precisely the element of *balanced* horror and comedy that defines the grotesque.[24] Lacking it, the grotesque shades off into either broad and harmless comedy or unadulterated horror. Whether the comedy or the horror prevails, however, is once again largely a matter of reader response. The grotesque, like irony, is a sort of no man's land between comedy and tragedy, as it is in a deeper sense between both of them and the absurd. Tragedy represents a world of order, where any infraction is summarily judged; comedy, in both its benign and derisive forms, also asserts the primacy of order; the grotesque represents the incursion of disorder, typically associated with physical abnormalities, deformations, and perversions. Though the grotesque may thus be used in a harmless or playful sense for ornamental purposes, as Rabelais and Sterne frequently do, for example, it is essentially a major mode of entropic comedy, an expression—like irony, however different they otherwise may be—of Beckett's intellectual laugh aimed at that which is not true. To quote Kayser once again, the grotesque is the opposite of the sublime in that the sublime guides our view towards the true and the good, while the grotesque points to the inhuman and the abyss.[25] Henninger, as we have noted, sees black humour as reaching its highest and most appropriate expression as it approaches ever closer to that abyss. I would argue, however, as Thomson does for the grotesque, that once the comic element disappears we have left the realm of black humour. One of the decisive factors in maintaining the element of comedy is precisely the interaction of the grotesque and the ironic modes that we find, for example, in the placid reasonableness of Swift's advocacy of cannibalism, or the detached interest with which Kafka observes Gregor Samsa's desperate attempts to roll out of bed. The sense of disorientation generated by the stylistic misalliance in such cases produces an exhilaration dependent upon the diametrically opposed nature of its two constituent principles.

The satiric mode of entropic comedy, as we have seen, unsuccessfully urges the necessity of reconciling the real and the ideal, while the ironic mode watches the gap become unbridgeable. The grotesque mode goes further in that it undermines the autonomy of the real, and by extension the validity of the guarantee implied by the notion of a linkage between real and ideal. The absurd mode, in turn, registers the disappearance of the ideal altogether, an event commemorated in modern times by Zarathustra's advertisement of the death of God, which simultaneously marks the achievement of self-awareness on the part of entropic humour. 'Wer auf den höchsten Berg steigt, der lacht über alle Trauer-Spiele und Trauer-Ernste,' proclaims Zarathustra. 'Das Lachen sprach ich heilig; ihr höheren Menschen, lernt mir—lachen.'[26] The absurd laugh is the 'risus purus ... the saluting of the highest joke,' the dianoetic laugh, as Beckett calls it, and in spite of its venerable pedigree reaching back to Ecclesiastes and Democritus of Abdera, it has never been as widely laughed as in the last half-century, and the humour of disorientation, though by no means peculiar to the last century, has never before been as widespread. Satire and irony cross the line dividing self-confident humour from black humour only in extremis; the grotesque is usually a form of black humour; the absurd finally, insofar as it is a comic rather than a tragic mode, is always an expression of black humour, and even in its tragic emphasis remains a fertile source of latent entropic humour. All the forms of black humour discussed so far, in short, tend ultimately towards the absurd, towards the dianoetic laugh. All that is left of our play of real and ideal is the gap in the centre, the yawn, the hiatus—the common root of these three variations on emptiness also informs a fourth: 'chaos.'

The dianoetic laugh has two registers, however, one transcending the other, though Beckett does not specifically distinguish them. These two registers are not mutually exclusive; indeed one always implies the other, and by differentiating between them we are able to extend our spectrum of humour a further step to the point where we can begin to see the spectrum curving back on itself. Our spectrum so far contains three varieties of humour, subdivided into two groups: on the one hand benign and derisive humour, on the other black or entropic humour. Benign and derisive humour combine to form a higher class in that they express together the humour of cosmos, benign humour characterized by unthreatened values and the celebration of order, derisive humour characterized by the sense of threatened values and the aggressive rejection of potential disorder. They are, in fact, the passive and active sides respectively of the comedy of cosmos. The comedy of entropy, of black humour, may usefully be seen in similar terms. On the passive side we have black humour in all its modes of expression discussed so far, characterized implicitly by the sense of values lost and the apparent acceptance of total disorder. On the active side we have a form of entropic humour which we may call 'metahumour,' characterized by the sense of values parodied and the transvaluation of 'modes of ululation' into the parodic and paradoxical celebration of entropy.

The term 'metahumour' is appropriate in this context not least in that it is usefully suggestive of a range of meaning corresponding to the gradations of Beckett's dianoetic laugh, 'the laugh laughing at the laugh,' a range which in terms of our model includes not only the absurd mode but also its deconstructive counterpart, the mode of entropic parody. In a broader sense, indeed, all black humour contains the seeds of metahumour in that by its nature it includes its own critique, but in the fullest sense metahumour finds expression in that form of entropic comedy which is highly self-conscious, self-reflexive, and essentially marked by parody, as in, for example, Borges' *Ficciones*, Nabokov's *Pale Fire*, Robbe-Grillet's *Maison de rendez-vous*, Calvino's *Cosmicomiche*, Handke's *Die Hornissen*. All of these, in their various ways, laugh the dianoetic laugh, but in each case it is not the passive laughter of simply acknowledging the existence of the 'highest joke,' it is an active laughter of connivance, of keeping up the joke, marked by an essential inauthenticity. This is the humour of parodic norms, flaunted fictivity, gratuitous constructs. Here, in the realm of the game, as satire gives way to parody, is Breton's 'révolte supérieure de l'esprit,' worked into iridescent counter-worlds beyond the dianoetic laugh. Metahumour in its full parodic sense is a play with paradox, self-deconstructive in that it is joyously affirmative though what it affirms is nothingness: for in these structurations of uncertainty we discover that the spectrum of humour is inscribed on a Möbius strip, circling back on itself until the celebration of entropy becomes a paradoxical celebration of order, cosmos regained, but through the looking glass.

The dissonance and schizophrenia of entropic humour have traditionally centred on borderland areas of the imagination: taboo and insanity, dream and fantasy, mirror-worlds at the lip of the abyss, realms of the hypothetical, the ostentatiously fictive or surrealist. Metahumour teases disorder into parodic order in its own borderland, in the play of re-creative fictivity. Parody and paradox are the mode of being of these narcissistic antiworlds, and in their play with chaos they emphasize precisely form, shapeliness, structuration in an exhilarated, euphoric flaunting of artifice.[27] Black humour is the humour of disorientation; metahumour is the humour of parodic re-orientation. Metahumour, one may add, finds pervasive expression in modern

narrative fiction, and coming to the latter by a different route Robert
Scholes classifies it as metafiction. The echo is appropriate, for this
is both self-parodic fiction and self-parodic humour, fiction about
fiction, humour about humour. Or, to put it in Alfred Jarry's terms,
metahumour is applied pataphysics.[28]

* * *

Is there any critical advantage in using an integrated concept of
black humour in the approach to appropriate texts? I believe there is,
and for corroboration one could point once again to the re-evaluation
of Shakespeare's humour or Cervantes' humour that took after the
theoretical recognition of benign humour in the eighteenth century.
The whole area of literary humour is still in need of comprehensive
mapping, and false signposts abound. In spite of the fact, for example,
that comedy has largely taken over the traditional role of tragedy in our
time, the tenacious view that tragedy is somehow a 'higher' genre than
comedy has by no means disappeared, and black humorists are regularly attacked on the basis of this and similar arguments. Our model
provides a useful tool in such a discussion in that it suggests a tradition and a context against which approaches as apparently different
as the satire of de Sade or Swift on the one hand and the parody of
Borges or Nabokov on the other may be seen to be correlative.

Some interesting large questions suggest themselves concerning
the extent and frontiers of the tradition of entropic comedy. One
of the largest would concern the degree to which twentieth-century
experimentalism is the product of an attitude which is best classifi-
able as entropic humour. Breton forecast the growing importance
of black humour as an attitude, and one only has to turn to our
dominant modern faith, science, to see something of what he meant:
the terrifying and exhilarating world of sub-atomic particle physics,
antiworlds, time warps, black holes, cloning, microtechnology, and so
on is a world of pure black humour, as if invented by Flann O'Brien's
mad philosopher De Selby. For the modern writer, to quote Robbe-
Grillet, there is every reason to suppose that '"the improbable" and the
"true-to-type" are no longer remotely capable of serving as criteria.
Indeed, it is very much as if the *false*—that is to say the possible,
the impossible, the hypothesis, the lie, etc.—had become one of the
privileged themes' of modern writing.[29] Not all twentieth-century

experimentation, of course, is fuelled by black humour, but one could argue that large tracts of it certainly are.

In the lyric, for example, one could point to the development of the long tradition of nonsense verse. Nonsense, of course, is not always primarily an expression of the absurd: it can in fact reinforce our sense of superiority over the contingencies of logic and quotidian reality. There is always a latent suggestion of the absurd, however, and as the suggestion becomes stronger we find absurd forms evolving to mirror thematic absurdity, as we see in the contrast of, say, Lewis Carroll or Edward Lear or Christian Morgenstern on the one hand and Dada or the Surrealism of the twenties on the other. In the theatre, what Martin Esslin dubbed the Theatre of the Absurd is clearly enough the major expression of black humour. There were antecedents, of course, notably in the *commedia dell'arte*, in some Shakespearean scenes, especially in *King Lear* and *Hamlet*, for example, and in the grotesque piling up of corpses in the final scenes of certain Jacobean dramas. But while we are frequently jolted by thematic incongruities in such earlier 'dark comedies,'[30] it is only in the Theatre of the Absurd, as Esslin has shown, that we find the refusal to treat tragic materials tragically adequately reflected by formal devices which show us absurdity rather than telling us about it. In fiction the situation is similar. Robert Scholes sees modern black humour fiction as deriving ultimately from the satirical fantasies of the eighteenth century and the picaresque fiction of the sixteenth and seventeenth centuries, and one could push its origins further back to medieval and Renaissance jestbooks and the Classical tradition of what Frye calls Menippean satire. Black humour, however, is only one of many strands, and frequently a relatively unimportant one, in these antecedents; as in the lyric and the theatre the formal consequences of the increasing sway of black humour become most apparent in the twentieth century. As the Theatre of the Absurd of the fifties drew on the formal resources of Surrealism, so it contributes in turn to the major emergence of black humour fiction in the sixties, though the way had already been paved as early as the thirties by Beckett and Raymond Queneau, Flann O'Brien and Alfred Döblin.[31]

We can take modern fiction as a more specific test of the applicability of the model, bearing in mind, of course, that not all texts classified as black humour fiction necessarily demonstrate their blackness or their humour in every sentence, any more than one would expect every phrase of a stage comedy to be relentlessly comic. In one text black humour will flare episodically, while in another it will smoulder pervasively. Thus Lautréamont's *Chants de Maldoror* is black from start to finish; so is Grass's *Blechtrommel* though in an entirely different register; García Márquez's *Cien anos de soledad* is so in large part; Nabokov's *Pale Fire* thematically hardly at all at first blush but essentially so in that its essence is disorientation and its expression the perfect mirror. The mirror is a highly polished one here, as it is also in Robbe-Grillers *Maison de rendez-vous*, for example; but less brilliant reflections can be equally effective, as in Heller's *Catch-22* or even the Alice books.

Central disorientation finds expression in such thematic areas as the portrayal of the existential labyrinth (Borges, Grass), with such sub-motifs as solitude (Beckett, García Márquez), circularity and stasis (Beckett, Queneau's *Le Chiendent*), entropy (Pynchon). The present is a waste land (*Catch-22*), a technetronic desert (Pynchon); the past is an historical nightmare (Grass, García Márquez, Queneau, Döblin's *Babylonische Wandrung*); the future appears in terms of comic dystopia (Burgess's *Clockwork Orange*) or of comic apocalypse (Vonnegut's *Cat's Cradle*). Central to the vision of the black humorist is the epistemological dilemma of the impotent, imploded self: Beckett's *Murphy*, Cortazar's *Rayuela*, Thomas Bernhard's *Das Kalkwerk*. Formally the self-consuming metahumorous construct is probably the most striking example of modern fictional black humour; others would include the devaluation of plot and character, and the whole area of parodic linguistic experiment, whether as the polyvalent nonsense of the Jabberwocky or *Finnegans Wake* or Arno Schmidt's *Zettels Traum* or as the linguistic 'baffle' deliberately obstructing the reader in *Le Chiendent* or *Clockwork Orange*.

In terms of our articulatory model one finds such works as *Catch-22*, *Die Blechtrommel*, and *Clockwork Orange* marked predominantly by black humour in the form of satire; the works of Borges and Pynchon are marked rather by irony; Döblin's *Babylonische Wandrung* as well as most of Kafka's works are marked by the grotesque; those of Beckett and Cortazar by the absurd; those of Nabokov, Robbe-Grillet, and Calvino by parody. These pedantic distinctions refer, of course, only to predominant emphases: literature rarely sleeps in such Procrustean beds. Awareness of a coherent tradition of black humour and its modal articulation, however, *can* suggest useful and interesting class relationships, and even on the level of the individual text this awareness can lead to fresh angles of vision, as when, for example, we look at Kafka's *Verwandlung* as one of a class that also includes not only *Murphy* and *Rayuela* but also *Pale Fire*.

One concluding point needs to be made. The scholarly analysis of humour smacks all too much of academic humourlessness, and we must not lose sight of what in the final analysis is the most important aspect of black humour as it is of all humour: it allows us to envisage the facelessness of the void and yet be able to laugh rather than despair. Entropic humour, which in the end is seen to be simply an intensification of the disturbing dynamics common to all humour, comes in many shapes and forms, and our laughter may contain many degrees of bitterness and hollowness, mirthlessness and parody and pain, but in the end—we do laugh, and while we laugh there's hope. The last century has seen the loss of belief in our selves, in our societies, and in our gods. The comedy of entropy accepts the absurd as its birth-right, and we are invited to share its descent to a no longer believed-in hell as well as its resurrection towards a nonexistent heaven. Laughing at oneself, indeed, may not necessarily be a sign of psychic good health—but we should not forget either that comedy, like tragedy, began its career as part of a fertility rite. The element of joy, of delight in language and design and structure, is everywhere apparent in modern literary black humour, born though it may be of despair and formlessness and silence. 'To become conscious of what is horrifying and to laugh at it,' wrote Ionesco, echoing Zarathustra, 'is to become master of that which is horrifying.[32] Or to put it another way, as Valéry is reported to have said once, Sisyphus goes on rolling his stone, but at least he ends up with a remarkable set of muscles. All humour, like all art and all literature, is Janus-faced, looking in one direction towards cosmos and in the other towards chaos. All humour, and *a fortiori* all literary humour, black or otherwise, must ultimately be affirmative of life and a celebration of the victory of the embattled spirit over the void. This is hardly a modern discovery: the Hindu sage knew it about twenty-two centuries ago when he wrote in the *Ramayana* that 'there are three things which are real: God, human folly, and laughter. Since the first two pass our comprehension, we must do what we can with the third.'[33]

NOTES

1. A.J. Chapman and H.C. Foot, eds., *It's a Funny Thing, Humour* (Oxford: Pergamon 1911).
2. Bruce Jay Friedman, ed., *Black Humor* (New York: Bantam 1965) viii-x.
3. Ibid., xi. For a similar opinion see Douglas M. Davis. *The World of Black Humor* (New York: Dutton 1967).
4. Max F. Schulz, *Black Humor Fiction of the Sixties* (Athens: Ohio University Press 1973) 11.
5. Cristóbal Serra's *Antologia del humor negro español* (Barcelona: Tusquets 1976) will not be discussed here since it essentially follows Breton in its conception of black humour—though it extends the tradition backwards in time to include *Lazarillo de Tormes* as well as Cervantes, Quevedo, and Gracián.
6. André Breton, *Anthologie de l'humour noir* (Paris: J.J. Pauvert 1939; 3rd ed. 1966) 12.
7. Northrop Frye's theory of mythos would place these in the sixth phase of satire/irony, that is to say on the very border of tragedy. Cf. *Anatomy of Criticism* (1957; New York: Atheneum 1966) 238. Though Frye does not use the term 'black humour,' he would seem to locate its typical thematic expressions in the first three phases of satire (ibid., 226–34)—but ultimately, since all of reality is grist to the mill of humour it cannot be broken on Frye's mythical wheel.
8. Gerd Henninger, *Brevier des schwarzen Humors* (Munich: dtv 1966) 5–13; see also his 'Zur Genealogie des schwarzen Humors,' *Neue Deutsche Hefte* 13, 2 (1966) 18–34, especially 19–22.
9. For example, Robert Scholes, *Fabulation and Metafiction* (New Haven: Yale University Press 1979) 142.
10. For a useful recent survey of humour theories see J.H. Goldstein and P.E. McGhee, eds., *The Psychology of Humor* (New York: Academic Press 1972).
11. Stuart Tave, *The Amiable Humorist: A Study in the Comic Theory of Criticism of the Eighteenth and Early Nineteenth Centuries* (Chicago: University of Chicago Press 1960)
12. Ibid, ix.

13. Ronald A. Knox. 'On Humour and Satire,' from Ronald Paulson, ed. *Essays in Satire* (1928), rpt. in *Satire: Modern Essays in Criticism* (Englewood Cliffs, N.J.: Prentice-Hall 1971) 52–65.

14. Goldstein and McGhee, 20.

15. See Max Brod, *Franz Kafka: A Biography* (New York: Schocken 1968) 178.

16. Cf. Louis Cazamian, *The Development of English Humor* (Durham, N.C.: Duke University Press 1952). See also Luigi Pirandello's *L'umorismo* (1908), translated by Antonio Illiano and Daniel P. Testa as *On Humor* (Chapel Hill, N.C.: University of North Carolina Press 1974), and Ferdinand Baldensperger, 'Les Definition de l'humour,' in his *Etudes d'histoire littéraire* (Paris 1907) 176–222.

17. Henninger (fn 8) 'Zur Genealogie . . . ,' 17

18. Paul Hazard, *La Crise de la conscience européenne*, 1680–1715 (Paris: Boivin 1935).

19. Tave, 37.

20. Cazamian, 103.

21. Samuel Beckett, *Watt* (New York: Grove Press 1959) 48.

22. Frye, 35.

23. Wolfgang Kayser, *Das Groteske* (1957); trans. Ulrich Weisstein, *The Grotesque in Art and Literature* (New York: McGraw-Hill 1963) 188.

24. Philip Thomson, *The Grotesque.* The Critical Idiom, 24 (London, Methuen 1972) 21.

25. Kayser, 58.

26. Friedrich Nietzche, *Also sprach Zarathustra* (München: Goldmann n.d.) 33, 227.

27. The phrase is borrowed from Patricia Merivale's 'The Flaunting of Artifice in Vladimir Nabokov and Jorge Luis Borges,' in L.S. Dembo, ed., *Nabokov: The Man and his Work* (Madison: University of Wisconsin Press 1967) 209–24.

28. Alfred Jarry defined the concept of pataphysics in his *Gestes et opinions du docteur Faustroll* (posthumously published in 1911): 'La pataphysique est la science des solutions imaginaires, qui accorde symboliquement aux linéaments les propriétés des objets décrits par leur virtualité' *(Oeuvres complétes,* I, 217). Pataphysics in one sense is simply the power of the imagination, and its predominance in the modern black humour tradition would

seem to be adequate refutation of Johan Huizinga's suggestion in *Homo Ludens* (1944) of the atrophy of the play-element in twentieth-century art and literature.

29. Alain Robbe-Grillet, *Pour un nouveau roman* (Paris: Minuit 1963) 139–40; quoted in Vivian Mercier's *The New Novel from Queneau to Pinget* (New York: Farrar, Straus and Giroux 1971) 43.

30. J.L. Styan's *The Dark Comedy: The Development of Modern Comic Tragedy* (Cambridge: Cambridge University Press 1962) is a comprehensive survey.

31. One major developmental distinction between the Theatre of the Absurd and the black humour fiction of the next decade is that the former tended, as Esslin has shown, to devalue language, while in the latter, as Robert Scholes, for example, has shown in *Fabulation and Metafiction*, language is everywhere primary.

32. Eugène Ionesco, 'La Dèmystification par l'humour noir,' *Avant-Scène* (Paris), 15 February 1959; quoted by Martin Esslin, *The Theatre of the Absurd* (1961; Garden City: Anchor Books 1969) 158.

33. *The Ramayana*, trans. A. Menen (New York: Scribner 1954) 276; quoted Goldstein and McGhee, 191.

DIVINE COMEDY
(DANTE ALIGHIERI)

"Elements of Dark Humor in Dante's *Divine Comedy*"
by Lauren P. De La Vars,
St. Bonaventure University

The title of *The Divine Comedy* is a puzzle to modern readers who are unaware of how the term "comedy" has evolved over the centuries since Dante Alighieri wrote his masterpiece in the first decade of the 1300s. Dante's *The Divine Comedy* is a three-part work that recounts the poet's journey through Hell and Purgatory and his eventual arrival in Heaven. It is "divine" (an adjective applied to the *Comedy* not by Dante, but possibly first by Boccaccio, Dante's earliest biographer) because it takes place not in the ordinary human world but in the destinations of human souls after death: Hell, Purgatory, and Heaven (*Inferno, Purgatorio*, and *Paradiso*, in Dante's Italian). It is "comedy" because its plot trajectory is from misery, hatred, and discord to joy, love, and peace. For Dante, the truly comic is cosmic: *The Divine Comedy* is a comedy because it ends in transcendence, in the happiest possible way, with the protagonist experiencing the ineffable joy of oneness with the Divine.

Definitions of comedy derived from Greek and Roman literature stress the satiric, didactic, and ethical aspects of comedy, qualities directed toward the improvement of society. The comic catharsis is laughter, and the laughter is usually at the expense of a ridiculous or ludicrous character (L. Cowan 3). Readers and playgoers may be impelled to amend their own foolish behavior so that they will not provoke others' laughter.

As a medieval Christian, Dante had much different comic intentions. A surviving letter to an Italian patron named Can Grande della Scala shows us an early statement of Dante's purpose in *The Divine Comedy*. The letter expounds a distinctly medieval view of comedy. For medieval writers—and, indeed, for later Christian writers as well—a comic hero's progression from adversity to prosperity is the model of the pilgrim's progress toward God, through grace, from this fallen world to the celestial Paradise. As the protagonist, Dante the traveler learns and grows in knowledge and understanding as Virgil guides him through Hell and Purgatory and St. Bernard of Clairvaux and Beatrice guide him into Heaven and to God.

The letter to Can Grande states two reasons for Dante's work being defined as a comedy. First, it has a happy ending: indeed, its plot moves toward the greatest possible happiness. Secondly, it is written in Italian—the language of ordinary modern people—and not in Latin, the language of classical epic poetry like Virgil's *Æneid*. According to the letter to Can Grande, comedy

> differs from tragedy in its matter, in that tragedy is tranquil and conducive to wonder at the beginning, but foul and conducive to horror at the end, or catastrophe.... Comedy, on the other hand, introduces a situation of adversity, but ends its matter in prosperity.... Tragedy uses an elevated and sublime style, while comedy uses an unstudied and low style.... So from this it should be clear why the present work is called the *Comedy*. For, if we consider the matter, it is, at the beginning, that is, in Hell, foul and conducive to horror, but at the end, in Paradise, prosperous, conducive to pleasure, and welcome. And if we consider the manner of speaking, it is unstudied and low, since its speech is the vernacular, in which even women communicate. (Dante, "Letter" 100–101)

Commentators on Dante's masterwork have agreed with its assignment to the comic mode, even if its genre often seems more epic (Haller xxxvi). Literary critic Louise Cowan argues that the three locations of *The Divine Comedy* "represent the three possible regions of the comic terrain" (11). If the *Paradiso*, with its final vision of the soul's loving union with God, depicts the *Comedy*'s perfect happy ending, then the *Inferno* and the *Purgatorio* show the wastelands that Dante must cross in his quest for meaning. Perversions of the comic spirit, bitter irony, and gallows humor abound in the *Inferno*. Dante's Hell, where malice and selfishness reign, is not a place for wholehearted laughter. Smiles of fellow feeling do occur in the *Purgatorio*, however, as in Canto 21, when Dante grins at Statius's effusive hero worship of Virgil. Later, Bernard's and Beatrice's beatific smiles in Paradise merge into what seems to Dante to be "the smile of the universe" in Canto 27. Dante's journey takes him from dark humor, the kind that finds its material in the worst traits of humanity, to the bright, light, open paradise of cosmic unity.

In the *Inferno*, Dante's darkest humor can be classified very generally into two types: Dante the poet's grim inventions of appropriate punishments for unrepentant sinners, and Dante the pilgrim's false steps as he learns to negotiate this alien milieu. Some of Dante's dark humor comes from his fondness for ironic juxtaposition: "Dante the storyteller is fond of using images that suggest cosiness [sic] and idyllic surroundings in order to illustrate horrible and tragic events" (Lagercrantz 13). Some also comes from his unsparing sarcasm about political corruption in his hometown of Florence. For instance, he begins Canto 26 in the thieves' section of Hell, thus: "Rejoice, O Florence, since you are so great that over sea and land you beat your wings, and your name is spread through Hell! Among the thieves I found five of your citizens, such that shame comes to me—and you rise thereby to no great honor" (26:1–3).

For many readers, the suitability of the punishments fitting the crimes (what Dante refers to as *contrapasso*, or retribution) is the most memorable feature of Dante's imaginative depiction of Hell. For instance, the aptness of Canto 20's fortunetellers having their heads twisted around for eternity (as punishment for having looked too far ahead in life) may give the reader a kind of grim satisfaction. Another appropriate punishment is the one meted out to adulterous Francesca da Rimini and her lover: being blown about forever in a strong wind that mirrors the wayward lust to which they gave themselves on Earth (Canto 5). Insincere flatterers have not only their noses caked brown with excrement but their bodies perpetually drenched in it. Dante recognizes someone he knows in the open sewer of Canto 18:

> I beheld one whose head was so befouled with ordure that it
> did not appear whether he was layman or cleric. He bawled

to me, "Why are you so greedy to look more at me than at the other filthy ones?" And I to him, "Because if I rightly recall, I have seen you before with your hair dry, and you are Alessio Interminei of Lucca. . . ." And he, then, beating his pate, "Down to this the flatteries wherewith my tongue was never cloyed have sunk me." (18:116–126)

Such precisely retributive justice is darkly humorous. The souls of suicides are condemned to spend eternity inhabiting trees, "for it is not just that a man have what he robs himself of" (13:105). Money-lenders who charged exorbitant rates of interest are frozen forever hunched over, as if counting their ill-gotten gains. Thieves have their entrails searched and plundered by snakes (Canto 24); one of them, Vanni Fucci, obstinate in his sin, makes an obscene (and ridiculously useless) gesture toward heaven as he curses God (Canto 25). Bertran de Born, who Dante believed had sowed discord between King Henry II of England and his son, should have been beheaded for treason in life. Now he roams the ninth ditch of Malebolge, the eighth circle of Hell: "a trunk without the head going along . . . and it was holding the severed head by the hair, swinging it in hand like a lantern, and it was gazing at us and saying: 'O me!'" (28:119–123).

The ironic appropriateness of another *contrapasso* is many-layered. Pope Nicholas III, a nepotist and simoniac, is being punished head down, stuck in a stone tube with only his calves and his flaming, kicking feet protruding (Canto 19). He is just one of many corrupt popes thus entombed. Everything about the situation is topsy-turvy. Popes, the heirs of the first pope, Peter (renamed by Jesus with a name that means "rock" in Greek), should be the solid bedrock of the church, not trapped within the bedrock of Hell. These simoniac popes, who used their power for personal worldly gain, are upside down to represent their willing inversion of God's moral order. Their intellects and talents should have been used for heavenly purposes but instead served their ignoble material desires. Instead of the glorious flame of the Holy Spirit descending on their heads, as had happened to Peter and the other apostles on Pentecost, these corrupt popes are tormented by the ghoulish flames scorching their feet (Scott 198–199).

As a living human being, the only one ever to visit Hell, Dante the traveler experiences a full range of human emotions while observing and interacting with the demons and sinners of Hell. He swings from outrage to sympathy, from utter terror to the pure relief of seeing the stars again at long last. Thomas G. Bergin inventories the wealth of the traveler's experience in the *Inferno*:

> Dante has seen one hundred and twenty-eight sinners specifically mentioned by name (not counting the vast armies of the unnamed) and has had conversations with thirty-seven of them. He has met thirty monsters and five hybrid creatures. He has had two boat rides; he has ridden a centaur and a winged dragon. He has twice fainted. He has been exposed to excessive heat, bitter cold, strong winds, fearful sights, terrifying sounds, and foul odors. To this catalogue of physical trials must be added a complete stock of emotional and psychological experiences. He has felt compassion, pity, scorn, resentment, anger, vindictiveness, courage, and even, once in a while, a touch of amusement. And all these emotions are superimposed on the constants of terror, wonder, and lively curiosity. (221)

Dante's emotional volatility adds to the wry humor, as Dante the storyteller comments on his own foibles and reports Virgil's occasional chidings. At first, Dante the traveler is too disoriented to do anything but faint from terror and blindly follow Virgil's lead. But he becomes involved emotionally with the condemned sinners, beginning with his sympathetic request in Canto 5 to hear Francesca's story. In Canto 8 his indignant response to the unrepentant Filippo Argenti elicits Virgil's praise. Filippo, bogged down in the swamp that harbors the wrathful, tries to board the travelers' boat, weeping crocodile tears about his plight. Virgil fends him off, and Dante, recognizing him from his earthly days, sputters, "I should like well to see him soused in this soup, before we quit the lake." Dante's vindictive wish is granted: "A little after this I saw such rending of him by the muddy folk that I still praise and thank God for it. All cried, 'At Filippo Argenti!'—and the irascible Florentine spirit turned on himself with his teeth" (8:52–54, 58–63). The bleakly comic effect is triple: first, that Dante, heretofore compassionate and sensitive, should explode in sudden anger at a condemned soul being punished for anger; next, that the serene Virgil should approve of his pupil's outburst; and last, that a condemned soul being punished for anger should become so angry that he starts to gnaw on himself with his own teeth.

Virgil likewise approves of Dante's 27 line Scripture-quoting tirade against Pope Nicholas III, the upside-down simoniac in Canto 19, and his response is to swoop Dante up in a warm hug. But Virgil reproves Dante for his open-mouthed interest in Canto 30's battle of insults between the counterfeiter Master Adam and the liar Sinon: "Now just you keep on looking a little more and I will quarrel with you!" (30:131–132). The gentle humor here resides in Dante's shame and embarrassment at being caught goggling and in the vehemence of Virgil's rebuke.

Dante was indebted to the medieval dramatic tradition of farce. Leo Spitzer calls Cantos 21 to 23 "a whimsical inclusion . . . a farcical interlude" (86). This particular section of Hell—the fifth ditch of Malebolge, the eighth circle—lends itself to a lighter touch than any other place in Hell. Its sinners are guilty of barratry, the crime of political graft, or embezzlement, or the illicit bartering of public offices. Barratry is not exactly a funny sin. Certainly it impoverishes governments and their citizens. But it is considerably less violent and less gruesome than many others Dante has already described or will describe, so this episode is a welcome reprieve from the otherwise unbroken horror of Dante and Virgil's descent through the circles of Hell.

Dante may well have been hypersensitive to charges of political corruption, as barratry was precisely the crime for which the Florentine government had condemned him to death. Had Dante wished to skewer his enemies, this would have been the perfect episode to do so: He could have savored the moment of plunging them into the boiling tar and exposing their crimes to his audience. Surely he had included other enemies, even those still living at the time of his writing, in other circles of Hell. But he resisted the temptation to personalize any vendetta in this episode, for he had a different, comic goal in mind (Spitzer, 86–87, n. 5): to remind readers of God's omnipotence even in Hell. Hell's demons, as terrifying as they may seem, are ultimately ineffectual and can thus be laughed at.

The devils in this scene are depicted as oafish, comic villains whose mischief backfires. In medieval Christian drama, the devil "is regularly represented as a comic character, precisely because he is conquered in principle by the Good" (Spitzer 87). These elemental fiends, called the Malebranche ("evil claws"), have ludicrous nicknames that resist easy translation into English, but here are approximations, some by Dorothy L. Sayers: Badtail, Crinklebeard, Grizzly, Hellkin, Deaddog, Pigtusk, Dragonsnort, Catclaw, Cramper, and Crazyred (Gallagher 45).

This fifth ditch of Malebolge is filled with thick, acrid tar at a rolling boil. It is guarded by a squad of black gargoyle devils who use their pitchforks to poke the barrators back down under: "Just so[,] cooks make their scullions plunge the meat down into the cauldron with their forks, that it may not float" (21:55–57).

Dante the traveler's impulse in these cantos is to flee, not just because the devils are evil but because they are rude and crude. Because his and Virgil's visit are ordained by God, he knows that they are safe from physical torture. Nevertheless, as Spitzer comments, "it seems clear that he is experiencing a real terror of the defiling contact of vulgarity" (86). Dante's squeamish stiffness is that of the prude who cannot escape from the gross humor of the farcical situation into which he has been thrown. He and Virgil are the unwilling straightmen in this slapstick routine. Sticky tar that adheres to everything it contacts is an excellent metaphor for Hell's contaminating touch.

Virgil assures him that he has dealt with these fiends before and he knows how to handle them. Reminding them that he is in Hell by God's will, Virgil secures safe passage through the ditch with an escort of 10 devils for himself and Dante. Dante reports with comic understatement, "I drew near to my leader, pressing in close to him, and did not turn my eyes from their looks, which were not good" (21: 97–99). One of the devils lowers his pitchfork at Dante, jesting that he will nick him in the bottom. Dante protests feebly that he would rather not have any such escort, but Virgil reassures him and the contingent sets off for the exit with a vulgar "trumpet-blast" from the squad leader's rump. At this crude noise, Dante primly notes that he has never been subjected to such indecorousness anywhere in the world, not even among military troops or sailors.

As they make their way along the margin of the tar pit, one of the boiling sinners, a Spanish embezzler, eases his back up into the air to cool down for just a moment. He is seized by his sticky hair and dragged out by the Malebranche, who threaten to skin him and actually do puncture him with a tusk and tear off part of his arm with a grappling hook. The Spaniard's blasé reaction is comical: In the midst of being savaged by the demons, he casually glances at his mutilated arm and keeps on gossiping with Virgil and Dante about Italians who share his boiling tar bath.

The Spaniard promises to trick several Italians into surfacing for a chat, if only the Malebranche would back away from the edge for a moment. Duped, the demons step back. The Spaniard dives back in, away from their vengeful forks and hooks: Being boiled is preferable to being dismembered. Dante and Virgil scoot out of range, and the demons, cheated of their prey, wrangle among themselves. As Dante and Virgil savor their escape, they look back to see some of the demons fishing their mates out of the tar where they had fallen in the fray. The episode ends with Virgil and Dante in a most undignified position, clutching each other and sliding down a cliff as if it were a toboggan run, chased by the furious parboiled and tar-encrusted demons. The travelers are saved because the demons cannot leave their zone.

This episode of the fifth ditch of the Malebolge is the longest single episode in the *Inferno*. Obviously, Dante meant it and its grotesque humor to be a highlight of the journey through Hell, a farcical reminder of the limitations of evil. The Malebranche gargoyles are quarrelsome dolts, easily tricked, and just as imprisoned as their charges. Even their leader, Satan, the dark lord of Hell, is bound and impotent, frozen solid at Hell's center. God, not evil, rules the universe.

But why is there no dark humor in the *Purgatorio* or the *Paradiso*? Thomas G. Bergin notes the different modes of Dante the traveler's experience in the three parts of the *Divine Comedy*. In the *Inferno*, Dante is a "spectator . . . and the spectacles are memorable" (233). He feels a dizzying array of emotions, from revulsion to pity, for the lost souls he meets. He never identifies himself as their equal. He never engages them long in conversation. They "have after all only one thing to teach him" (233). In this disequilibrium is the potential for humor. With the denizens of Purgatory, though, Dante feels a sense of "Christian kinship" and a sense of participation in the aspirants' desire for Heaven. Additionally, the *contrapasso* undergone by souls in Purgatory is elective, not imposed. No dark or cynical humor is to be found in the situation of sinners earnestly and willingly undergoing suffering in order to reverse their sinful earthly predilections and achieve the bliss of Heaven. For instance, on the first terrace of Mount Purgatory Dante sees the formerly proud being humbled as they bend under heavy loads. Having ascended to the next terrace (where the formerly envious are punished for their jealous stares by having their eyes sewn shut), he is still troubled by the method chosen for the purgation of pride. Talking with Sapia of Siena, Dante the pilgrim winces to think of the heavy weight of stone he might bear in Purgatory after his own death, to atone for his own besetting sin of pride (13:136–138). He has identified himself as a future resident of Purgatory, the equal of those he meets. Any humor here is tinged with regret but is ultimately hopeful, not dark.

If the opposite of dark humor is bright humor, then bright humor, a dazzling, colorful, joyous "smile of the universe," is the prevailing mode of the *Paradiso*. "'Glory be the Father, to the Son, and to the Holy Spirit!' all Paradise began, so that the sweet song held me rapt. What I saw seemed to me a smile of the universe, so that my rapture entered both by hearing and by sight. O joy! O ineffable gladness! O life entire of love and of peace!" (27:1–8). The antithesis of the selfishness and malice that energize Hell is Dante's final vision of the light and love that power the universe (Canto 33).

WORKS CITED

Alighieri, Dante. *Inferno*. 1: Italian Text and Translation. *The Divine Comedy*. Trans. Charles S. Singleton. Bollingen Series LXXX. Princeton: Princeton UP, 1989.

———. "The Letter to Can Grande." *Literary Criticism of Dante Alighieri*. Trans. and ed. Robert S. Haller. Lincoln: U of Nebraska P, 1973. 95–111.

———. *Paradiso*. 1: Italian Text and Translation. *The Divine Comedy*. Trans. Charles S. Singleton. Bollingen Series LXXX. Princeton: Princeton UP, 1991.

———. *Purgatorio*. 1: Italian Text and Translation. *The Divine Comedy*. Trans. Charles S. Singleton. Bollingen Series LXXX. Princeton: Princeton UP, 1991.

Bergin, Thomas G. *Dante*. New York: Orion, 1965.

Cowan, Bainard. "Dante, Hegel, and the Comedy of History." *The Terrain of Comedy*. Ed. Louise Cowan. Dallas: Dallas Institute of Humanities and Culture, 1984. 89–109.

Cowan, Louise. "Introduction: The Comic Terrain." *The Terrain of Comedy*. Ed. Louise Cowan. Dallas: Dallas Institute of Humanities and Culture, 1984. 1–18.

Gallagher, Joseph. *To Hell and Back with Dante: A Modern Reader's Guide to* The
    Divine Comedy. Liguori, Missouri: Triumph Books, 1996.
Haller, Robert S. Introduction. *Literary Criticism of Dante Alighieri.* Trans. and
    ed. Robert S. Haller. Lincoln: U of Nebraska P, 1973. ix-xlvii.
Lagercrantz, Olof. *From Hell to Paradise: Dante and His Comedy.* New York:
    Washington Square, 1966.
Scott, John A. *Understanding Dante.* Notre Dame: U of Notre Dame P, 2004.
Spitzer, Leo. "The Farcical Elements in *Inferno*, Cantos XXI-XXIII." *Modern
    Language Notes* 59 (1944): 83–88.

THE DUMBWAITER
(HAROLD PINTER)

"When Farce Turns into Something Else: Harold Pinter's *The Dumb Waiter*"
by Scott Walters, University of North Carolina at Asheville

In 1958, London theater critic Irving Wardle fatefully referred to Harold Pinter's play *The Birthday Party* as a "comedy of menace," and the phrase stuck. Originally a subtitle to an otherwise forgotten play by David Campton that premiered the previous year, Wardle's (and Campton's) clever twist on the literary term "comedy of manners" sutured together two seemingly contradictory words to form, Frankenstein-monster-like, a composite idea that perfectly captured Pinter's world of nameless threat and quotidian absurdity. Pinter himself, in a phrase he would later try to dismiss as a joke but which attached itself to his work just as permanently as Wardle's literary tattoo, described his own plays as being about "the weasel under the cocktail cabinet." Like comedy of menace, it is an image made up of equal parts danger, ridiculousness, and middle-class domesticity. *The Dumb Waiter*, which Pinter wrote in 1957 a year before *The Birthday Party*, compresses those same elements into a one-act play that seems a cross between Samuel Beckett's *Waiting for Godot* (which premiered in England two years earlier) and an Abbott and Costello film.

Pinter's two central characters, the hitmen Ben and Gus, are often compared to Samuel Beckett's two tramps, Vladimir and Estragon, and at first glance the comparison seems apt. Yet for all the similarities between the characters' actions, the context in which they act is vastly different. While both resemble baggy-pants clowns following the tradition of comic duos like Laurel and Hardy, Abbott and Costello, or the British team Jewel and Warriss, the Beckett pair's antics are set against the backdrop of an uncaring, empty universe that pays no attention to them whatsoever, no matter what they do. Pinter's characters, on the other hand, exist within an actively hostile environment that hears everything they say and sees everything they do—and does so with malice. The danger is real, and it has real consequences.

From the first moments of *The Dumb Waiter*, long before Pinter reveals the criminal occupations of his central characters, the audience is encouraged to see Gus and Ben as clowns. The play begins with a wordless set piece, easily imagined as taking place within a Laurel and Hardy film, in which Gus establishes himself as the childlike "innocent" and Ben as the irritable "grown-up."

> GUS *ties his laces, rises, yawns, and begins to walk slowly to the door, left. He stops, looks down, and shakes his foot.*
>
> BEN *lowers his paper and watches him. GUS kneels and unties his shoe-lace and slowly takes off the shoe. He looks inside it and brings out a flattened matchbox. He shakes it and examines it. Their eyes meet. BEN rattles his paper and reads. GUS puts the matchbook in his pocket and bends down to put on his shoe. He ties his lace, with difficulty. BEN lowers his paper and watches him. GUS walks to the door, left, stops, and shakes his other foot. He kneels, unties his shoe-lace, and slowly takes off the shoe. He looks inside it and brings out a flattened cigarette packet. He shakes it and examines it. Their eyes meet. BEN rattles his paper and reads. GUS puts the packet in his pocket, bends down, puts on his shoe and ties the lace.*
>
> He wanders off, left.
>
> BEN *slams the paper down on the bed and glares after him. He picks up the paper and lies on his back, reading.* (85)

Pinter was an actor himself, one who appeared in many a farce, and the care with which he describes this silent sequence demonstrates an actor's understanding of what makes something work as comedy. The comedic "rule of three," for instance, which is the generally accepted notion that comic business should be repeated three times with the final repetition being a variation on the previous two, is explicitly followed as Gus checks his shoes and Ben reacts. One can sense the deliberate pace of this opening scene from the stage direction's short declarative sentences, metronome-like, a pace that is necessary both for comic effect and for the audience to have time at the beginning of the play to orient themselves to the characters. When the next sound that is heard is that of a lavatory chain being pulled "twice . . . but the lavatory does not flush," and then Gus re-enters "scratching his head," we know that the world into which we've entered is ruled by the God of Comedy, not of Tragedy.

This sense of absurdity continues as the dialogue begins and Ben, outraged by what he read in his newspaper, shares the "unbelievable" story of an 87-year-old man who was run over by a truck he crawled under as he attempted to cross the street during a traffic jam (86). Gus echoes Ben's incredulity and then leaves to pull the lavatory chain, unsuccessfully yet again, like some sort of comic punctuation. When he returns, the conversation turns to making tea and the nice crockery that "he's laid on," the first mention of the man who employs them. However, this topic is changed yet again by Ben's discovery of another "bloody ridiculous" story, this one of an 8-year-old girl who killed a cat and her 11-year-old brother who witnessed the killing and who Gus and Ben believe is the actual murderer, despite there being no evidence in the story to support their hypothesis (88). "What about that, eh?" Ben demands, slamming down the paper. "A kid of eleven killing a cat and blaming it on his little sister of eight! It's enough to—" and he picks the paper up, disgusted, and clearly on the look out for yet another shocking example of social degeneracy (88).

We come to recognize that these two men hanging about in a basement room, for reasons yet unclear, seem to be following a set pattern of behavior, as if they know their lines and their roles and are playing them flawlessly. It's patter, a comic routine. However, plays are rarely about days when nothing happens, and *The Dumb Waiter* is no exception.

Gus, who is the play's protagonist, has something on his mind, a question that he wants to ask Ben that keeps getting delayed, first by questions about the tea, then by the cat-killing newspaper article. When he finally does get Ben's attention by making a move "to the foot of BEN's bed," which is clearly a violation of standard operating procedure, Ben's irritated "What?" causes Gus to chicken out (88). "Have you noticed," he stammers, "the time that tank takes to fill?" One can imagine Ben blinking at Gus in disbelief as they discuss the "deficient ballcock" that is the likely culprit in the lavatory's flushing problem.

It isn't until after a discussion concerning a photograph of an unidentified cricket team and the lack of windows in the room they're in that Gus finally gets back to the question he wants to ask: "Don't you ever get a bit fed up?" It is a tentative question, somewhat timid, and yet Ben's reply shuts the door in Gus's face. "Fed up?" Ben asks incredulously. "What with?" The answer, according to the stage direction, is "Silence" (90). This is followed, as if in response, by the lavatory at last flushing offstage. One gets the sense that to Ben, Gus's question deserves such a response.

Nevertheless, Gus is not to be deterred. After a few more moments of small talk, he finally blurts out, "Eh, I've been meaning to ask you. . . . Why did you stop the car this morning in the middle of the road?" From Ben's careful non-answer, it is clear that he has been caught off guard and must proceed with caution. "You did stop, didn't you?" Gus insists, and his question, like his earlier one about being fed up, is met once again with silence. Yet Gus presses on, describing what he witnessed and concluding that it looked "like you were waiting for something." Ben instantly denies this hypothesis, only to contradict himself the next moment by saying, "We were too early" (92). After which he again clams up, leaving Gus to conjecture with what little information he has been given. Ben tries to change the subject to another newspaper outrage, but Gus refuses to be pulled back into his role and instead hints that another question is forthcoming.

Pinter eventually became famous for his pauses, and in the case of *The Dumb Waiter*, what remains unspoken is far more important than what has been said aloud. Between the lines of vaudeville patter one senses a shadow lurking beneath the surface, an uneasiness we detect in both characters' behavior. That Ben is hiding something becomes abundantly clear when Gus catches him in another contradiction. This time, Ben denies having been at a soccer game with Gus, only to unwittingly acknowledge his presence by arguing with him about the validity of a penalty at the end of the game. It isn't that the actual circumstances are important but rather that Ben at first denied a shared experience that he clearly remembered. Why? Gus's unspoken question echoes within the "pause" that follows Ben's slip-up. Something is wrong, and it seems as if Gus is doggedly trying to remind Ben of their shared history, their friendship. When he suggests that they see a game the next day, Ben "tonelessly" informs him, illogically, that every team is playing away (95).

It is at this moment—the moment when Ben has clearly established his inability to lie without getting caught—that something alarming happens: An envelope slides under the door into the room. Gus and Ben freeze in apprehension, uncertain how to proceed, and immediately they slip back into their roles as comic bunglers. Treating the envelope as if it were filled with explosives, Ben tells Gus to open it, and they find that it is filled with 12 matches. When Ben instructs Gus to "open the door and see if you can catch anyone outside," we get the first clue as to their real reason for being there: Gus "goes to his bed and brings a revolver from under the pillow" (96). A revolver! In an instant, everything in the play is retroactively transformed. Our comic bunglers reveal a more sinister side, and the environment, which heretofore had been unremarkable in the extreme, is suddenly filled with mystery and menace. By the time they finally look, there is no longer anyone in the hall, and the purpose of the envelope remains unexplained. As will be true throughout the play, neither Gus nor Ben discusses the significance of what has occurred. In fact, Gus pretends as if this were an everyday occurrence, indeed an especial convenience given that he lacks matches of his own. "Well," he announces casually, "they'll come in handy" (96).

With the arrival of the matches, and Gus's and Ben's comic reactions to them, the play shifts from nonchalant situation comedy to out-and-out farce. Farces, according to Albert Bermel, "share several family traits: unreality (some farcical actions don't quite lend themselves to explanation, even to dream interpretation), brutality, and objectivity." The brutality, however, is "unreal" (Bermel 22). What follows is the most-discussed scene in the play, one that starts the play's acceleration into brutal unreality:

> BEN: Go and light it.
> GUS: Light what?
> BEN: The kettle.
> GUS: You mean the gas.

BEN: Who does?

GUS: You do.

BEN: (*his eyes narrowing*) What do you mean, I mean the gas?

GUS: Well, that's what you mean, don't you? I mean the gas?

BEN: (*powerfully*) If I say go and light the kettle I mean go and light the kettle.

GUS: How can you light a kettle?

BEN: It's a figure of speech! Light the kettle! It's a figure of speech!

GUS: I've never heard it.

BEN: Light the kettle! It's common usage!

GUS: I think you've got it wrong.

BEN: (*menacing*) What do you mean?

GUS: They say put on the kettle.

BEN: (*taut*) Who says?

(*They stare at each other, breathing hard.*)

(*Deliberately.*) I have never in all my life heard anyone say put on the kettle.

GUS: I bet my mother used to say it.

BEN: Your mother? When did you last see your mother?

GUS: I don't know, about—

BEN: Well, what are you talking about your mother for?

(*They stare.*)

Gus, I'm not trying to be unreasonable. I'm just trying to point out something to you.

GUS: Yes, but—

BEN: Who's the senior partner here, me or you?

GUS: You.

BEN: I'm only looking after your interests, Gus. You've got to learn, mate.

GUS: Yes, but I've never heard—

BEN: (*vehemently*) Nobody says light the gas! What does the gas light?

GUS: What does the gas—?

BEN: (*grabbing him with two hands by the throat, at arm's length*) THE KETTLE, YOU FOOL!

(*GUS takes the hands from his throat.*)

GUS: All right, all right. (97–8)

From a comic standpoint, we have moved from Laurel and Hardy to the Three Stooges, from gentle absurdity to comic violence. So many clues label this short scene as farce. For instance, the "strangling" of Gus "at arm's length," which Pinter so explicitly describes, is ineffectual, physically awkward, and patently ridiculous. If you visualize that moment, or better yet get someone to help you stage it, its absurdity springs instantly to life. The straight-arm strangling is a broad comedy mainstay, as is the careful removal of Ben's hands from Gus's throat.

Similarly, the subject matter is trivial, and the intensity of Ben's reaction is completely out of proportion to what is at stake. The argument builds, with Ben going from speaking "powerfully" to "taut" to "vehemently" just before attacking Gus physically. With Gus's stubborn rejoinder, "I bet my mother used to say it," this argument between two dangerous hit men transforms into a playground scuffle between second-graders (96).

Despite its farcical appearance, however, there is a great deal at stake. As Pinter noted in an interview, Ben and Gus "deliberately go into this argument as an evasion of the issue. The issue being that they are both in fact frightened of their condition, of their situation, of their state" (quoted in Knowles 28). The deliberateness is most dramatically illustrated by a single detail that is easily missed in forward motion of the performance: Precisely three lines before the start of this argument over proper usage, Gus says about the appearance of the matches, "I can light the kettle now" (97). Not light the gas; light the kettle. Not only has Gus heard the contested phrase, but he has used it recently and in conversation with Ben himself, a fact that is never acknowledged. Furthermore, when the argument is over, Ben wearily tells Gus, "Put on the bloody kettle, for Christ's sake." After which the stage direction reads, "BEN goes to his bed, but, realizing what he has said, stops and half turns. They look at each other" (99).

These simple details, combined with Ben's previous bungled attempts at lying, should raise questions in the minds of the audience as to just what is going on. Was Gus deliberately baiting Ben? And was Ben doing the same to Gus? Forgotten, perhaps intentionally so, in this tussle over word usage is a much more disturbing question that remains unanswered: Who slid those matches under the door, and why? When Gus comes back from the kitchen, deadpanning that he has successfully lit "the stove," the arrival of the matches is never raised again (99). It is as if there has been an unspoken agreement to avoid that unsettling subject.

However, the routine has been broken, or at least Gus refuses to return to it. With increasing intensity, and despite Ben's angry command that he "stop wondering" (99), Gus begins asking inappropriate questions about the coming job: Who's it going to be? When is Wilson, their boss, going to arrive? Wilson owns this place, doesn't he? Gus starts wondering why nobody ever hears what they do and complains that Wilson sometimes doesn't even bother to show up. Ben continues to stonewall until suddenly Gus blurts out the subject of his real concern: "I've been thinking about the last one. . . . I was just thinking about that girl, that's all." What follows is one of the most casually grisly speeches in modern drama. Gus says,

> She wasn't much to look at, I know, but still. It was a mess, though, wasn't it? What a mess. Honest, I can't remember a mess like that one. They don't seem to hold together like men, women. A looser texture, like. Didn't she spread, eh? She didn't half spread. Kaw! But I've been meaning to ask you. Who clears up after we're gone? . . . (103)

Perhaps for the first time, Gus has expressed moral questions over his own and Ben's actions. As if on cue, Gus's musings are interrupted by the loud clatter of the dumb waiter behind them. At this moment, with the play threatening to tip over into disturbing seriousness, the appearance of a new "character" forces the action back into the realm of farce.

Bermel, in a segment of *Farce* he titles "The Object as Antagonist," writes that in farce "many objects acquire intelligence of a sort, they appear malevolent; they are out to get people" (Bermel 27). As if to acknowledge this concept, both Gus and Ben jump up and grab their revolvers, leveling them at the wall behind them. When they throw open the door of the dumb waiter, they discover it empty save for a note: an order of "Two braised steak and chips. Two sago puddings. Two teas without sugar" (103). The men are baffled. "That's a bit— that's a bit funny, isn't it?" Gus suggests. To which Ben responds, "No. It's not funny." They're both right.

In the sequence that follows, the two men try their best, like Charlie Chaplin working in the factory in *Modern Times*, to respond to the increasingly impossible demands of the dumb waiter as it arrives with ever more elaborate food orders. In farce, Bermel writes, "machines make trouble by opposing the human character [when] they go on working normally when it's important that they stop" (31). In this case, the dumb waiter is relentless. Desperate, Ben and Gus scamper to and fro, improbably filling the dumb waiter with the little snacks Gus brought with him for the job, shouting desperately up the chute what they are sending up. But they are finally defeated by the third order (the rule of three again): "Macaroni Pastitsio. Ormitha Macarounada" (108). It's hopeless. There is nothing that can be done. The philosopher Henri Bergson, in his classic essay "Laughter," writes that the "attitudes, gestures and movements of the human body are laughable in exact proportion as that body reminds us of a mere machine" (79). Both Ben and Gus have become machines, subservient to another machine. And they've just broken down.

However, a dumb waiter does not run independently; it requires someone at the other end to operate it, in the same way that matches do not suddenly appear under a door through their own power. "There are innumerable comedies," Bergson writes in describing a comic technique he calls the "dancing jack," in which "one of the characters thinks he is speaking and acting freely ... whereas, viewed from a certain standpoint, he appears to be a mere toy in the hands of another, who is playing with him" (111). Ben and Gus behave as if their life depends on pleasing an unidentified person at the other end of the dumb waiter, one who is clearly toying with them. What starts out laughable becomes frightening the more desperate the characters become.

When Gus discovers a speaking tube, the opportunity presents itself to finally communicate with the person upstairs. While Gus bluntly informs him that "the larder's bare," Ben grabs the tube and deferentially explains that "We sent up all we had" (111). The voice at the other end informs him that everything they sent up was spoiled; their efforts are unappreciated. However, as the conversation ends, Ben puts down the speaking tube and triumphantly announces, "You know what he said? Light the kettle! Not put on the kettle! Not light the gas! But light the kettle!" Ben has been redeemed—the powers that be are on his side (112).

Wearily, Ben insists on going through the instructions of how he and Gus are to kill their victims, even though they do it the same way every time. Billington notes the "double-act device of having one partner rehearse instructions which the other subtly misunderstands" (91), but in this case the misunderstanding is more serious than comic: Ben forgets to tell Gus to take out his gun. Gus is disturbed: "You've never missed that out before, you know that?" (116). When Ben has concluded, Gus asks, "What do we do if it's a girl?" "We do exactly the same," Ben responds. Gus "shivers" and exits (116).

When he returns, Gus has solved the mystery of who is upstairs: Wilson. And Gus is furious. "Well, what's he playing all these games for? What's he doing it for?" he demands. In response, the dumb waiter clatters down again with a final, one-word order: "Scampi" (118). Gus has had enough. "WE'VE NOTHING LEFT!" he shouts at the top of his voice into the speaking tube. They've given all they have.

Gus exits to the kitchen to get a drink of water, and in his absence the speaking tube whistles and Ben answers. He is informed by the voice that the victim has arrived and "will be coming straight away. The normal method to be employed . . . Sure, we're ready," Ben assures the unseen boss (120). At last, the killing that we've been waiting for throughout the play is about to happen.

"The conventional device for creating farcical instability," Bermel writes, "is a profusion of stage entrances and exits, swiftly executed" (33). In this play, there are two doors: one to the kitchen where Gus has gone, and the other to the outside through which the victim is to arrive. In a brilliant coup de theatre, Ben hangs up the speaking tube and goes to the door to the kitchen to call Gus. Suddenly, the other door "opens sharply. BEN turns, his revolver leveled at the door. GUS stumbles in. He is stripped of his jacket, waistcoat, tie, holster and revolver. He stops, body stooping, his arms at his sides. He raises his head and looks at BEN. A long silence. They stare at each other" (121). This is the final image of the play. Things are no longer funny.

"One of the clauses," Bermel writes, "in an unwritten contract between farceurs and their audiences used to state that the characters will . . . come out of their ordeals unscathed, because the audience must be permitted to laugh. When that clause was not honored," he concludes, "the play ceased to be farce—for the moment, at any rate—and turned into something else" (23).

That something else, one might suggest, is comedy of menace.

WORKS CITED

Bergson, Henri. "Laughter." 1901. In *Comedy: "An Essay on Comedy" by George Meredith; "Laughter" by Henri Bergson*. Ed. Wylie Sypher. Baltimore: Johns Hopkins University Press, 1980.

Bermel, Albert. *The Comprehensive and Definitive Account of Farce: One of the World's Funniest Art Forms*. New York: Simon and Schuster, 1982.

Billington, Michael. *The Life and Work of Harold Pinter*. London: Faber and Faber, 1996.

Knowles, Ronald. *Understanding Harold Pinter*. Columbia, S.C.: University of South Carolina Press, 1995.

Pinter, Harold. *The Caretaker and The Dumb Waiter; Two Plays*. Rev. New York: Grove Press, 1965.

The Stories of
Nikolai Gogol and *Lolita*
(Vladimir Nabokov)

"Observations on Black Humor
in Gogol and Nabokov"
by W. Woodin Rowe, in *The Slavic
and East European Journal* (1974)

Introduction

Indicating how "Nabokov and Gogol persistently, and often rather playfully, touch upon subjects generally considered improper, indelicate, even taboo," W. Woodwin Rowe argues that both writers employ dark humor in a similar fashion. For Rowe, "Such humor, by twisting or reversing generally accepted attitudes and values, tends to undermine the reader's world." Thus, dark humor enables both to comment upon the reality of the social world and the reality of the human condition.

Discussions of black humor or black comedy often feature the works of Vladimir Nabokov but rarely those of Nikolaj Gogol. For example, Max Schulz in "Toward a Definition of Black Humor"[1] refers to Nabokov repeatedly. No doubt one reason for neglect of Gogol is his relative unfamiliarity for English readers. Yet numerous effects of

---

Rowe, W. Woodin "Observations on Black Humor in Gogol and Nabokov." *The Slavic and East European Journal*. 18.4 (Winter 1974): 392–399.

dark humor produced by these two very different writers are strikingly similar, Nabokov's disclaimers notwithstanding.[2]

To begin with, both Nabokov and Gogol favor what I have elsewhere ("Gogolesque Reversals," 111–13) termed reversal words, and these are often darkly humorous. In Gogol's *The Government Inspector*, Dobčinskij makes a request to Xlestakov "regarding a certain very delicate circumstance."[3] His eldest son, he explains, was conceived before the marriage. But this was done just as "perfectly," he hastens to add, as if the marriage had already taken place. Now, having legalized the situation, he desires permission to call his "lawful" son "Dobčinskij." The dark humor of "perfectly" (does marriage render conception any more perfect?) seems enhanced by what we have learned earlier: Dobčinskij's belatedly legalized son may well be the judge's (p. 64). The "very delicate circumstance" is therefore doubly indelicate. In Nabokov's *Lolita*, Humbert refers to the girl as his "aging mistress."[4] Lolita is indeed aging (especially in view of Humbert's predilection for nymphets), but this description ironically reminds us how disturbingly young this mistress really is.

Doctors, sickness, and hospitals readily lend themselves to effects of dark humor; consider for instance the hospital scenes in Joseph Heller's *Catch 22* and the gynecologist lampoon in Southern and Hoffenberg's *Candy*. In *The Government Inspector* the patients at the hospital are said to be "getting well like flies" (p. 45). The implications are both humorous and disturbing. Not only do the flies reversely suggest "dying like," they also suggest unsanitary hospital conditions. Less playful is Nabokov's frequent depiction of outrageous attitudes of human beings toward one another. Scheming to have Lolita, Humbert imagines for Charlotte (in order to get her out of the way) "a nice Caesarean operation and other complications in a safe maternity ward" (p. 82). The words "nice" and "safe" reverse their meanings when considered from Charlotte's point of view.[5] With Gogol the effect occurs more playfully and less often. Špon'ka is told by his aunt that he, as a baby, almost soiled her dress, but "fortunately" she handed him to the nurse just in time (I, 295). Here "fortunately" reverses itself if we picture the plight of the nurse. When Kovalëv (in "The Nose") returns home after failing to place an ad in the newspaper, he finds his lackey Ivan lying on his back and spitting "rather successfully" at a spot on the ceiling (III, 64). Clearly, the word "successfully" reverses itself in context as gravity takes effect.

The last two examples focus on human excreta. Both Nabokov and Gogol repeatedly refer to corporeal functions. In result, the appetites, creations, and eliminations of the human body often seem uneasily animalistic. Coprological detail is typical. In Nabokov's *Despair*, Hermann discovers in the place where the tramp Felix had been "that pathetically impersonal trace which the unsophisticated wanderer is wont to leave under a bush: one large, straight, manly piece and a thinner one coiled over it" (p. 27). The word "manly" is oddly associated with thickness in this description, and moreover it appears just when man is, like an animal, detectable only by his trace. In *Pale Fire* Kinbote frequently employs "manly" to suggest homosexual activities. Evoking an interest between men, "manly" ironically reverses its customary meaning.

John Barth's Todd Andrews bursts out laughing when he sees himself making love in a large bedroom mirror. "Nothing," he writes, "to me, is so consistently, profoundly, earth-shakingly funny as we animals in the act of mating."[6] In Nabokov's *King, Queen, Knave*, Franz is said to lift up a strand of Martha's hair "with a nose-wrinkling horse-nuzzle."[7] The relationship between these two is purely physical, and the image of a nuzzling horse seems quite apt for amorous Franz. In Gogol's "The Carriage" Čertokuckij (awakened by his wife) lets out "a low mooing sound, like a calf emits when seeking with its muzzle the teats of its mother." He then mutters: "Mm ... Stretch out your little neck, sugar plum. I'll kiss you." (III, 187.) The amorous husband likened to a calf seeking its mother is not merely animalistic; the description also reminds us that a woman's body accommodates both her lover and her offspring. In *Dead Souls* Čičikov's carriage collides with another in chapter 5. Inside we see a golden-haired girl whose face is compared to a freshly laid egg (VI, 90). The idea of giving birth seems rather uneasily introduced here, although there is a certain logic, however unusual in context, in associating male–female relationships with giving birth and nursing.

In Gogol's "The Diary of a Madman," Popriščin's developing madness evinces a near logic which is strangely anticipatory. Dreaming of becoming an important person, he writes: "Just wait ... I'll yet be a colonel myself, and God willing perhaps something even higher" (III, 198). Later when he believes himself to be the King of Spain, these words acquire a rather biting irony, especially the phrase "God willing." Popriščin ingeniously construes his painful treatments at the insane asylum as quaint ceremonies honoring the new Spanish King. Nabokov has also treated insanity, with dark humor, as almost frighteningly logical. A favored manifestation of this is termed "referential mania," and it occurs most vividly in *The Defense* and in the short story "Signs and Symbols."

Both Nabokov and Gogol persistently feature taboo topics. *Ada* chronicles incest; *Lolita*, pedophilia. Humbert craftily describes an imaginary adultery to convince the nosy Farlows that Lolita is really his own daughter. She is allegedly the fruit of "a mad love affair" (p. 102) between him and Charlotte, so that after Charlotte's death it is perfectly proper for Lolita to live with Humbert. As he leaves to pick up Lolita at camp, Jean Farlow says, "Kiss your daughter for me" (p. 106).[8]

In Gogol's "The Soročincy Fair," we see Xavron'ja leading the priest's son to the hut where she is staying. At this point she is termed Solopij's "mistress." The term is of course apt, yet it also suggests Xavron'ja's intended relationship with another man. The taboo focus is intensified by the fact that her would-be lover is the priest's son. At the hut he mentions "offerings," adding that only from Xavron'ja can one receive truly delectable offerings. "Here are some offerings for you," answers Xavron'ja, "placing wooden bowls on the table and coyly buttoning up her apparently unintentionally unbuttoned blouse." She goes on to enumerate the doughy foods in the bowls (I, 122). The words "apparently unintentionally" of course suggest an intentional display. "Offerings" with reference to food for a priest's son is ironic. Moreover, before the doughy "offerings" are named the focus playfully shifts to Xavron'ja's revealing blouse. The priest's son then says that his heart craves for sweeter foods from Xavron'ja. When she feigns not to understand what food he has in mind, he replies: "Of your love."

The appetite for food is associated with sexual appetite also in *Lolita*. Near the town of Kasbeam, Humbert remarks that Lolita "craved for fresh fruits" (p. 214). He then goes into town to buy her some bananas while she stays at the motel and makes love with Quilty. In view of Lolita's relationship with Humbert the phrase "craved for fresh fruits" expands in meaning as we realize that she had planned to meet Quilty near Kasbeam. Indeed, Humbert seems to realize what has happened as he watches her eat one of the bananas (p. 217).

With both Nabokov and Gogol, the natural functions of the human body are seen in disharmony with social convention. Humbert describes Charlotte as follows: "Oh, she was very genteel: she said 'excuse me' whenever a slight burp interrupted her flowing speech" (p. 77). In *Dead Souls* we learn how "extremely precise and genteel in their words and expressions" the ladies of N are: "They never said, 'I blew my nose,' 'I sweated,' or 'I spat,' but rather conveyed this by 'I relieved my nose' or 'I had to make use of my handkerchief'" (VI, 158–59).[9] Both writers add their own verbal twists to this pattern. Čičikov impresses a servant at the inn: "In the gestures of this gentleman there was something quite solid, and he blew his nose exceedingly loudly" (VI, 10). The nose-blowing is comically glorified as gentlemanly and the word "solid" is used to suggest a quite unsolid procedure. Of Nabokov's hero Pnin we read: "The zipper a gentleman depends on most would come loose in his puzzled hand at some nightmare moment of haste and despair."[10] Here "gentleman" seems in humorous disharmony with the physical need being referred to, no matter how much the hypothetical gentleman depends on his zipper.

Summarizing the aesthetic strategies of black humor, Schulz notes a careful blurring of the distinction between narrator and author. This allows, he writes, "for the introduction of authorial responses to the narrator's vision not verified by the experience of the narrative" (p. 130). As an example Schulz offers the ending of *Lolita*. From Gogol's works we may adduce the endings of *Dead Souls* (part 1), the "Ivans" tale, and *The Government Inspector*, wherein the narrative (or stage directive) consciousness abruptly soars above what precedes it, leaving the reader (or spectator) with the strange feeling that the point of view to which he has previously been exposed is only one of several possible perspectives. The effect is ironically vivifying, bringing to mind Barbara Monter's phrase "an illusion of *unreality*."[11]

Both Nabokov and Gogol favor a descriptive technique whereby someone or something is inaccurately labeled, promoting the reader's creative participation. Early in *Dead Souls*, for example, we see a window apparently containing two samovars, except that "one samovar," as Gogol puts it, has a pitch-black beard; quick deduction tells us that the word "samovar" refers to a face which, however, resembles a samovar. We also learn in *Dead Souls* that Manilov's son Femistokljus wants to be an ambassador when he grows up. Then at table a servant wipes "the ambassador's" nose to prevent a large drop from falling into his soup (VI, 31).

Evocative inaccurate labeling is employed by both Nabokov and Gogol to suggest furtive sex. In "May Night, or The Drowned

Maiden," we read that the village head "was a widower, but in his house lived his sister-in-law" (I, 161). The woman is repeatedly called "sister-in-law," while the reader becomes increasingly certain that her role is other than that of a sister-in-law. Another example may be seen in "Špon'ka" when the aunt informs her nephew that a certain Stepan Kuz'mic allegedly deeded him some land. This man, the aunt tells Špon'ka, "began to visit your mother when you were not yet in the world; true, at times when your father was not at home" (I, 295). Typically, Gogol has the aunt say "your father" just as we learn that Špon'ka's father was perhaps someone else.

During the bedroom scene at the Enchanted Hunters, Lolita talks in her sleep and calls Humbert (who is stealthily approaching the bed) "Barbara." We then read: "Barbara, wearing my pajamas which were much too tight for her, remained poised motionless over the little sleep-talker" (p. 130). Here both "Barbara" and "her" are vividly inaccurate. Moreover Nabokov's wording graphically suggests the physical contrast between males and females. Gogol, in Špon'ka's dream, brings out this contrast still more sharply by having him discover that "his wife was not a person at all but some kind of woolen material" (I, 307). Such a wife, we learn, is usually measured and cut by a merchant. Špon'ka has already exclaimed that he would not know what to do with a wife (p. 306). His nightmare realization that a female which is a flat woolen area that is measured and cut is "not a person at all" is thus darkly humorous.

In part 2 of *Dead Souls*, when Čičikov reflects that it may be possible to avoid repaying the money he has borrowed from Kostanzoglo, we are told: "A strange thought presented itself; it was not as if Čičikov had conceived it himself, but it suddenly, all on its own, appeared, teasing, smirking, and winking at him" (VII, 89). As Humbert plans to drug Lolita in order to fondle her at night, we read: "Other visions of venery presented themselves to me swaying and smiling" (p. 73). In both descriptions the unsavory ideas seem to come from outside, seductively approaching Čičikov and Humbert, whose guilt seems faintly, humorously diminished.

When Čičikov buys Xlobuev's estate, he pays 10,000 rubles in cash, and another 5,000 are "promised" for delivery the next day, "that is, promised; it was planned to bring three, the rest later, maybe in two or three days, and if possible to postpone it yet somewhat more" (VII, 86–87). At this point the word "promised" has been humorously reversed; the money seems almost to appear and then vanish. In *Laughter in The Dark* the following is offered through the eyes of Axel Rex: "They could have given him a better room for his money (which, he thought, they might never see)."[12] As with Čičikov, the payment seems to appear only to be canceled by subsequent wording.

Both writers employ the device of the inaccurate label to create a tinge of dark humor when death is concerned. As Akakij's mother ("The Overcoat") tries to decide upon a name for him, she is repeatedly termed "the deceased" (III, 142). In *King, Queen, Knave*, Martha and Franz plot to kill Dreyer. As their schemes unfold, he is called "my late husband," "my deceased," and "the deceased" while still alive (pp. 156, 158). "The deceased used to sleep on that bed there," Martha tells Franz. And since two of their schemes entail shooting Dreyer, we are told that (according to the second plan) Franz would be waiting behind a tree with the "reloaded" revolver (p. 179). Nabokov even develops the idea further: "When they had again killed" Dreyer, Franz would "again" take his wallet (179–80). In *Pale Fire* Kinbote casually mentions a "self-made widow."[13]

Today it may be difficult to see *Dead Souls* as assaulting a religious taboo, yet the title was originally banned by the censor because of the church's position that souls are eternal and thus cannot be termed dead.[14] But Gogol went still further. Korobocka, we recall, has the eerie presence of mind to wonder if dead souls might be useful in some way around the house. She also inquires if Čičikov wishes to dig the dead souls up out of the ground (VI, 51). Later there is speculation about the difficulty of resettling Čičikov's souls, including fear of an uprising by such a "restless lot" (VI, 155). In part 2 Tentetnikov speculates that Čičikov is a professor traveling about in search of plants, or perhaps fossilized objects (VII, 27). Čičikov is of course still seeking to acquire dead souls. The word *iskopaemye* (here rendered "fossilized objects") suggests through its root meaning "dug up things." Also in part 2, Platonov is plagued by intense boredom. Čičikov sympathetically, and hopefully, suggests that this boredom may have been caused by the deaths of many serfs (VII, 52).

Nabokov derives much of his dark humor about death from suicide. In *Pale Fire* Kinbote writes: "There are purists who maintain that a gentleman should use a brace of pistols, one for each temple" (p. 157). He proceeds to term vein-tapping in one's bath a "fancy release" but "uncertain and messy." "Air comfort" (in jumping from high buildings) is also discussed. "The ideal drop," he concludes, "is from an aircraft, your muscles relaxed ... your packed parachute shuffled off, cast off, shrugged off—farewell, *shootka!*" This Zemblan word is translated by Kinbote as "little chute." Also aptly, it is spelled like the English word *shoot*. Still another play of meaning derives from Russ. *šutka* 'joke': the implication is that life itself may be a joke which is shrugged off by the gesture of suicide. Indeed Kinbote's mockingly glorified tone ("purists," "ideal drop") seems mixed with disturbing suggestions of pleasure, of escape ("fancy release," "air comfort," "muscles relaxed"). If life is seen as a temporary, deceptive condition limited by the range of normal conscious perception, the idea of release or escape can turn grimly serious. In *Speak, Memory* Nabokov writes: "The prison of time is spherical and without exits. Short of suicide, I have tried everything."[15] And if death is apparently viewed by Nabokov as an escape, or release, we may recall that in Gogol's "The Overcoat" Akakij finally "releases" his ghostly soul (*ispustil dux*; III, 168).

In sum, both Nabokov and Gogol persistently, and often rather playfully, touch upon subjects generally considered improper, indelicate, even taboo. This has produced some strikingly similar effects of dark humor. Such humor, by twisting or reversing generally accepted attitudes and values, tends to undermine the reader's world. Sex, insanity, and death are uneasily featured. With both writers the natural functions of the human body are seen in disharmony with social convention. Ultimately human life and even its termination are viewed from a faintly alien perspective. The process is reinforced by ironic reversals of individual words. Additional perspectives are abruptly added by what Schulz terms "authorial responses to the narrator's vision not verified by the experience of the narrative." And the technique of inaccurate labeling promotes the reader's vivifying participation. Despite these various similarities, we may note some differences in emphasis. Nabokov more frequently depicts an outrageous attitude of one human being towards another. With Nabokov the human body seems more animalistic; medical care is more grimly undermined. With Gogol insanity seems a relatively playful (though nonetheless painful) internal disorder; Nabokov presents it as a sinister conspiracy from without. Gogolian humor relating to death seems relatively muted and capricious; Nabokov insinuates a disturbing attraction towards suicide. We may also discern a difference in overall effect. Dark humor seems more consciously contrived by Nabokov. It seems more basic to the world view promoted by his writing—a view however from which he seeks to dissociate himself. With Gogol even the most similar effects seem less pessimistic, though they may condition a more resigned perspective on human life. In short, one can discern Gogol's sad smile as he walks hand in hand with his characters,[16] whereas Nabokov's characters, as he has claimed, are indeed galley slaves.[17]

NOTES

1. *Southern Review*, 9 (1973), 117–34. Schulz refers to Nabokov four times in proposing "six kinds of deployment" relating to "the aesthetic strategies of Black Humor" (p. 130). See also Mathew Winston, "*Humour noir* and Black Humor," in Harry Levin, ed., *Veins of Humor* (Cambridge, Mass.: Harvard Univ. Press, 1972), 269–84. Winston focuses on Nabokov in describing "grotesque," as opposed to "absurd" black humor. And the grotesque, via Victor Erlich's *Gogol* (New Haven: Yale Univ. Press, 1969), surely reminds us of Gogol. Winston notes that his label "grotesque" roughly corresponds to Robert Scholes's "picaresque," as distinguished from "satirical" black humor (p. 277). Schulz has found that Scholes minimizes the Black humorists' "seriousness" when he characterizes them "as playful or artful" in some respects (p. 133). As noted below, the playful and artful humor of both Nabokov and Gogol can turn quite serious. (Robert Scholes especially characterizes "satirical" black humor as "playful" and "artful"; *The Fabulators* [New York: Oxford Univ. Press, 1967], 41.) (See also Douglas M. Davis, ed., *The World of Black Humor* (New York: E. P. Dutton, 1967), 17, and Joyce Carol Oates, "Whose Side Are You On," *New York Times Book Review*, 4 June 1972, p. 63.

2. See my "Gogolesque Perception-Expanding Reversals in Nabokov," *Slavic Review*, 30 (1971), 110–20, where I discuss several similar mechanisms as well as Mr. Nabokov's disclaimers. Several of the examples below are treated somewhat differently in my *Nabokov's Deceptive World* (New York: New York Univ. Press, 1971) and in my forthcoming book-length study of Gogol's works.

3. N. V. Gogol, *Polnoe sobranie sočinenij* (14 vols.; M.: AN SSSR, 1937–52), IV, 66. Volume and page references given parenthetically in the text are to this edition.

4. Vladimir Nabokov, *Lolita* (New York: G. P. Putnam's Sons, 1955), 192.

5. Similarly, Hermann tells us that he was "winding up the brief series of preparatory caresses" in lovemaking that his wife "was supposed to be entitled to." Vladimir Nabokov, *Despair* (New York: G. P. Putnam's Sons, 1966), 37.

6. John Barth, *The Floating Opera* (New York: Doubleday, 1967), 124.

7. Vladimir Nabokov, *King, Queen, Knave* (New York: McGraw-Hill, 1968), 155.

8. The well-known ending of *Candy* ("Good grief, it's daddy!") also focuses on sexual intimacy between a father and daughter. In Gogol's works, Katerina's father ("The Terrible Vengeance") desires her incestuously; in "The Soročincy Fair," when Paraska and her father dance together, thinking they are alone, Cybulja interrupts them by remarking: "Well, that's fine, the father and daughter have fixed up a wedding here all by themselves!" (I, 135).

9. This sort of dark humor reaches its peak—or nadir—in J. P. Donleavy's *The Gingerman* (New York: Berkeley, 1959) when Sebastian Dangerfield (whom Douglas Davis terms "perhaps the best case study" of black humor heroes, p. 18) defends his friend Kenneth to his wife Marian: "Kenneth's a gentleman in every respect. Have you ever heard him fart?" (p. 42.)

10. Vladimir Nabokov, *Pnin* (New York: Atheneum, 1965), 14.

11. Barbara Heldt Monter, "'Spring in Fialta': The Choice that Mimics Chance," *TriQuarterly*, 17 (Winter 1970), 133.

12. Vladimir Nabokov, *Laughter in the Dark* (New York: Berkeley, 1966), 78.

13. Vladimir Nabokov, *Pale Fire* (New York: Lancer, 1966), 60. Somewhat similarly Charles Addams has shown a multitude of gravestones for sale and the sign, "Special! Do-it-yourself kit." In J. P. Donleavy's *A Fairy Tale of New York* (New York: Delacorte, 1973), 85, the hero dreams of building "an empire of bargain-priced self-service funeral parlors." And in John Barth's *The Floating Opera* there is a 90-year-old lady "who buys her

one-a-day vitamin pills in the smallest bottles—for her, the real economy size" (p. 50).

14. See Gogol's letter to P. A. Pletnev, 7 Jan. 1842 (XII, 28).
15. Vladimir Nabokov, *Speak, Memory* (New York: G. P. Putnam's Sons, 1966), 20. The Russian version reads: "Kažetsja, krome samoubijstva, ja pereproboval vse vyxody." Vladimir Nabokov, *Drugie berega* (New York: Čexov, 1954), 10.
16. Gogol suggests this early in chapter 7 of *Dead Souls* (VI, 134).
17. "The Art of Fiction, XL: Vladimir Nabokov, an Interview," *Paris Review*, 41 (summer–fall 1967), 96.

"A Good Man Is Hard to Find"
(Flannery O'Connor)

"Clichés, Superficial Story-Telling, and the Dark Humor of Flannery O'Connor's 'A Good Man Is Hard to Find'"
by Robert C. Evans,
Auburn University at Montgomery

In one of her most memorable and most often quoted comments about why she wrote such strangely violent, grotesque, and darkly humorous fiction, Flannery O'Connor explained that

> When you can assume that your audience holds the same beliefs you do, you can relax a little and use more normal means of talking to it; when you have to assume that it does not, then you have to make your vision apparent by shock—to the hard of hearing you shout, and for the almost-blind you draw large and startling figures. (*Mystery and Manners* 34)

Certainly no story by O'Connor better illustrates these methods than her tragically comic (or comically tragic) masterpiece "A Good Man Is Hard to Find." This story describes an ill-fated vacation trip to Florida by a family from Georgia—a family consisting of a spry old grandmother; her ill-tempered son Bailey; Bailey's silent and compliant wife; two grossly ill-mannered children named John Wesley and June Star; and an innocent and pleasant baby. The trip goes reasonably well until the family, on a deserted road, accidentally encounters a trio of escaped convicts consisting of an intelligent and thoughtful killer called The Misfit and his two dimwitted henchmen, Hiram and Bobby Lee. The first half of the story is consistently funny and ridiculous, although the humor often has a real edge and ironic bite. By the time the story ends, however, the previously ridiculous family from Georgia suddenly seem (with the possible exception of June Star, the little girl) pitiful and almost tragic figures. This is especially true of the grandmother, who must stand by and suffer while her son, daughter-in-law, and three grandchildren are all taken off into the woods and shot. The grandmother herself is then executed in the last paragraphs of the story—a story that brims with grim humor and shocking violence but one that also (paradoxically) can be said to display a highly comic or happy ending.

Few works of literature better illustrate the effectiveness of dark humor than this one. One reason O'Connor employs this sort of shockingly black comedy is to make a clear contrast between her own kind of writing and the other, far more stale and predictable styles in which language generally tends to be used, especially in modern society. She goes out of her way to draw striking contrasts between her own kind of storytelling (and artistic craftsmanship) and the kinds of stories that occupy the attention of the characters featured in her text. Those characters tend to use language in ways that are hackneyed, unoriginal, and clichéd and to appreciate kinds of writing or works of art that are stale, predictable, and highly conventional. O'Connor, by contrast, uses her special brand of dark humor to shake her readers awake and keep them alert.

As its very title already suggests, "A Good Man Is Hard to Find" (like much of O'Connor's fiction) is very much concerned with satirizing stale and clichéd uses of language. The characters who use clichés in many of O'Connor's stories (such as Julian's mother in "Everything That Rises Must Converge," or Mrs. Turpin in "Revelation," or Mrs. Hopewell and her daughter Hulga in "Good Country People," with its obviously clichéd title) are all characters who tend to speak (and, more importantly, to think) in highly conventional and unoriginal ways. When O'Connor's characters mouth clichés (and many of them do), that is usually a sign that they have ceased to think for themselves, if in fact they ever possessed any original thoughts to begin with. O'Connor's use of dark humor is one means by which she keeps her own fiction from becoming similarly stale and predictable. It is one means by which she keeps her readers alert and forces them to think.

In "A Good Man Is Hard to Find," the characters who most obviously speak clichés are the grandmother and Red Sammy Butts, the owner of a ramshackle barbecue restaurant whom the grandmother talks to during the trip. Indeed, the encounter between these two characters is almost a festival of clichés, and it begins with Red Sammy's very first words: "'You can't win,' he said. 'You can't win,' and he wiped his sweating red face off with a gray handkerchief. 'These days you don't know who to trust,' he said. 'Ain't that the truth?'" (141). Every single one of his opening phrases is a commonplace platitude, but each of those phrases also manages to communicate more about Red Sammy's personality than he probably intends. Thus "You can't win" implies that he thinks of himself as being in competition with other persons; "you don't know who to trust" suggests that he looks upon other people with innate suspicion, perhaps because he is not entirely trustworthy himself; while "Ain't that the truth" implies that he looks to other people simply to ratify what he already thinks rather than to challenge him in any thoughtful or provocative ways.

Of course, challenging and provoking readers is O'Connor's goal, and one of the ways she achieves that goal is by mimicking (and thereby mocking) the clichéd words and thoughts of her own characters. The grandmother, however, has no such provocative intentions when she responds to Red Sammy; she is more than happy merely to agree immediately with practically everything he says. Her first response to his opening flood of clichés is to offer one of her own: "'People are certainly not nice like they used to be'" (141). She then immediately flatters Red Sammy by telling him, in another clichéd phrase, that he is a "'good man,'" but then Sammy's wife instantly undercuts such sunny optimism with an observation of her own: "'It isn't a soul in this green world of God's that you can trust,' she said. 'And I don't count nobody out of that, not nobody,' she repeated, looking at Red Sammy" (142). Red Sammy's much-put-upon wife has a clearer and sharper insight into his selfish character than does the grandmother, who has just met him. By allowing the wife to speak, O'Connor typically—and comically—undercuts the grandmother's perfunctory flattery with a bit of dark and biting humor. This technique—a technique of puncturing complacent clichés—is one that O'Connor uses again and again throughout the story. Indeed, one of the most important purposes of the whole encounter between the grandmother and Red Sammy is to draw a stark contrast between the old woman's utterly predictable conversations with Red Sammy and her later unnerving and disturbing discussions with the Misfit, whose words and behavior are consistently surprising and entirely out of her control.

In the meantime, Red Sammy is more than happy to mouth more clichés: "'A good man is hard to find,'" Red Sammy said. 'Everything is getting terrible. I remember the day you could go off and leave your screen door unlatched. Not no more'" (142). Likewise, the grandmother comments that "in her opinion Europe was entirely to blame for the way things were now. She said the way Europe acted you would think we were made of money and Red Sam said it was no use talking about it, she was exactly right" (142). Each of her phrases, as well as Red Sammy's response, is a cliché, and the crucial phrase is the claim that there is "no use talking about it." The grandmother and Red Sammy feel no need to talk about their assertions, because they have ceased to think. They merely repeat the words and ideas that they (and most of their contemporaries) take for granted. A major purpose of the story will be to shake most of the characters (especially the grandmother), as well as O'Connor's readers, out of this kind of smug complacency. Ironically, the grandmother will greatly benefit (at least spiritually) by the end of the story when she discovers that clichéd thinking and clichéd phrases will not help her deal with the Misfit.

One of the most striking examples of O'Connor's use of dark, unexpected humor to puncture clichés occurs in the memorably funny encounter between Red Sammy's wife and June Star. When she first meets the girl (whose sharp tongue has already been turned against her own grandmother), Red Sammy's wife tries to be friendly by mouthing the usual clichés: "'Ain't she cute?' Red Sam's wife said, leaning over the counter. 'Would you like to come be my little girl?'" But June Star responds with the same kind of brutal honesty often employed by O'Connor: "'No I certainly wouldn't,' June Star said. 'I wouldn't live in a broken-down place like this for a million bucks!'" (141). To this, Red Sam's wife can only respond by reiterating her cliché, although this time with obvious strain: "'Ain't she cute?' the woman repeated, stretching her mouth politely." Of course, the honest answer to the woman's question is that June Star is *anything* but "cute," but this whole encounter is a perfect example of the way O'Connor uses biting humor to puncture stale conventions. Inevitably, when the story is taught, June Star's line gets one of the biggest laughs, precisely because it is so unexpected, so shocking, so honest, and so wickedly impolite. June Star doesn't play games, and she certainly doesn't play by anyone else's rules. O'Connor depicts her (and, to a lesser extent, John Wesley) as a mean, selfish, and utterly inconsiderate child, thereby violating the standard fictional rule that children should be presented as innocent, naïve, and "cute." O'Connor is often most darkly humorous—and most honest—when describing the behavior of children.

It would be easy enough to cite other examples in which characters in this story speak in clichés ("'I just know you're a good man,'" the grandmother later says as she desperately pleads with the Misfit) only to have those clichés implicitly or explicitly undercut ("'Nome, I ain't a good man,' The Misfit said after a second *as if he had considered her statement carefully*" [emphasis added]; 148). By now, however, the basic point is clear: O'Connor consistently presents characters who speak, think, and act without giving their words, thoughts, or behavior any real or careful consideration, and then she often subverts their empty words and their thoughtless thinking in ways that surprise us, shock us, and often make us laugh, even if her humor is dark and our laughter is often painful. O'Connor's art is deliberately provocative in every sense of those two words: It is designed to shake us up and (as the Misfit says in another context) it is intended to throw everything "'off balance'" (152). O'Connor writes not in order to confirm conventional ways of thinking but to undermine them and throw them into question. Merely funny or "comic" humor would not have the same effect; it would be shallow and superficial. Simple comedy usually confirms—rather than undercuts—standard prejudices or common assumptions. The purpose of O'Connor's dark humor, however, is precisely to make us think.

O'Connor constantly calls attention to kinds of artwork, writing, or storytelling whose purposes are significantly at odds with her own. It hardly seems an accident, for instance, that the story opens with descriptions of both the grandmother and Bailey reading the newspaper. In the fourth sentence of the story, Bailey is described "sitting on the edge of his chair at the table, bent over the orange sports section of the *Journal*" (137). Bailey reads, apparently, mainly for entertainment and amusement. He is not (for instance) reading the opinion pages (which might make him think) but is merely reading accounts of superficial, ultimately unimportant wins and losses. He reads, probably, about baseball, the national pastime. Indeed, passing the time is primarily how Bailey has spent most of his life. Later, right before he dies, he will be described in terms that might be appropriate to the sports pages: "He was squatting in the position of a runner about to sprint forward but he didn't move" (147). For the moment, however, Bailey is engaged in reading one of the most entertaining but ultimately least significant parts of the newspaper. There is certainly nothing darkly comical about sports writing, and so O'Connor already begins to make a distinction between the kind of writing appreciated by people like Bailey and the kind of writing she herself intends to offer.

That the grandmother reads the news pages already suggests a significant distinction between the old lady and her son: The grandmother is a more serious character than Bailey, and she is not only more concerned with significant events but is (ultimately) more capable of meaningful thought. Nevertheless, the fact that she concentrates on the most sensational aspects of the day's news—the escape of a killer from the "'Federal Pen'" (137)—suggests that she reads the paper partly to inject some excitement into her otherwise uneventful life. Of course, her life will later become far more exciting and eventful than she would wish when the family happens to encounter the criminal she now only reads about, and O'Connor already begins indulging in her typically dark humor when she makes the grandmother proclaim, "'I wouldn't take my children in any direction with a criminal like that aloose in it. I couldn't answer to my conscience if I did'" (137). It goes without saying that it will be the grandmother who will later inadvertently lead her family exactly to the Misfit and thus to destruction—a fact that is meant to be both funny and painful.

Meanwhile, the two children, like their grandmother and father, seem fixated on superficial forms of reading and entertainment. No sooner is John Wesley introduced, for instance, than O'Connor tells us that he "and the little girl, June Star, were reading the funny papers on the floor" (137). Here as well as later, the children read to amuse themselves and to pass the time; the effect would be entirely different if they were studying Sunday school lessons or Scripture. Like their father, the children think of reading as a way to enjoy themselves rather than as a means of stimulating real thought. It is hardly surprising that June Star is familiar with another form of popular entertainment—the television (and/or radio) game show "Queen for a Day." When John Wesley rudely suggests that if his grandmother doesn't want to go to Florida with the rest of the family she might want to stay at home by herself, June Star even more rudely remarks, "'She wouldn't stay at home to be queen for a day'" (137). She thereby alludes (in her typically darkly comical way) to an enormously popular radio and television show, a show in which elderly women competed against each other by enumerating their sufferings. The one who had had the hardest luck (as judged by audience applause) was crowned "Queen for a Day" and was then given various prizes, such as refrigerators and furniture. This allusion to "Queen for a Day" is relevant to the rest of the story in numerous ways, but one of the most obvious aspects of its relevance is that it shows how June Star and the others spend much of their time: They watch television (or listen to the radio) and fantasize about worldly prosperity. By the very end of the story the grandmother will have achieved (thanks to the shocking provocation provided by the Misfit) an altogether truer and higher kind of ennoblement than could be achieved on "Queen for a Day." For the moment, however, the allusion—along with the reference to the "funny papers"—helps confirm our sense that this family looks to reading and other forms of entertainment as sources of simple plea-sure rather than as sources of provocative thought. There is nothing darkly comic about either the "funny papers" or "Queen for a Day," but the allusions to both of those pastimes are part of the underlying dark humor of O'Connor's story. Throughout her tale, O'Connor constantly alludes to forms of entertainment that are far less serious, probing, and unsettling than her own.

She implies in passing, for instance, that the grandmother is familiar with the light comic operas of Gilbert and Sullivan by revealing that the grandmother has named her cat "Pitty Sing" (a name almost identical to the name of a character in *The Mikado* [138]). O'Connor later emphasizes once more that John Wesley and June Star spend much of their time reading "comic magazines" (139)—that is, magazines that may be humorous but not in any dark or disturbing ways. Likewise, right after the grandmother refers to impoverished black children as "'little niggers,'" O'Connor immediately reports that "The children exchanged comic books" (139). This juxtaposition of a crude and insensitive (if historically credible) comment and an exchange of "comic books" is meant to imply something about the superficial, shallow nature of much of the entertainment (and much of the thinking) common in contemporary culture. The grandmother and the rest of her family tend to look at each other, and especially at other people, as the kind of uncomplicated, two-dimensional figures one might indeed find in comic books. The grandmother cannot appreciate the real deprivation and misfortune that nearly-naked "little niggers" might be suffering. Indeed, when she spots the small black child standing outside his shack, she instantly exclaims, "'Oh look at the cute little pickaninny!'" (This statement immediately follows her comment that in the good old days, people "'did right'".) And, no sooner does she treat the child as a crude stereotype (rather than as a real human being) than she then proclaims, concerning him, "'If I could paint, I'd paint that picture'" (139). The kind of picture she would paint would, surely, depict the boy as superficially "cute." It is easy to imagine him, in her painting, as wide-eyed, smiling, and waving. That, indeed, is how he appears in O'Connor's story, but in the story the impact of his appearance is ironic and darkly humorous. In the story, the boy, by his mere presence, reminds us of the racism and injustice of a society in which he is written off simply as a "cute little pickanniny" and "little nigger." Later, at the very end of the story, the grandmother will be shaken out of her complacency to such a degree that she will be able to reach out even to the murderous Misfit as if he is one of her "own children" (152). For the moment, however, she can still only see the little black boy merely as "cute" (and inferior).

The grandmother's attitudes toward the world have been shaped by the kind of repeated exposure to entertaining but unrealistic popular culture that is implied by her passing reference to Margaret Mitchell's famous and immensely popular novel *Gone With the Wind* (139). That novel, of course, also became one of the most popular films of all time, and it (and other examples of nostalgic pop culture like it) seems to have colored the way the grandmother thinks of herself and presents herself to the rest of society. She dresses primly and properly, wants to be considered a "lady" (especially if found dead on the side of a road; (138)), remembers fondly how she was "courted" when she was a "maiden lady" (140), and fantasizes about seeing once more "an old plantation that she had visited ... once when she was a young lady" (142). The grandmother, in other words, almost sees herself as the heroine of an old-time romance novel rather than as an elderly and somewhat neglected woman from a lower-middle-class Southern family, and her tendency to live in an appealing fantasy world rather than to face reality squarely is memorably (and very humorously) suggested even when she reacts to the pain she feels after the family's car runs off the road: "'I believe I have injured an organ'" (145). Scarlett O'Hara could not have said it better herself, and it is not really until the entrance of the Misfit and the slow and methodical killing of each person in her family that the grandmother is gradually stripped of all her romantic pretenses and all her appealing illusions. O'Connor's fiction (unlike pop culture) does not confirm illusions; it explodes them. Almost until the very conclusion of the story, the grandmother thinks she may be able to script the sort of conventional happy ending she most desires. In that desired ending, the grandmother would, at the very least, survive and return more or less unchanged to her old way of life (even if shorn of the rest of her family). O'Connor, however, in her darkly humorous way, has a different ending in mind—an ending in which the grandmother dies a violent, bloody death, but in which the joke, finally and surprisingly, is on the Misfit. When the grandmother reaches out to the Misfit in the last split second of her life and touches him in a gesture of genuine but wholly unpredictable love and compassion, the grandmother (or at least O'Connor) gets the last laugh. Yes, the grandmother is instantly killed by the Misfit, but the final lines of the story strongly imply that the grandmother is the one who triumphs. Like the behavior of Jesus (who was also killed despite, and even because of, the depth of his love), the grandmother's gesture of compassion throws "'everything off-balance'" (152). At the end of the story, the grandmother is clearly the spiritual winner (as she half-sits and half-lies "in a puddle of blood with her legs crossed under her like a child's and her face smiling up at the cloudless sky"), while the Misfit (whose eyes seem "red-rimmed and pale and defenseless-looking") is the obvious loser (152–153). In spite of the grandmother's best efforts to remain a character in a superficial Southern romance novel, O'Connor, through her use of dark humor, has turned her into the oddly triumphant central figure of a modern morality play. Like the great medieval morality play *Everyman*, O'Connor's story begins with worldly humor but ends with otherworldly transcendence. Death comes to the grandmother as it comes to us all, but by unexpectedly (and probably even unintentionally) tossing aside the normal script, the grandmother becomes a true "lady" in ways neither she nor we might have expected could happen.

WORKS CITED OR CONSULTED

Harris, Carole K. "The Echoing Afterlife of Clichés in Flannery O'Connor's 'Good Country People.'" *Flannery O'Connor Review* 5 (2007): 56–66.

O'Connor, Flannery. "A Good Man Is Hard to Find." *Flannery O'Connor: Collected Works*. Ed. Sally Fitzgerald. New York: Library of America, 1988. 137–153.

———. *Mystery and Manners: Occasional Prose*. Ed. Sally Fitzgerald. New York: Noonday, 1970.

HENRY IV, PARTS ONE AND TWO
(WILLIAM SHAKESPEARE)

"The Rejection of Falstaff"
by A.C. Bradley, in
Oxford Lectures on Poetry (1909)

INTRODUCTION

In this lecture delivered in 1902, influential Shakespeare critic A.C. Bradley explores the bard's characterization of Falstaff and speculates on the artistic motivations behind his ignominius end in *Henry V*. According to Bradley, such speculation is inevitable, since audiences identify and empathize so completely with Falstaff and his humorous antics that Henry's treatment of him seems unjustified and cruel. Posing this question, Bradley then launches into a discussion of why audiences are drawn to Falstaff's dark humor which, he asserts, is not that of an "object of mirth," but of a "humorist of genius." "Instead of being comic to you and serious to himself, he is more ludicrous to himself than to you; and he makes himself out more ludicrous than he is, in order that he and others may laugh." The "enemy of everything that would interfere with his ease, and therefore of anything serious, and especially of everything respectable and moral," Falstaff uses humor to maintain his freedom, presenting to audiences

Bradley, A.C. "The Rejection of Falstaff." *Oxford Lectures on Poetry,* 2nd Ed. 1909. New York: MacMillan, 1917. 247–275.

the comic triumphs of a man trying to remain unfettered by
responsibility and mortality.

∿

Of the two persons principally concerned in the rejection of Falstaff,
Henry, both as Prince and as King, has received, on the whole, full
justice from readers and critics. Falstaff, on the other hand, has been in
one respect the most unfortunate of Shakespeare's famous characters.
All of them, in passing from the mind of their creator into other minds,
suffer change; they tend to lose their harmony through the dispropor-
tionate attention bestowed on some one feature, or to lose their uniqueness by being conventionalised into types already familiar. But Falstaff
was degraded by Shakespeare himself. The original character is to be
found alive in the two parts of *Henry IV,* dead in *Henry V,* and nowhere
else. But not very long after these plays were composed, Shakespeare
wrote, and he afterwards revised, the very entertaining piece called *The
Merry Wives of Windsor.* Perhaps his company wanted a new play on a
sudden; or perhaps, as one would rather believe, the tradition may be
true that Queen Elizabeth, delighted with the Falstaff scenes of *Henry
IV,* expressed a wish to see the hero of them again, and to see him in love.
Now it was no more possible for Shakespeare to show his own Falstaff
in love than to turn twice two into five. But he could write in haste—the
tradition says, in a fortnight—a comedy or farce differing from all his
other plays in this, that its scene is laid in English middle-class life, and
that it is prosaic almost to the end. And among the characters he could
introduce a disreputable fat old knight with attendants, and could call
them Falstaff, Bardolph, Pistol, and Nym. And he could represent this
knight assailing, for financial purposes, the virtue of two matrons, and in
the event baffled, duped, treated like dirty linen, beaten, burnt, pricked,
mocked, insulted, and, worst of all, repentant and didactic. It is horrible.
It is almost enough to convince one that Shakespeare himself could
sanction the parody of Ophelia in the *Two Noble Kinsman.* But it no
more touches the real Falstaff than Ophelia is degraded by that parody.
To picture the real Falstaff befooled like the Falstaff of the *Merry Wives*
is like imagining Iago the gull of Roderigo, or Becky Sharp the dupe of
Amelia Osborne. Before he had been served the least of these tricks he
would have had his brains taken out and buttered, and have given them
to a dog for a New Year's gift. I quote the words of the impostor, for
after all Shakespeare made him and gave to him a few sentences worthy

of Falstaff himself. But they are only a few—one side of a sheet of note-paper would contain them. And yet critics have solemnly debated at what period in his life Sir John endured the gibes of Master Ford, and whether we should put this comedy between the two parts of *Henry IV,* or between the second of them and *Henry V.* And the Falstaff of the general reader, it is to be feared, is an impossible conglomerate of two distinct characters, while the Falstaff of the mere playgoer is certainly much more like the impostor than the true man.

The separation of these two has long ago been effected by criticism, and is insisted on in almost all competent estimates of the character of Falstaff. I do not propose to attempt a full account either of this character or of that of Prince Henry, but shall connect the remarks I have to make on them with a question which does not appear to have been satisfactorily discussed—the question of the rejection of Falstaff by the Prince on his accession to the throne. What do we feel, and what are we meant to feel, as we witness this rejection? And what does our feeling imply as to the characters of Falstaff and the new King?

1.

Sir John, you remember, is in Gloucestershire, engaged in borrowing a thousand pounds from Justice Shallow; and here Pistol, riding helter-skelter from London, brings him the great news that the old King is as dead as nail in door, and that Harry the Fifth is the man. Sir John, in wild excitement, taking any man's horses, rushes to London; and he carries Shallow with him, for he longs to reward all his friends. We find him standing with his companions just outside Westminster Abbey, in the crowd that is waiting for the King to come out after his coronation. He himself is stained with travel, and has had no time to spend any of the thousand pounds in buying new liveries for his men. But what of that? This poor show only proves his earnestness of affection, his devotion, how he could not deliberate or remember or have patience to shift himself, but rode day and night, thought of nothing else but to see Henry, and put all affairs else in oblivion, as if there were nothing else to be done but to see him. And now he stands sweating with desire to see him, and repeating and repeating this one desire of his heart—'to see him.' The moment comes. There is a shout within the Abbey like the roaring of the sea, and a clangour of trumpets, and the doors open and the procession streams out.

FAL. God save thy grace, King Hal! my royal Hal!

PIST. The heavens thee guard and keep, most royal imp of fame!

FAL. God save thee, my sweet boy!

KING. My Lord Chief Justice, speak to that vain man.

CH. JUST. Have you your wits? Know you what 'tis you speak?

FAL. My King! my Jove! I speak to thee, my heart!

KING. I know thee not, old man: fall to thy prayers;

  How ill white hairs become a fool and jester!

  I have long dream'd of such a kind of man,

  So surfeit-swell'd, so old and so profane;

  But being awaked I do despise my dream.

  Make less thy body hence, and more thy grace;

  Leave gormandizing; know the grave doth gape

  For thee thrice wider than for other men.

  Reply not to me with a fool-born jest:

  Presume not that I am the thing I was;

  For God doth know, so shall the world perceive,

  That I have turn'd away my former self;

  So will I those that kept me company.

  When thou dost hear I am as I have been,

  Approach me, and thou shalt be as thou wast,

  The tutor and the feeder of my riots:

  Till then, I banish thee, on pain of death,

  As I have done the rest of my misleaders,

  Not to come near our person by ten mile.

  For competence of life I will allow you,

  That lack of means enforce you not to evil:

  And, as we hear you do reform yourselves,

  We will, according to your strengths and qualities,

  Give you advancement. Be it your charge, my lord,

  To see perform'd the tenour of our world.

  Set on.

The procession passes out of sight, but Falstaff and his friends remain. He shows no resentment. He comforts himself, or tries to comfort himself—first, with the thought that he has Shallow's thousand pounds, and then, more seriously, I believe, with another thought. The King, he sees, must look thus to the world; but he will be sent for in private when night comes, and will yet make the fortunes of his friends. But even as he speaks, the Chief Justice, accompanied by Prince John, returns, and gives the order to his officers:

> Go, carry Sir John Falstaff to the Fleet;
> Take all his company along with him.

Falstaff breaks out, 'My lord, my lord,' but he is cut short and hurried away; and after a few words between the Prince and the Chief Justice the scene closes, and with it the drama.

What are our feelings during this scene? They will depend on our feelings about Falstaff. If we have not keenly enjoyed the Falstaff scenes of the two plays, if we regard Sir John chiefly as an old reprobate, not only a sensualist, a liar, and a coward, but a cruel and dangerous ruffian, I suppose we enjoy his discomfiture and consider that the King has behaved magnificently. But if we *have* keenly enjoyed the Falstaff scenes, if we have enjoyed them as Shakespeare surely meant them to be enjoyed, and if, accordingly, Falstaff is not to us solely or even chiefly a reprobate and ruffian, we feel, I think, during the King's speech, a good deal of pain and some resentment; and when, without any further offence on Sir John's part, the Chief Justice returns and sends him to prison, we stare in astonishment. These, I believe, are, in greater or less degree, the feelings of most of those who really enjoy the Falstaff scenes (as many readers do not). Nor are these feelings diminished when we remember the end of the whole story, as we find it in *Henry V*, where we learn that Falstaff quickly died, and, according to the testimony of persons not very sentimental, died of a broken heart.[1] Suppose this merely to mean that he sank under the shame of his public disgrace, and it is pitiful enough: but the words of Mrs. Quickly, 'The king has killed his heart'; of Nym, 'The king hath run bad humours on the knight; that's the even of it'; of Pistol,

> Nym, thou hast spoke the right,
> His heart is fracted and corroborate,

assuredly point to something more than wounded pride; they point to wounded affection, and remind us of Falstaff's own answer to Prince Hal's question, 'Sirrah, do I owe you a thousand pound?' 'A thousand pound, Hal? a million: thy love is worth a million: thou owest me thy love.'

Now why did Shakespeare end his drama with a scene which, though undoubtedly striking, leaves an impression so unpleasant? I will venture to put aside without discussion the idea that he meant us throughout the two plays to regard Falstaff with disgust or indignation, so that we naturally feel nothing but pleasure at his fall; for this idea implies that kind of inability to understand Shakespeare with which it is idle to argue. And there is another and a much more ingenious suggestion which must equally be rejected as impossible. According to it, Falstaff, having listened to the King's speech, did not seriously hope to be sent for by him in private; he fully realised the situation at once, and was only making game of Shallow; and in his immediate turn upon Shallow when the King goes out, 'Master Shallow, I owe you a thousand pound,' we are meant to see his humorous superiority to any rebuff, so that we end the play with the delightful feeling that, while Henry has done the right thing, Falstaff, in his outward overthrow, has still proved himself inwardly invincible. This suggestion comes from a critic who understands Falstaff, and in the suggestion itself shows that he understands him.[2] But it provides no solution, because it wholly ignores, and could not account for, that which follows the short conversation with Shallow. Falstaff's dismissal to the Fleet, and his subsequent death, prove beyond doubt that his rejection was meant by Shakespeare to be taken as a catastrophe which not even his humour could enable him to surmount.

Moreover, these interpretations, even if otherwise admissible, would still leave our problem only partly solved. For what troubles us is not only the disappointment of Falstaff, it is the conduct of Henry. It was inevitable that on his accession he should separate himself from Sir John, and we wish nothing else. It is satisfactory that Sir John should have a competence, with the hope of promotion in the highly improbable case of his reforming himself. And if Henry could not trust himself within ten miles of so fascinating a companion, by all means let him be banished that distance: we do not complain. These arrangements would not have prevented a satisfactory ending: the King could have communicated his decision, and Falstaff could have accepted it, in a private interview rich in humour and merely touched with pathos. But Shakespeare has so contrived matters that Henry could not send a private warning to Falstaff even if he wished to, and in their public meeting Falstaff is made to behave in so infatuated and outrageous a manner that great sternness on the King's part was unavoidable.

And the curious thing is that Shakespeare did not stop here. If this had been all we should have felt pain for Falstaff, but not, perhaps, resentment against Henry. But two things we do resent. Why, when this painful incident seems to be over, should the Chief Justice return and send Falstaff to prison? Can this possibly be meant for an act of private vengeance on the part of the Chief Justice, unknown to the King? No; for in that case Shakespeare would have shown at once that the King disapproved and cancelled it. It must have been the King's own act. This is one thing we resent; the other is the King's sermon. He had a right to turn away his former self, and his old companions with it, but he had no right to talk all of a sudden like a clergyman; and surely it was both ungenerous and insincere to speak of them as his 'misleaders,' as though in the days of Eastcheap and Gadshill he had been a weak and silly lad. We have seen his former self, and we know that it was nothing of the kind. He had shown himself, for all his follies, a very strong and independent young man, deliberately amusing himself among men over whom he had just as much ascendency as he chose to exert. Nay, he amused himself not only among them, but at their expense. In his first soliloquy—and first soliloquies are usually significant—he declares that he associates with them in order that, when at some future time he shows his true character, he may be the more wondered at for his previous aberrations. You may think he deceives himself here; you may believe that he frequented Sir John's company out of delight in it and not merely with this cold-blooded design; but at any rate he *thought* the design was his one motive. And, that being so, two results follow. He ought in honour long ago to have given Sir John clearly to understand that they must say good-bye on the day of his accession. And, having neglected to do this, he ought not to have lectured him as his misleader. It was not only ungenerous, it was dishonest. It looks disagreeably like an attempt to buy the praise of the respectable at the cost of honour and truth. And it succeeded. Henry *always* succeeded.

You will see what I am suggesting, for the moment, as a solution of our problem. I am suggesting that our fault lies not in our resentment at Henry's conduct, but in our surprise at it; that if we had read his character truly in the light that Shakespeare gave us, we should have been prepared for a display both of hardness and of policy at this point in his career. And although this suggestion does not suffice to solve the problem before us, I am convinced that in itself it is true.

Nor is it rendered at all improbable by the fact that Shakespeare has made Henry, on the whole, a fine and very attractive character, and that here he makes no one express any disapprobation of the treatment of Falstaff. For in similar cases Shakespeare is constantly misunderstood. His readers expect him to mark in some distinct way his approval or disapproval of that which he represents; and hence where *they* disapprove and *he* says nothing, they fancy that he does *not* disapprove, and they blame his indifference, like Dr. Johnson, or at the least are puzzled. But the truth is that he shows the fact and leaves the judgment to them. And again, when he makes us like a character we expect the character to have no faults that are not expressly pointed out, and when other faults appear we either ignore them or try to explain them away. This is one of our methods of conventionalising Shakespeare. We want the world's population to be neatly divided into sheep and goats, and we want an angel by us to say, 'Look, that is a goat and this is a sheep,' and we try to turn Shakespeare into this angel. His impartiality makes us uncomfortable: we cannot bear to see him, like the sun, lighting up everything and judging nothing. And this is perhaps especially the case in his historical plays, where we are always trying to turn him into a partisan. He shows us that Richard II was unworthy to be king, and we at once conclude that he thought Bolingbroke's usurpation justified; whereas he shows merely, what under the conditions was bound to exist, an inextricable tangle of right and unright. Or, Bolingbroke being evidently wronged, we suppose Bolingbroke's statements to be true, and are quite surprised when, after attaining his end through them, he mentions casually on his death-bed that they were lies. Shakespeare makes us admire Hotspur heartily; and accordingly, when we see Hotspur discussing with others how large his particular slice of his mother-country is to be, we either fail to recognise the monstrosity of the proceeding, or, recognising it, we complain that Shakespeare is inconsistent. Prince John breaks a tottering rebellion by practising a detestable fraud on the rebels. We are against the rebels, and have heard high praise of Prince John, but we cannot help seeing that his fraud is detestable; so we say indignantly to Shakespeare, 'Why, you told us he was a sheep'; whereas, in fact, if we had used our eyes we should have known beforehand that he was the brave, determined, loyal, cold-blooded, pitiless, unscrupulous son of a usurper whose throne was in danger.

To come, then, to Henry. Both as prince and as king he is deservedly a favourite, and particularly so with English readers, being, as he is, perhaps the most distinctively English of all Shakespeare's men. In *Henry V* he is treated as a national hero. In this play he has lost much of the wit which in him seems to have depended on contact with Falstaff, but he has also laid aside the most serious faults of his youth. He inspires in a high degree fear, enthusiasm, and affection; thanks to his beautiful modesty he has the charm which is lacking to another mighty warrior, Coriolanus; his youthful escapades have given him an understanding of simple folk, and sympathy with them; he is the author of the saying, 'There is some soul of goodness in things evil'; and he is much more obviously religious than most of Shakespeare's heroes. Having these and other fine qualities, and being without certain dangerous tendencies which mark the tragic heroes, he is, perhaps, the most *efficient* character drawn by Shakespeare, unless Ulysses, in *Troilus and Cressida*, is his equal. And so he has been described as Shakespeare's ideal man of action; nay, it has even been declared that here for once Shakespeare plainly disclosed his own ethical creed, and showed us his ideal, not simply of a man of action, but of a man.

But Henry is neither of these. The poet who drew Hamlet and Othello can never have thought that even the ideal man of action would lack that light upon the brow which at once transfigures them and marks their doom. It is as easy to believe that, because the lunatic, the lover, and the poet are not far apart, Shakespeare would have chosen never to have loved and sung. Even poor Timon, the most inefficient of the tragic heroes, has something in him that Henry never shows. Nor is it merely that his nature is limited: if we follow Shakespeare and look closely at Henry, we shall discover with the many fine traits a few less pleasing. Henry IV describes him as the noble image of his own youth; and, for all his superiority to his father, he is still his father's son, the son of the man whom Hotspur called a 'vile politician.' Henry's religion, for example, is genuine, it is rooted in his modesty; but it is also superstitious—an attempt to buy off supernatural vengeance for Richard's blood; and it is also in part political, like his father's projected crusade. Just as he went to war chiefly because, as his father told him, it was the way to keep factious nobles quiet and unite the nation, so when he adjures the Archbishop to satisfy him as to his right to the French throne, he knows very well that the Archbishop *wants* the war, because it will defer and perhaps prevent what he considers the spoliation of the Church. This same strain of policy is what Shakespeare marks in the first soliloquy in *Henry IV*, where the prince describes his riotous life as a mere scheme to win him glory later. It implies that readiness to use other people as means to his own ends which is a conspicuous feature in his father; and it reminds us of his father's plan of keeping himself out of the people's sight while Richard was making himself cheap by his incessant public appearances. And if I am not mistaken there is a further likeness. Henry is kindly and pleasant to every one as Prince, to every one deserving as King; and he is so not merely out of policy: but there is no sign in him of a strong affection for any one, such an affection as we recognise at a glance in Hamlet and Horatio, Brutus and Cassius, and many more. We do not find this in *Henry V*, not even in the noble address to Lord Scroop, and in *Henry IV* we find, I think, a liking for Falstaff and Poins, but no more: there is no more than a liking, for instance, in his soliloquy over the supposed corpse of his fat friend, and he never speaks of Falstaff to Poins with any affection. The truth is, that the members of the family of Henry IV have love for one another, but they cannot spare love for anyone outside their family, which stands firmly united, defending its royal position against attack and instinctively isolating itself from outside influence.

Thus I would suggest that Henry's conduct in his rejection of Falstaff is in perfect keeping with his character on its unpleasant side as well as on its finer; and that, so far as Henry is concerned, we ought not to feel surprise at it. And on this view we may even explain the strange incident of the Chief Justice being sent back to order Falstaff to prison (for there is no sign of any such uncertainty in the text as might suggest an interpolation by the players). Remembering his father's words about Henry, 'Being incensed, he's flint,' and remembering in *Henry V* his ruthlessness about killing the prisoners when he is incensed, we may imagine that, after he had left Falstaff and was no longer influenced by the face of his old companion, he gave way to anger at the indecent familiarity which had provoked a compromising scene on the most ceremonial of occasions and in the presence alike of court and crowd, and that he sent the Chief Justice back to take vengeance. And this is consistent with the fact that in the next play we find Falstaff shortly afterwards not only freed from prison, but unmolested in his old haunt in Eastcheap, well within ten miles of Henry's person. His anger had soon passed, and he knew that the requisite effect had been produced both on Falstaff and on the world.

But all this, however true, will not solve our problem. It seems, on the contrary, to increase its difficulty. For the natural conclusion is that Shakespeare *intended* us to feel resentment against Henry. And yet that cannot be, for it implies that he meant the play to end disagreeably; and no one who understands Shakespeare at all will consider that supposition for a moment credible. No; he must have meant the play to end pleasantly, although he made Henry's action consistent. And hence it follows that he must have intended our sympathy with Falstaff to be so far weakened when the rejection-scene arrives that his discomfiture should be satisfactory to us; that we should enjoy this sudden reverse of enormous hopes (a thing always ludicrous if sympathy is absent); that we should approve the moral judgment that falls on him; and so should pass lightly over that disclosure of unpleasant traits in the King's character which Shakespeare was too true an artist to suppress. Thus our pain and resentment, if we feel them, are wrong, in the sense that they do not answer to the dramatist's intention. But it does not follow that they are wrong in a further sense. They may be right, because the dramatist has missed what he aimed at. And this, though the dramatist was Shakespeare, is what I would suggest. In the Falstaff scenes he overshot his mark. He created so extraordinary a being, and fixed him so firmly on his intellectual throne, that when he sought to dethrone him he could not. The moment comes when we are to look at Falstaff in a serious light, and the comic hero is to figure as a baffled schemer; but we cannot make the required change, either in our attitude or in our sympathies. We wish Henry a glorious reign and much joy of his crew of hypocritical politicians, lay and clerical; but our hearts go with Falstaff to the Fleet, or, if necessary, to Arthur's bosom or wheresomever he is.[3]

In the remainder of the lecture I will try to make this view clear. And to that end we must go back to the Falstaff of the body of the two plays, the immortal Falstaff, a character almost purely humorous, and therefore no subject for moral judgments I can but draw an outline, and in describing one aspect of this character must be content to hold another in reserve.

2.

Up to a certain point Falstaff is ludicrous in the same way as many other figures, his distinction lying, so far, chiefly in the mere abundance of ludicrous traits. *Why* we should laugh at a man with a huge belly and corresponding appetites; at the inconveniences he suffers on a hot day, or in playing the footpad, or when he falls down and there are no levers at hand to lift him up again; at the incongruity of his unwieldy bulk and the nimbleness of his spirit, the infirmities of his age and his youthful lightness of heart; at the enormity of his lies and wiles, and the suddenness of their exposure and frustration; at the contrast between his reputation and his real character, seen most absurdly when, at the mere mention of his name, a redoubted rebel surrenders to him—*why*, I say, we should laugh at these and many such things, this is no place to inquire; but unquestionably we do. Here we have them poured out in endless profusion and with that air of careless ease which is so fascinating in Shakespeare; and with the enjoyment of them I believe many readers stop. But while they are quite essential to the character, there is in it much more. For these things by themselves do not explain why, beside laughing at Falstaff, we are made happy by him and laugh *with* him. He is not, like Parolles, a mere *object* of mirth.

The main reason why he makes us so happy and puts us so entirely at our ease is that he himself is happy and entirely at his ease. 'Happy' is too weak a word; he is in bliss, and we share his glory. Enjoyment—no fitful pleasure crossing a dull life, nor any vacant convulsive mirth—but a rich deep-toned chuckling enjoyment circulates continually through all his being. If you ask *what* he enjoys, no doubt the answer is, in the first place, eating and drinking, taking his ease at his inn, and the company of other merry souls. Compared with these things, what we count the graver interests of life are nothing to him. But then, while we are under his spell, it is impossible to consider these graver interests; gravity is to us, as to him, inferior to gravy; and what he does enjoy he enjoys with such a luscious and good-humoured zest that we sympathise and he makes us happy. And if anyone objected, we should answer with Sir Toby Belch, 'Dost thou think, because thou art virtuous, there shall be no more cakes and ale?'

But this, again, is far from all. Falstaff's ease and enjoyment are not simply those of the happy man of appetite;[4] they are those of the humorist, and the humorist of genius. Instead of being comic to you and serious to himself, he is more ludicrous to himself than to you; and he makes himself out more ludicrous than he is, in order that he and others may laugh. Prince Hal never made such sport of Falstaff's person as he himself did. It is *he* who says that his skin hangs about him like an old lady's loose gown, and that he walks before his page like a sow that hath o'erwhelmed all her litter but one. And he jests at himself when he is alone just as much as when others are by. It is the same with his appetites. The direct enjoyment they bring him is scarcely so great as the enjoyment of laughing at this enjoyment; and for all his addiction to sack you never see him for an instant with a brain dulled by it, or a temper turned solemn, silly, quarrelsome, or pious. The virtue it instils into him, of filling his brain with nimble, fiery, and delectable shapes— this, and his humorous attitude towards it, free him, in a manner, from slavery to it; and it is this freedom, and no secret longing for better things (those who attribute such a longing to him are far astray), that makes his enjoyment contagious and prevents our sympathy with it from being disturbed.

The bliss of freedom gained in humour is the essence of Falstaff. His humour is not directed only or chiefly against obvious absurdities; he is the enemy of everything that would interfere with his ease, and therefore of anything serious, and especially of everything respectable and moral. For these things impose limits and obligations, and make us the subjects of old father antic the law, and the categorical imperative, and our station and its duties, and conscience, and reputation, and other people's opinions, and all sorts of nuisances. I say he is therefore their enemy; but I do him wrong; to say that he is their enemy implies that he regards them as serious and recognises their power, when in truth he refuses to recognise them at all. They are to him absurd; and to reduce a thing *ad absurdum* is to reduce it to nothing and to walk about free and rejoicing. This is what Falstaff does with all the would-be serious things of life, sometimes only by his words, sometimes by his actions too. He will make truth appear absurd by solemn statements, which he utters with perfect gravity and which he expects nobody to believe; and honour, by demonstrating that it cannot set a leg, and that neither the living nor the dead can possess it; and law, by evading all the attacks of its highest representative and almost forcing him to laugh at his own defeat; and patriotism, by filling his pockets with the bribes offered by competent soldiers who want to escape service, while he takes in their stead the halt and maimed and the gaol-birds; and duty, by showing how he labours in his vocation—of thieving; and courage, alike by mocking at his own capture of Colvile and gravely claiming to have killed Hotspur; and war, by offering the Prince his bottle of sack when he is asked for a sword; and religion, by amusing himself with remorse at odd times when he has nothing else to do; and the fear of death, by maintaining perfectly untouched, in the face of imminent peril and even while he *feels* the fear of death, the very same power of dissolving it in persiflage that he shows when he sits at ease in his inn. These are the wonderful achievements which he performs, not with the sourness of a cynic, but with the gaiety of a boy. And, therefore, we praise him, we laud him, for he offends none but the virtuous, and denies that life is real or life is earnest, and delivers us from the oppression of such nightmares, and lifts us into the atmosphere of perfect freedom.

No one in the play understands Falstaff fully, any more than Hamlet was understood by the persons round him. They are both men of genius. Mrs. Quickly and Bardolph are his slaves, but they know not why. 'Well, fare thee well,' says the hostess whom he has pillaged and forgiven; 'I have known thee these twenty-nine years, come peas-cod time, but an honester and truer-hearted man—well, fare thee well.' Poins and the Prince delight in him; they get him into corners for the pleasure of seeing him escape in ways they cannot imagine; but they often take him much too seriously. Poins, for instance, rarely sees, the Prince does not always see, and moralising critics never see, that when Falstaff speaks ill of a companion behind his back, or writes to the Prince that Poins spreads it abroad that the Prince is to marry his sister, he knows quite well that what he says will be repeated, or rather, perhaps, is absolutely indifferent whether it be repeated or not, being certain that it can only give him an opportunity for humour. It is the same with his lying, and almost the same with his cowardice, the two main vices laid to his charge even by sympathisers. Falstaff is neither a liar nor a coward in the usual sense, like the typical cowardly boaster of comedy. He tells his lies either for their own humour, or on purpose to get himself into a difficulty. He rarely expects to be believed, perhaps never. He abandons a statement or contradicts it the moment it is made. There is scarcely more intent in his lying than in the humorous exaggerations which he pours out in soliloquy just as much as when others are by. Poins and the Prince understand this in part. You see them waiting eagerly to convict him, not that they may really put him to shame, but in order to enjoy the greater lie that will swallow up the less. But their sense of humour lags behind his. Even the Prince seems to accept as half-serious that remorse of his which passes so suddenly into glee at the idea of taking a purse, and his request to his friend to

bestride him if he should see him down in the battle. Bestride Falstaff!
'Hence! Wilt thou lift up Olympus?' Again, the attack of the Prince
and Poins on Falstaff and the other thieves on Gadshill is contrived,
we know, with a view to the incomprehensible lies it will induce him
to tell. But when, more than rising to the occasion, he turns two men
in buckram into four, and then seven, and then nine, and then eleven,
almost in a breath, I believe they partly misunderstand his intention,
and too many of his critics misunderstand it altogether. Shakespeare
was not writing a mere farce. It is preposterous to suppose that a
man of Falstaff's intelligence would utter these gross, palpable, open
lies with the serious intention to deceive, or forget that, if it was too
dark for him to see his own hand, he could hardly see that the three
misbegotten knaves were wearing Kendal green. No doubt, if he *had*
been believed, he would have been hugely tickled at it, but he no more
expected to be believed than when he claimed to have killed Hotspur.
Yet he is supposed to be serious even then. Such interpretations would
destroy the poet's whole conception; and of those who adopt them
one might ask this out of some twenty similar questions:—When
Falstaff, in the men in buckram scene, begins by calling twice at short
intervals for sack, and then a little later calls for more and says, 'I am
a rogue if I drunk to-day,' and the Prince answers, 'O villain, thy lips
are scarce wiped since thou drunk'st last,' do they think that *that* lie
was meant to deceive? And if not, why do they take it for granted
that the others were? I suppose they consider that Falstaff was in
earnest when, wanting to get twenty-two yards of satin on trust from
Master Dombledon the silk-mercer, he offered Bardolph as security;
or when he said to the Chief Justice about Mrs. Quickly, who accused
him of breaking his promise to marry her, 'My lord, this is a poor
mad soul, and she says up and down the town that her eldest son
is like you'; or when he explained his enormous bulk by exclaiming,
'A plague of sighing and grief! It blows a man up like a bladder'; or
when he accounted for his voice being cracked by declaring that he
had 'lost it with singing of anthems'; or even when he sold his soul on
Good-Friday to the devil for a cup of Madeira and a cold capon's leg.
Falstaff's lies about Hotspur and the men in buckram do not essentially differ from these statements. There is nothing serious in any of
them except the refusal to take anything seriously.

This is also the explanation of Falstaff's cowardice, a subject on
which I should say nothing if Maurice Morgann's essay,[5] now more

than a century old, were better known. That Falstaff sometimes behaves in what we should generally call a cowardly way is certain; but that does not show that he was a coward; and if the word means a person who feels painful fear in the presence of danger, and yields to that fear in spite of his better feelings and convictions, then assuredly Falstaff was no coward. The stock bully and boaster of comedy is one, but not Falstaff. It is perfectly clear in the first place that, though he had unfortunately a reputation for stabbing and caring not what mischief he did if his weapon were out, he had not a reputation for cowardice. Shallow remembered him five-and-fifty years ago breaking Scogan's head at the court-gate when he was a crack not thus high; and Shallow knew him later a good back-swordsman. Then we lose sight of him till about twenty years after, when his association with Bardolph began; and that association implies that by the time he was thirty-five or forty he had sunk into the mode of life we witness in the plays. Yet, even as we see him there, he remains a person of consideration in the army. Twelve captains hurry about London searching for him. He is present at the Council of War in the King's tent at Shrewsbury, where the only other persons are the King, the two princes, a nobleman and Sir Walter Blunt. The messenger who brings the false report of the battle to Northumberland mentions, as one of the important incidents, the death of Sir John Falstaff. Colvile, expressly described as a famous rebel, surrenders to him as soon as he hears his name. And if his own wish that his name were not so terrible to the enemy, and his own boast of his European reputation, are not evidence of the first rank, they must not be entirely ignored in presence of these other facts. What do these facts mean? Does Shakespeare put them all in with no purpose at all, or in defiance of his own intentions? It is not credible.

And when, in the second place, we look at Falstaff's actions, what do we find? He boldly confronted Colvile, he was quite ready to fight with him, however pleased that Colvile, like a kind fellow, gave himself away. When he saw Henry and Hotspur fighting, Falstaff, instead of making off in a panic, stayed to take his chance if Hotspur should be the victor. He *led* his hundred and fifty ragamuffins where they were peppered, he did not *send* them. To draw upon Pistol and force him downstairs and wound him in the shoulder was no great feat, perhaps, but the stock coward would have shrunk from it. When the Sheriff came to the inn to arrest him for an offence whose penalty was death, Falstaff, who was hidden behind the arras, did not stand there quaking for fear, he immediately fell asleep and snored. When he stood in the battle reflecting on what would happen if the weight of his paunch should be increased by that of a bullet, he cannot have been in a tremor of craven fear. He *never* shows such fear; and surely the man who, in danger of his life, and with no one by to hear him, meditates thus: 'I like not such grinning honour as Sir Walter hath. Give me life: which if I can save, so; if not, honour comes unlooked-for, and there's an end,' is not what we commonly call a coward.

'Well,' it will be answered, 'but he ran away on Gadshill; and when Douglas attacked him he fell down and shammed dead.' Yes, I am thankful to say, he did. For of course he did not want to be dead. He wanted to live and be merry. And as he had reduced the idea of honour *ad absurdum*, had scarcely any self-respect, and only a respect for reputation as a means of life, naturally he avoided death when he could do so without a ruinous loss of reputation, and (observe) with the satisfaction of playing a colossal practical joke. For *that* after all was his first object. If his one thought had been to avoid death he would not have faced Douglas at all, but would have run away as fast as his legs could carry him; and unless Douglas had been one of those exceptional Scotchmen who have no sense of humour, he would never have thought of pursuing so ridiculous an object as Falstaff running. So that, as Mr. Swinburne remarks, Poins is right when he thus distinguishes Falstaff from his companions in robbery: 'For two of them, I know them to be as true-bred cowards as ever turned back; and for the third, if he fight longer than he sees reason, I'll forswear arms.' And the event justifies this distinction. For it is exactly thus that, according to the original stage-direction, Falstaff behaves when Henry and Poins attack him and the others. The rest run away at once; Falstaff, here as afterwards with Douglas, fights for a blow or two, but, finding himself deserted and outmatched, runs away also. Of course. He saw no reason to stay. *Any* man who had risen superior to all serious motives would have run away. But it does not follow that he would run from mere fear, or be, in the ordinary sense, a coward.[6]

3.

The main source, then, of our sympathetic delight in Falstaff is his humorous superiority to everything serious, and the freedom of soul enjoyed in it. But, of course, this is not the whole of his character.

Shakespeare knew well enough that perfect freedom is not to be gained in this manner; we are ourselves aware of it even while we are sympathising with Falstaff; and as soon as we regard him seriously it becomes obvious. His freedom is limited in two main ways. For one thing he cannot rid himself entirely of respect for all that he professes to ridicule. He shows a certain pride in his rank: unlike the Prince, he is haughty to the drawers, who call him a proud Jack. He is not really quite indifferent to reputation. When the Chief Justice bids him pay his debt to Mrs. Quickly for his reputation's sake, I think he feels a twinge, though to be sure he proceeds to pay her by borrowing from her. He is also stung by any thoroughly serious imputation on his courage, and winces at the recollection of his running away on Gadshill; he knows that his behaviour there certainly looked cowardly, and perhaps he remembers that he would not have behaved so once. It is, further, very significant that, for all his dissolute talk, he has never yet allowed the Prince and Poins to *see* him as they saw him afterwards with Doll Tearsheet; not, of course, that he has any moral shame in the matter, but he knows that in such a situation he, in his old age, must appear contemptible—not a humorist but a mere object of mirth. And, finally, he has affection in him—affection, I think, for Poins and Bardolph, and certainly for the Prince; and that is a thing which he cannot jest out of existence. Hence, as the effect of his rejection shows, he is not really invulnerable. And then, in the second place, since he is in the flesh, his godlike freedom has consequences and conditions; consequences, for there is something painfully wrong with his great toe; conditions, for he cannot eat and drink for ever without money, and his purse suffers from consumption, a disease for which he can find no remedy.[7] As the Chief Justice tells him, his means are very slender and his waste great; and his answer, 'I would it were otherwise; I would my means were greater and my waist slenderer,' though worth much money, brings none in. And so he is driven to evil deeds; not only to cheating his tailor like a gentleman, but to fleecing Justice Shallow, and to highway robbery, and to cruel depredations on the poor woman whose affection he has secured. All this is perfectly consistent with the other side of his character, but by itself it makes an ugly picture.

Yes, it makes an ugly picture when you look at it seriously. But then, surely, so long as the humorous atmosphere is preserved and the humorous attitude maintained, you do not look at it so. You no more regard Falstaff's misdeeds morally than you do the much more atrocious misdeeds of Punch or Reynard the Fox. You do not exactly ignore them, but you attend only to their comic aspect. This is the very spirit of comedy, and certainly of Shakespeare's comic world, which is one of make-believe, not merely as his tragic world is, but in a further sense—a world in which gross improbabilities are accepted with a smile, and many things are welcomed as merely laughable which, regarded gravely, would excite anger and disgust. The intervention of a serious spirit breaks up such a world, and would destroy our pleasure in Falstaff's company. Accordingly through the greater part of these dramas Shakespeare carefully confines this spirit to the scenes of war and policy, and dismisses it entirely in the humorous parts. Hence, if *Henry IV* had been a comedy like *Twelfth Night*, I am sure that he would no more have ended it with the painful disgrace of Falstaff than he ended *Twelfth Night* by disgracing Sir Toby Belch.[8]

But *Henry IV* was to be in the main a historical play, and its chief hero Prince Henry. In the course of it his greater and finer qualities were to be gradually revealed, and it was to end with beautiful scenes of reconciliation and affection between his father and him, and a final emergence of the wild Prince as a just, wise, stern, and glorious King. Hence, no doubt, it seemed to Shakespeare that Falstaff at last must be disgraced, and must therefore appear no longer as the invincible humorist, but as an object of ridicule and even of aversion. And probably also his poet's insight showed him that Henry, as he conceived him, *would* behave harshly to Falstaff in order to impress the world, especially when his mind had been wrought to a high pitch by the scene with his dying father and the impression of his own solemn consecration to great duties.

This conception was a natural and a fine one; and if the execution was not an entire success, it is yet full of interest. Shakespeare's purpose being to work a gradual change in our feelings towards Falstaff, and to tinge the humorous atmosphere more and more deeply with seriousness, we see him carrying out this purpose in the Second Part of *Henry IV*. Here he separates the Prince from Falstaff as much as he can, thus withdrawing him from Falstaff's influence, and weakening in our minds the connection between the two. In the First Part we constantly see them together; in the Second (it is a remarkable fact) only once before the rejection. Further, in the scenes where Henry appears apart from Falstaff, we watch him growing more and more grave, and awakening more and more poetic interest; while Falstaff, though his humour scarcely flags to the end, exhibits more and more of his seamy side. This is nowhere turned to the full light in Part I; but in Part II we see him as the heartless destroyer of Mrs. Quickly, as a ruffian seriously defying the Chief Justice because his position as an officer on service gives him power to do wrong, as the pike preparing to snap up the poor old dace Shallow, and (this is the one scene where Henry and he meet) as the worn-out lecher, not laughing at his servitude to the flesh but sunk in it. Finally, immediately before the rejection, the world where he is king is exposed in all its sordid criminality when we find Mrs. Quickly and Doll arrested for being concerned in the death of one man, if not more, beaten to death by their bullies; and the dangerousness of Falstaff is emphasised in his last words as he hurries from Shallow's house to London, words at first touched with humour but at bottom only too seriously meant: 'Let us take any man's horses; the laws of England are at my commandment. Happy are they which have been my friends, and woe unto my Lord Chief Justice.' His dismissal to the Fleet by the Chief Justice is the dramatic vengeance for that threat.

Yet all these excellent devices fail. They cause us momentary embarrassment at times when repellent traits in Falstaff's character are disclosed; but they fail to change our attitude of humour into one of seriousness, and our sympathy into repulsion. And they were bound to fail, because Shakespeare shrank from adding to them the one device which would have ensured success. If, as the Second Part of *Henry IV* advanced, he had clouded over Falstaff's humour so heavily that the man of genius turned into the Falstaff of the *Merry Wives*, we should have witnessed his rejection without a pang. This Shakespeare was too much of an artist to do—though even in this way he did something—and without this device he could not succeed. As I said, in the creation of Falstaff he overreached himself. He was caught up on the wind of his own genius, and carried so far that he could not descend to earth at the selected spot. It is not a misfortune that happens to many authors, nor is it one we can regret, for it costs us but a trifling inconvenience in one scene, while we owe to it perhaps the greatest comic character in literature. For it is in this character, and not in the judgment he brings upon Falstaff's head, that Shakespeare asserts his supremacy. To show that Falstaff's freedom of soul was in part illusory, and that the realities of life refused to be conjured away by his humour—this was what we might expect from Shakespeare's unfailing sanity, but it was surely no achievement beyond the power of lesser men. The achievement was Falstaff himself, and the conception of that freedom of soul, a freedom illusory only in part, and attainable only by a mind which had received from Shakespeare's own the inexplicable touch of infinity which he bestowed on Hamlet and Macbeth and Cleopatra, but denied to Henry the Fifth.

NOTES

1. See on this and other points Swinburne, *A Study of Shakespeare*, p. 106 ff.
2. Rötscher, *Shakespeare in seinen höchsten Charaktergebilden*, 1864.
3. That from the beginning Shakespeare intended Henry's accession to be Falstaff's catastrophe is clear from the fact that, when the two characters first appear, Falstaff is made to betray at once the hopes with which he looks forward to Henry's reign. See the First Part of *Henry IV*, Act I., Scene ii.
4. Cf. Hazlitt, *Characters of Shakespear's Plays*.
5. [Morgann, Maurice. *An Essay on the dramatic character of Sir John Falstaff*. 1777.]
6. It is to be regretted, however, that in carrying his guts away so nimbly he 'roared for mercy'; for I fear we have no ground for rejecting Henry's statement to that effect, and I do not see my way to adopt the suggestion (I forget whose it is) that Falstaff spoke the truth when he swore that he knew Henry and Poins as well as he that made them.
7. Panurge too was 'naturally subject to a kind of disease which at that time they called lack of money'; it was a 'flux in his purse' (Rabelais, Book II., chapters xvi., xvii.).
8. I seem to remember that, according to Gervinus, Shakespeare did disgrace Sir Toby—by marrying him to Maria!

"THE LOVE SONG OF J. ALFRED PRUFROCK"
(THOMAS STEARNS ELIOT)

"'Almost Ridiculous': Dark Humor in Eliot's 'The Love Song of J. Alfred Prufrock'"
by Robert C. Evans,
Auburn University at Montgomery

Garrison Keillor, the popular literary humorist, storyteller, and author, recalled in an early 2007 blog entry that when he was young,

> most major American writers seemed to be alcoholic or suicidal or both, and we students absorbed the notion that the true sign of brilliance is to be seriously screwed up. The true poet is haunted by livid demons, brave, doomed, terribly wounded, and if one was (as I was) relatively unscratched, you concealed this and tried to impersonate doom.
>
> The prime minister of high culture was T.S. Eliot, who suffered from a lousy marriage and hated his job and so wrote "The Love Song of J. Alfred Prufrock," a small, dark mopefest of a poem in which old Pru worries about whether to eat a peach or roll up his trousers. This poem pretty much killed off the pleasure of poetry for millions of people who got dragged through it in high school.

Keillor, of course, was simply tossing off, in passing, a brief impressionistic recollection, not offering extended literary analysis, but he was soon challenged by another blogger named Linda Sue Grimes, a Ph.D. in literature who argued that it "is funny that Keillor, whose own banter and reportage is laced with humor, does not see the humor in 'Old Pru.'" The titular speaker of Eliot's poem (Grimes contends) is "a ridiculous character, utterly laughable." He is "merely a conglomeration of all the ridiculous traits of humankind at any time; therefore, readers cannot take him seriously. Readers are free to simply enjoy the inane things he thinks and says by laughing at them." The poem, Grimes suggests, is "too funny to be a 'dark mopefest,'" and Prufrock himself "becomes a caricature who instead of drawing sympathy draws derision from the reader."

Somewhere between the opinions of Keillor and Grimes lies something like the truth. Prufrock is not as utterly laughable and completely ridiculous a character as Grimes seems to suggest; certainly any survey of the commentary the poem has elicited shows that Prufrock has frequently been read as far more than a figure of mere fun or simple ridicule. In fact, the poem has often been interpreted as a provocative meditation on such highly serious themes (to list merely a few in alphabetical order) as alienation from nature and others, antiheroism, anxiety and frustration, boredom or *ennui*, bourgeois decadence, the corruptions of cities, damnation and redemption, the decline of Western civilization, the deconstruction of personality, disillusionment and passivity, failure of will, fear of old age, fear of sex, intense self-consciousness, the loss of youth, metaphysical distress, the perils of indecision, personal weakness in an ugly world, psychological insecurity, romantic despair, self-division, self-disgust, social isolation, solipsism, the sordidness of daily existence, spiritual emptiness and sterility, and turpitude and evil (Blalock 53–83). No wonder young Keillor was depressed! Nevertheless, despite the often gloomy tone of the poem and the often persuasively gloomy ways in which it has been interpreted, the work does contain obvious elements of humor, irony, satire, parody, self-mockery, and burlesque. To the extent that it is indeed a humorous poem, then, its humor is dark; but its humor is also more complicated and subtle than Grimes seems to allow. Prufrock is not a figure who seems "utterly laughable," nor is he simply a target of readers' superior "derision." He is, instead, a figure who is perfectly capable of mocking himself and who even (partly for that reason) earns a hard-won measure of the reader's sympathy. If Prufrock were less self-aware, he might also be more laughable and more simply funny.

Almost everyone would agree that one of the most obviously humorous aspects of the poem is its very title. The name "J. Alfred Prufrock" sounds stiff, formal, pretentious, and affected; to imagine that a character with such a name might be either the subject or the author of a "love song" therefore seems (as Prufrock himself might put it) "almost ridiculous" (l. 118). The term "love song" will, of course, seem even more ironical and darkly comic as the poem develops, since this is a work that largely concerns the protagonist's inability either to find love or to express it. For the moment, though, the title suggests a more blatantly comic poem than Eliot eventually delivers, and the shift to a darker tone seems evident immediately in the unexpected quotation from Dante's *Inferno* that precedes the poem proper. Like so much else in this work, the precise import of the quotation is difficult to determine. The speaker, Guido da Montefeltro, is a liar who has been trapped as a flame in one of the lower circles of hell; he is willing to speak to Dante only because he assumes that his words will never be repeated or reported: "If I thought that my reply would be to one who would ever return to the world, this flame would stay without further movement; but since none has ever returned alive from this depth, if what I hear is true, I answer you without fear of infamy" (Baym 1420).

Guido, needless to say, is mistaken in his assumption that Dante will never be able to report what he is told; indeed, the words Guido speaks become embedded in one of the most famous and most widely read poems ever written. The same, of course, is also true of Prufrock's own confession. The joke, then, is on both Guido and Prufrock, or perhaps (if Prufrock himself is imagined as deliberately including the quotation from Dante in his "Love Song"), the joke is deliberately *by* Prufrock at his own expense. However the quotation from Dante is precisely interpreted, its import seems not only dark (since it implies that Prufrock is trapped in a kind of Hell) but also somewhat comic (since it calls attention to the fact that his embarrassed confessions are about to be made widely public). Nevertheless, in trying to determine the exact tone of the quotation from Dante, much depends on whether we assume that it is inserted by Eliot (the creator of Prufrock) or whether it is intentionally included by Prufrock himself. If the latter assumption seems persuasive, then Prufrock has already begun a process of self-mockery—a process that becomes even more undeniable and obvious as the poem proceeds.

Paradoxically, the more Prufrock is willing to openly mock himself, the less merely risible (because the more humble, sympathetic, and self-aware) he ultimately seems.

The very first words of the poem proper—"Let us go then, you and I" (l. 1)—are typically puzzling and may also, already, be characteristically ironic. Presumably the "I" is Prufrock himself, but who is the "you"? Commentators have disagreed greatly about the identity of this latter figure, but surely the "you" is in one sense the reader, who is about to accompany Prufrock (as Dante accompanied Virgil) on a tour through a kind of hell. The opening line of the poem implies, then, a purposeful journey with a companion—an implication that will seem somewhat ironic by the conclusion of the work, since Prufrock will ultimately arrive nowhere and will seem incapable of making or sustaining connections. Meanwhile, the poem's second line—"When the evening is spread out against the sky"—implies an already literally dark setting, although whether such darkness is meant to seem appealing or disturbing is as yet unclear. Only when we reach the third line—"Like a patient etherised upon a table"—does the tone suddenly and clearly seem both shocking and ironic. If the image seems darkly humorous (and it does often provoke surprised laughter during classroom discussions), it also seems surprisingly grotesque, suggesting a theme of figurative sickness that runs throughout the work. Is Prufrock, by using such an image, already suggesting his own capacity for a kind of grim and sardonic dark humor? And, if this is the case, should a man capable of such biting irony himself be treated as a figure of mere ridicule and derision? Here, as so often elsewhere, any humor the poem displays seems both dark and provocative, and the attitude we are meant to adopt toward Prufrock is by no means simple or obvious.

Humor—dark or otherwise—is not especially obvious in the first 30 lines or so of the poem. Instead, gloomy and depressing imagery tends to predominate, especially when the speaker proposes a journey "through certain half-deserted streets, / The muttering retreats / Of restless nights in one-night cheap hotels, / And saw-dust restaurants with oyster-shells" (ll. 4–7). Any humor here—even of a dark sort—is hardly blatant (to say the least). The references to "cheap hotels" and "saw-dust" restaurants may strike some readers as comically melancholy, as if Prufrock is a depressed, depressing person who is absolutely determined to be joyless. Likewise, his comment that the streets "follow like a tedious argument / Of *insidious* intent" (ll. 8–9;

emphasis added) may already contain a hint of comic paranoia, while his reference to an "overwhelming question" (l. 10) may perhaps imply that he takes himself and his humdrum existence far too seriously and is therefore already a target of ironic mockery by the poet. There may, too, be a touch of comic exasperation when Prufrock exclaims, concerning the supposedly "overwhelming" question, "Oh, do not ask, 'What is it?'" (l. 11), and there certainly seems more than a touch of comic incongruity in the abrupt shift reporting that "In the room the women come and go / Talking of Michelangelo" (ll. 13–14).

The sudden juxtaposition of these lines with the verse paragraph that precedes them must have struck Eliot's first readers, especially, as disorienting and nearly absurd, just as the equally sudden shift to the prolonged description of the "yellow fog" must have made many early readers (and many later ones, too) wonder what, exactly, the structure and point of the poem was supposed to be and how to interpret both its protagonist and its odd mixture of tones and strange combinations of images. Sometimes dark, sometimes almost lyrical, sometimes portentous and paradoxical ("There will be time to murder and create"; l. 28), sometimes exhibiting shrewd social insight ("There will be time, there will be time / To prepare a face to meet the faces that you meet"; ll. 26–27), the poem for much of its first 30 lines seems to waver between the serious and the absurd, with touches also of the grotesque. Not until we reach the oddly deflating reference to "the taking of a toast and tea" (l. 34)—which suddenly plunges us into a world of routine bourgeois domesticity—does the tone become overtly satirical and ironic.

From this point forward, the humor tends to be more blatant as the focus shifts more clearly to Prufrock himself. His repeated wondering—"'Do I dare?' and, 'Do I dare'" (l. 38)—suggests risible weakness, especially since he doesn't even "dare" to report clearly what is troubling him, and this impression of somewhat laughable fragility and comic self-consciousness is soon reinforced by other details: his uncertainty about whether or not to climb a stair (presumably to engage in a social encounter he partly dreads); his worry about the "bald spot of the middle of [his] hair"; his acute awareness of how others might respond to his appearance ("They will say: 'How his hair is growing thin! ... 'how his arms and legs are thin!'"); even his elaborately upper-middle-class style of dress ("My morning coat, my collar mounting firmly to the chin, / My necktie rich and modest, but asserted by a simple pin"; [ll. 39–44]). All these details make Prufrock a figure whom both he and others find hard to take seriously. But the mere fact that he is willing to honestly report his defects suggests that he is not entirely a figure of fun. Most people, if they are honest with themselves (as Prufrock apparently tries to be honest with himself) can relate, on some level, to the kinds of insecurities Prufrock expresses. Everyone dislikes being judged harshly by others; everyone dislikes the physical decay that accompanies aging; everyone has wished to avoid an unwanted social encounter. Merely laughing at Prufrock is too easy; it implies a position of unrealistic superiority, as if the laugher were entirely immune to the kinds of anxieties Prufrock expresses. What makes Prufrock a figure of dark humor is the fact that we *cannot* entirely distance ourselves from him or find him merely ridiculous. The anxieties and uncertainties that trouble him (and that make him partly comic) are ones that are by no means confined to Prufrock alone.

Prufrock is usually regarded, by himself and others, as both piti-fully and laughably weak, especially in his relations with the women who increasingly come to dominate his thoughts and expressions. He seems emasculated, and his social awkwardness both results from and enhances his social insecurities. The more uncomfortable he feels, the more ineptly he acts; and the more ineptly he acts, the more uncomfort-able he feels. There is, perhaps, a touch of comic paranoia in his focus on "The eyes that fix you in a formulated phrase" (l. 56), and there is, perhaps, a touch of risible self-pity when he imagines himself "formu-lated, sprawling on a pin" and then "pinned and wriggling on the wall" (l. 57–58). In lines like these, Prufrock does seem somewhat laugh-ably pathetic, but any laughter directed at him also seems partly cruel, especially since he is so aware of his own shortcomings. This is another sense, then, in which any comedy in "Prufrock" seems dark: laughing at Prufrock seems a bit like "kicking a man when he is down" (to use the old cliché), especially since no one is harder on Prufrock than Prufrock himself. He is highly aware of all his shortcomings and flaws; he seems full of genuine self-contempt; he doesn't seem, especially, to be seeking any pity or merely playing the role of victim to elicit sympathy; he doesn't try to hide, disguise, or make excuses for his flaws; and (most significantly) he also seems capable of genuinely sympathetic responses to others (as when he mentions that he has gone "at dusk through narrow streets / And watched the smoke that rises from the pipes / Of lonely men in shirt-sleeves, leaning out of windows"; ll. 70–72). For all these reasons, it seems difficult merely to laugh or jeer at Prufrock; his predicament, instead, arouses more complex responses—responses that should involve our own awareness of our own flaws and shortcomings. No one is more aware than Prufrock himself that he cuts a somewhat ridiculous figure, and his honesty in confessing his faults and foibles therefore makes him seem less a purely comic buffoon than a figure in a somewhat painful tragicomedy. Only an immensely self-assured and perhaps uncharitable person—only a person who might actually seem comically arrogant or even cruel—could entirely dismiss Prufrock as merely ridiculous. His predicament demands a more humble, more humane response, if only because we cannot entirely distance ourselves from the defects he displays.

Despite Prufrock's obvious weaknesses, he does exhibit a genuine ability to laugh at himself, and the mere fact that he puts his weaknesses on such public display suggests a kind of strength. It is Prufrock himself, after all, who imagines his "head (grown slightly bald) brought in upon a platter" (l. 82), and it is that unnecessary but added parenthetical phrase that makes especially obvious his genuine willingness to mock himself. This is a willingness he demonstrates again and again. It is Prufrock himself who imagines that the "eternal Footman" will "hold my coat, and snicker" (l. 85), just as it is Prufrock himself who repeatedly provides all the other details that make his life seem a continuous routine of incongruities and anti-climaxes that are described through a whole series of mock-serious allusions to such grand sources as the Bible and Shakespeare. For this reason, when Prufrock announces that he is "not Prince Hamlet, nor was meant to be," our first response is to think, *well, that's obvious*, but our second response should be to recall all the ways in which Prufrock does indeed resemble Hamlet, including in his melancholy, his indecisiveness, his self-contempt, and his sense of being woefully out of step with his complacently comfortable society. This is not to say that Prufrock is tragic; it is merely to say that he is not simply laughable. A similarly complex response is provoked when Prufrock, after dismissing any likeness between himself and Hamlet, implicitly compares himself instead to a figure like Polonius. Prufrock says that if he resembles any figure in a play, he is simply

> ... an attendant lord, one that will do
> To swell a progress, start a scene or two,

Advise the prince; no doubt, an easy tool,
Deferential, glad to be of use,
Politic, cautious, and meticulous;
Full of high sentence, but a bit obtuse;
At times, indeed, almost ridiculous–
Almost, at times, the Fool. (ll. 111–119)

Once more, however, the phrasing is double-edged, since the reference to obtuseness helps remind us of all the ways in which Prufrock is *not* obtuse. He is, if anything, painfully sensitive and self-aware, and the mere fact that he can mock himself as he does in the lines just quoted shows how far he is from entirely resembling Shakespeare's Polonius, whose key flaw is that he takes himself too seriously and cannot imagine himself as ridiculous in the ways he seems to others. Similarly ironic is Prufrock's comparison of himself to "the Fool" in an Elizabethan play. On the one hand, the comparison exhibits once more his humble (and/or perhaps masochistic) willingness to mock and denigrate himself in print; on the other hand, the comparison may also remind us that the fools in Shakespeare's plays are often the wisest characters, partly because they are also the most self-aware.

Here, then, as so often in Eliot's poem, Prufrock's phrasing cuts both ways. Prufrock never becomes a merely risible, entirely laughable figure. He is never the target of simple satire or uncomplicated irony—even his own. He is painfully self-aware of his weaknesses, his flaws, and his shortcomings, and honest readers will have to confess that Prufrock's flaws are not his alone. We cannot help but laugh sometimes at Prufrock, just as he insistently laughs at himself (especially in the latter half of the poem). Yet the joke, alas, is not entirely on Prufrock alone. He is, in many ways, the archetypal modern man, and conscientious readers will have to confess that in laughing at him, they laugh partly (and perhaps somewhat ruefully) at themselves.

WORKS CITED OR CONSULTED

Baym, Nina, ed. *The Norton Anthology of American Literature*. Sixth edition. Volume D. New York: Norton, 2003.

Blalock, Susan. *Guide to the Secular Poetry of T.S. Eliot*. New York: G.K. Hall, 1996.

Eliot, T.S. "The Love Song of J. Alfred Prufrock." Baym 1420–1423.

Grimes, Linda Sue. "Tricked by J. Alfred Prufrock: Learn to Laugh."
     November 7, 2007. http://american-poetry.suite101.com/article.cfm/
     tricked_by_j_alfred_prufrock. Accessed on October 16, 2008.
Keillor, Garrison. "The Old Scout: Choosing the Right Lunch Partners."
     February 20, 2007. http://prairiehome.publicradio.org/features/
     deskofgk/2007/02/27.shtml. Accessed on October 16, 2008.

A MODEST PROPOSAL
(JONATHAN SWIFT)

"Wood's Halfpence"
by Leslie Stephen, in *Swift* (1882)

INTRODUCTION

In this chapter from his late-nineteenth-century appraisal of Jonathan Swift's life and works, biographer Leslie Stephen discusses the political and social context that prompted such scathingly satirical works as *A Modest Proposal*. With "a passion the glow of which makes other passions look cold," Stephen argues that Swift's advocacy for the oppressed of Ireland occasioned his darkest and most humorous works. Commenting on the "superficial coolness" of *A Modest Proposal*'s tone, Stephen remarks that Swift's writing, "may be revolting to tender-hearted people, and has, indeed, led to condemnation of the supposed ferocity of the author almost as surprising as the criticisms which can see in it nothing but an exquisite piece of humour. It is, in truth, fearful to read even now."

In one of Scott's finest novels the old Cameronian preacher, who had been left for dead by Claverhouse's troopers, suddenly rises to

---

Stephen, Leslie. "Wood's Halfpence." *Swift*. 1882. London: MacMillan, 1898. 145–165.

confront his conquerors, and spends his last breath in denouncing the oppressors of the saints. Even such an apparition was Jonathan Swift to comfortable Whigs who were flourishing in the place of Harley and St. John, when, after ten years' quiescence, he suddenly stepped into the political arena. After the first crushing fall he had abandoned partial hope, and contented himself with establishing supremacy in his chapter. But undying wrath smouldered in his breast till time came for an outburst.

No man had ever learnt more thoroughly the lesson, "Put not your faith in princes;" or had been impressed with a lower estimate of the wisdom displayed by the rulers of the world. He had been behind the scenes, and knew that the wisdom of great ministers meant just enough cunning to court the ruin which a little common sense would have avoided. Corruption was at the prow and folly at the helm. The selfish ring which he had denounced so fiercely had triumphed. It had triumphed, as he held, by flattering the new dynasty, hoodwinking the nation, and maligning its antagonists. The cynical theory of politics was not for him, as for some comfortable cynics, an abstract proposition, which mattered very little to a sensible man, but was embodied in the bitter wrath with which he regarded his triumphant adversaries. Pessimism is perfectly compatible with bland enjoyment of the good things in a bad world; but Swift's pessimism was not of this type. It meant energetic hatred of definite things and people who were always before him.

With this feeling he had come to Ireland; and Ireland—I am speaking of a century and a half ago—was the opprobrium of English statesmanship. There Swift had (or thought he had) always before him a concrete example of the basest form of tyranny. By Ireland, I have said, Swift meant, in the first place, the English in Ireland. In the last years of his sanity he protested indignantly against the confusion between the "savage old Irish" and the English gentry, who, he said, were much better bred, spoke better English, and were more civilized than the inhabitants of many English counties.[1] He retained to the end of his life his antipathy to the Scotch colonists. He opposed their demand for political equality as fiercely in the last as in his first political utterances. He contrasted them unfavourably[2] with the Catholics, who had, indeed, been driven to revolt by massacre and confiscation under Puritan rule, but who were now, he declared, "true Whigs, in the best and most proper sense of the word," and thoroughly loyal to the house of Hanover. Had there been a danger of a Catholic revolt, Swift's feelings might have been different; but he always held that they were "as inconsiderable as the women and children," mere "hewers of wood and drawers of water," "out of all capacity of doing any mischief, if they were ever so well inclined."[3] Looking at them in this way, he felt a sincere compassion for their misery and a bitter resentment against their oppressors. The English, he said, in a remarkable letter,[4] should be ashamed of their reproaches of Irish dulness, ignorance, and cowardice. Those defects were the products of slavery. He declared that the poor cottagers had "a much better natural taste for good sense, humour, and raillery than ever I observed among people of the like sort in England. But the millions of oppressions they lie under, the tyranny of their landlords, the ridiculous zeal of their priests, and the misery of the whole nation, have been enough to damp the best spirits under the sun." Such a view is now commonplace enough. It was then a heresy to English statesmen, who thought that nobody but a Papist or a Jacobite could object to the tyranny of Whigs.

Swift's diagnosis of the chronic Irish disease was thoroughly political. He considered that Irish misery sprang from the subjection to a government not intentionally cruel, but absolutely selfish; to which the Irish revenue meant so much convenient political plunder, and which acted on the principle quoted from Cowley, that the happiness of Ireland should not weigh against the "least conveniency" of England. He summed up his views in a remarkable letter,[5] to be presently mentioned, the substance of which had been orally communicated to Walpole. He said to Walpole, as he said in every published utterance: first, that the colonists were still Englishmen, and entitled to English rights; secondly, that their trade was deliberately crushed, purely for the benefit of the English of England; thirdly, that all valuable preferments were bestowed upon men born in England, as a matter of course; and, finally, that in consequence of this the upper classes, deprived of all other openings, were forced to rack-rent their tenants to such a degree that not one farmer in the kingdom out of a hundred "could afford shoes or stockings to his children, or to eat flesh or drink anything better than sour milk and water twice in a year; so that the whole country, except the Scotch plantation in the north, is a scene of misery and desolation hardly to be matched on this side Lapland." A modern reformer would give the first and chief place to this social misery. It is characteristic that Swift comes to it as a consequence from the injustice to his own class: as, again, that he appeals to Walpole, not on the simple ground that the people are wretched, but on the ground that they will be soon unable to pay the tribute to England, which he reckons at a million a year. But his conclusion might be accepted by any Irish patriot. Whatever, he says, can make a country poor and despicable concurs in the case of Ireland. The nation is controlled by laws to which it does not consent; disowned by its brethren and countrymen; refused the liberty of trading even in its natural commodities; forced to seek for justice many hundred miles by sea and land; rendered in a manner incapable of serving the King and country in any place of honour, trust, or profit; whilst the governors have no sympathy with the governed, except what may occasionally arise from the sense of justice and philanthropy.

I am not to ask how far Swift was right in his judgments. Every line which he wrote shows that he was thoroughly sincere and profoundly stirred by his convictions. A remarkable pamphlet, published in 1720, contained his first utterance upon the subject. It is an exhortation to the Irish to use only Irish manufactures. He applies to Ireland the fable of *Arachne and Pallas*. The goddess, indignant at being equalled in spinning, turned her rival into a spider, to spin forever out of her own bowels in a narrow compass. He always, he says, pitied poor Arachne for so cruel and unjust a sentence, "which, however, is fully executed upon us by England with further additions of rigour and severity; for the greatest part of our bowels and vitals is extracted, without allowing us the liberty of spinning and weaving them." Swift of course accepts the economic fallacy equally taken for granted by his opponents, and fails to see that England and Ireland injured themselves as well as each other by refusing to interchange their productions. But he utters forcibly his righteous indignation against the contemptuous injustice of the English rulers, in consequence of which the "miserable people" are being reduced "to a worse condition than the peasants in France, or the vassals in Germany and Poland." Slaves, he says, have a natural disposition to be tyrants; and he himself, when his betters give him a kick, is apt to revenge it with six upon his footman. That is how the landlords treat their tenantry.

The printer of this pamphlet was prosecuted. The chief justice (Whitshed) sent back the jury nine times and kept them eleven hours before they would consent to bring in a "special verdict." The unpopularity of the prosecution became so great that it was at last dropped. Four years afterwards a more violent agitation broke out. A patent had been given to a certain William Wood for supplying Ireland with a copper coinage. Many complaints had been made, and in September, 1723, addresses were voted by the Irish Houses of Parliament, declaring that the patent had been obtained by clandestine and false representations; that it was mischievous to the country; and that Wood had been guilty of frauds in his coinage. They were pacified by vague promises; but Walpole went on with the scheme on the strength of a favourable report of a committee of the Privy Council; and the excitement was already serious when (in 1724) Swift published the *Drapier's Letters*, which give him his chief title to eminence as a patriotic agitator.

Swift either shared or took advantage of the general belief that the mysteries of the currency are unfathomable to the human intelligence. They have to do with that world of financial magic in which wealth may be made out of paper, and all ordinary relations of cause and effect are suspended. There is, however, no real mystery about the halfpence. The small coins which do not form part of the legal tender may be considered primarily as counters. A penny is a penny, so long as twelve are change for a shilling. It is not in the least necessary for this purpose that the copper contained in the twelve penny pieces should be worth or nearly worth a shilling. A sovereign can never be worth much more than the gold of which it is made. But at the present day bronze worth only twopence is coined into twelve penny pieces.[6] The coined bronze is worth six times as much as the uncoined. The small coins must have some intrinsic value to deter forgery, and must be made of good materials to stand wear and tear. If these conditions be observed, and a proper number be issued, the value of the penny will be no more affected by the value of the copper than the value of the banknote by that of the paper on which it is written. This opinion assumes that the copper coins cannot be offered or demanded in payment of any but trifling debts. The halfpence coined by Wood seem to have fulfilled these conditions, and as copper worth twopence (on the lowest computation) was coined into ten halfpence, worth fivepence, their intrinsic value was more than double that of modern halfpence.

The halfpence, then, were not objectionable upon this ground. Nay, it would have been wasteful to make them more valuable. It would have been as foolish to use more copper for the pence as to make the works of a watch of gold if brass is equally durable and convenient. But another consequence is equally clear. The effect of Wood's patent was that a mass of copper worth about 60,000*l.*[7] became worth 100,800*l.* in the shape of halfpenny pieces. There was, therefore, a balance of about *40,000l.* to pay for the expenses of coinage. It would have been waste to get rid of this by putting more copper in the coins; but, if so large a profit arose from the transaction, it would go to somebody. At the present day it would be brought into the national treasury. This was not the way in which business was done in Ireland. Wood was to pay 1000*l.* a year for fourteen years to the Crown.[8] But 14,000*l.* still leaves a large margin for profit. What was to become of it? According to the admiring biographer of Sir R. Walpole the patent had been originally given by Lord Sunderland to the Duchess of Kendal, a lady whom the King delighted to honour. She already received 3000*l.* a year in pensions upon the Irish Establishment, and she sold this patent to Wood for 10,000*l.* Enough was still left to give Wood a handsome profit; as in transactions of this kind every accomplice in a dirty business expects to be well paid. So handsome, indeed, was the profit that Wood received ultimately a pension of 3000*l.* for eight years—24,000*l.*, that is—in consideration of abandoning the patent. It was right and proper that a profit should be made on the transaction, but shameful that it should be divided between the King's mistress and William Wood, and that the bargain should be struck without consulting the Irish representatives, and maintained in spite of their protests. The Duchess of Kendal was to be allowed to take a share of the wretched halfpence in the pocket of every Irish beggar. A more disgraceful transaction could hardly be imagined, or one more calcu-lated to justify Swift's view of the selfishness and corruption of the English rulers.

Swift saw his chance, and went to work in characteristic fashion, with unscrupulous audacity of statement, guided by the keenest stra-tegical instinct. He struck at the heart as vigorously as he had done in the *Examiner*, but with resentment sharpened by ten years of exile. It was not safe to speak of the Duchess of Kendal's share in the transaction, though the story, as poor Archdeacon Coxe pathetically declares, was industriously propagated. But the case against Wood was all the stronger. Is he so wicked, asks Swift, as to suppose that a nation is to be ruined that he may gain three or four score thousand pounds? Hampden went to prison, he says, rather than pay a few shillings wrongfully; I, says Swift, would rather be hanged than have all my "property taxed at seventeen shillings in the pound at the arbitrary will and pleasure of the venerable Mr. Wood." A simple constitutional precedent might rouse a Hampden; but to stir a popular agitation it is as well to show that the evil actually inflicted is gigantic, independently of possible results. It requires, indeed, some audacity to prove that debasement of the copper currency can amount to a tax of seventeen shillings in the pound on all property. Here, however, Swift might simply throw the reins upon the neck of his fancy. Anybody may make any inferences he pleases in the mysterious regions of currency; and no inferences, it seems, were too audacious for his hearers, though we are left to doubt how far Swift's wrath had generated delusions in his own mind, and how far he perceived that other minds were ready to be deluded. He revels in prophesying the most extravagant consequences. The country will be undone; the tenants will not be able to pay their rents; "the farmers must rob, or beg, or leave the country; the shopkeepers in this and every other town must break or starve; the squire will hoard up all his good money to send to England and keep some poor tailor or weaver in his house, who will be glad to get bread at any rate."[9] Concrete facts are given to help the imagination. Squire Connolly must have 250 horses to bring his half-yearly rents to town; and the poor man will have to pay thirty-six of Wood's halfpence to get a quart of twopenny ale.

How is this proved? One argument is a sufficient specimen. Nobody, according to the patent, was to be forced to take Wood's halfpence; nor could any one be obliged to receive more than fivepence halfpenny in any one payment. This, of course, meant that the halfpence could only be used as change, and a man must pay his debts in silver or gold whenever it was possible to use a sixpence. It upsets Swift's statement about Squire Connolly's rents. But Swift is equal to the emergency. The rule means, he says, that every man must take fivepence halfpenny in every payment, *if it be offered*; which, on the next page, becomes simply in every payment; therefore, making an easy assumption or two, he reckons that you will receive 160*l*. a

year in these halfpence; and therefore (by other assumptions) lose
140*l*. a year.[10] It might have occurred to Swift, one would think, that
both parties to the transaction could not possibly be losers. But he
calmly assumes that the man who pays will lose in proportion to the
increased number of coins; and the man who receives, in proportion
to the depreciated value of each coin. He does not see, or think it
worth notice, that the two losses obviously counterbalance each other;
and he has an easy road to prophesying absolute ruin for everybody.
It would be almost as great a compliment to call this sophistry as to
dignify with the name of satire a round assertion that an honest man
is a cheat or a rogue.

The real grievance, however, shows through the sham argument.
"It is no loss of honour," thought Swift, "to submit to the lion; but
who, with the figure of a man, can think with patience of being
devoured alive by a rat?" Why should Wood have this profit (even if
more reasonably estimated) in defiance of the wishes of the nation? It
is, says Swift, because he is an Englishman and has great friends. He
proposes to meet the attempt by a general agreement not to take the
halfpence. Briefly, the halfpence were to be "Boycotted."

Before this second letter was written the English ministers had
become alarmed. A report of the Privy Council (July 24, 1724)
defended the patent, but ended by recommending that the amount to
be coined should be reduced to 40,000*l*. Carteret was sent out as Lord
Lieutenant to get this compromise accepted. Swift replied by a third
letter, arguing the question of the patent, which he can "never suppose,"
or, in other words, which everybody knew, to have been granted as a
"job for the interest of some particular person." He vigorously asserts
that the patent can never make it obligatory to accept the halfpence,
and tells a story much to the purpose from old Leicester experience.
The justices had reduced the price of ale to three-halfpence a quart.
One of them, therefore, requested that they would make another order
to appoint who should drink it, "for, by God," said he, "I will not."

The argument thus naturally led to a further and more important
question. The discussion as to the patent brought forward the question of right. Wood and his friends, according to Swift, had begun
to declare that the resistance meant Jacobitism and rebellion; they
asserted that the Irish were ready to shake off their dependence upon
the Crown of England. Swift took up the challenge and answered
resolutely and eloquently. He took up the broadest ground. Ireland,

he declared, depended upon England in no other sense than that in which England depended upon Ireland. Whoever thinks otherwise, he said, "I, M. B. despair, desire to be excepted; for I declare, next under God, I depend only on the King my sovereign, and the laws of my own country. I am so far," he added," from depending upon the people of England, that, if they should rebel, I would take arms and lose every drop of my blood to hinder the Pretender from being King of Ireland."

It had been reported that somebody (Walpole presumably) had sworn to thrust the halfpence down the throats of the Irish. The remedy, replied Swift, is totally in your own hands, "and therefore I have digressed a little ... to let you see that by the laws of God, of nature, of nations, and of your own country, you are and ought to be as free a people as your brethren in England." As Swift had already said in the third letter, no one could believe that any English patent would stand half an hour after an address from the English Houses of Parliament such as that which had been passed against Wood's by the Irish Parliament. Whatever constitutional doubts might be raised, it was, therefore, come to be the plain question whether or not the English ministers should simply override the wishes of the Irish nation.

Carteret, upon landing, began by trying to suppress his adversary. A reward of 300*l*. was offered for the discovery of the author of the fourth letter. A prosecution was ordered against the printer. Swift went to the levée of the Lord Lieutenant, and reproached him bitterly for his severity against a poor tradesman who had published papers for the good of his country. Carteret answered in a happy quotation from Virgil, a feat which always seems to have brought consolation to the statesman of that day:

> "Res dura et regni novitas me talia cogunt
> Moliri."

Another story is more characteristic. Swift's butler had acted as his amanuensis, and absented himself one night whilst the proclamation was running. Swift thought that the butler was either treacherous or presuming upon his knowledge of the secret. As soon as the man returned he ordered him to strip off his livery and begone. "I am in your power," he said, "and for that very reason I will not stand your insolence." The poor butler departed, but preserved his fidelity; and Swift, when the tempest had blown over, rewarded him by appointing him verger in the cathedral. The grand jury threw out the bill against the printer in spite of all Whitshed's efforts; they were discharged; and the next grand jury presented Wood's halfpence as a nuisance. Carteret gave way, the patent was surrendered, and Swift might congratulate himself upon a complete victory.

The conclusion is in one respect rather absurd. The Irish succeeded in rejecting a real benefit at the cost of paying Wood the profit which he would have made, had he been allowed to confer it. Another point must be admitted. Swift's audacious misstatements were successful for the time in rousing the spirit of the people. They have led, however, to a very erroneous estimate of the whole case. English statesmen and historians[11] have found it so easy to expose his errors that they have thought his whole case absurd. The grievance was not what it was represented; therefore it is argued that there was no grievance. The very essence of the case was that the Irish people were to be plundered by the German mistress; and such plunder was possible because the English people, as Swift says, never thought of Ireland except when there was nothing else to be talked of in the coffee-houses.[12] Owing to the conditions of the controversy this grievance only came out gradually, and could never be fully stated. Swift could never do more than hint at the transaction. His letters (including three which appeared after the last mentioned, enforcing the same case) have often been cited as models of eloquence, and compared to Demosthenes. We must make some deduction from this, as in the case of his former political pamphlets. The intensity of his absorption in the immediate end deprives them of some literary merits; and we, to whom the sophistries are palpable enough, are apt to resent them. Anybody can be effective in a way, if he chooses to lie boldly. Yet, in another sense, it is hard to over-praise the letters. They have in a high degree the peculiar stamp of Swift's genius: the vein of the most nervous common-sense and pithy assertion, with an undercurrent of intense passion, the more impressive because it is never allowed to exhale in mere rhetoric.

Swift's success, the dauntless front which he had shown to the oppressor, made him the idol of his countrymen. A Drapier's Club was formed in his honour, which collected the letters and drank toasts and sang songs to celebrate their hero. In a sad letter to Pope, in 1737, he complains that none of his equals care for him; but adds that as he walks the streets he has "a thousand hats and blessings upon old scores which those we call the gentry have forgot." The people received him as their champion. When he returned from England, in 1726, bells were rung, bonfires lighted, and a guard of honour escorted him to the deanery. Towns voted him their freedom and received him like a prince. When Walpole spoke of arresting him a prudent friend told the minister that the messenger would require a guard of ten thousand soldiers. Corporations asked his advice in elections, and the weavers appealed to him on questions about their trade. In one of his satires[13] Swift had attacked a certain Serjeant Bettesworth:

> "Thus at the bar the booby Bettesworth,
> Though half-a-crown o'erpays his sweat's worth."

Bettesworth called upon him with, as Swift reports, a knife in his pocket, and complained in such terms as to imply some intention of personal violence. The neighbours instantly sent a deputation to the Dean, proposing to take vengeance upon Bettesworth; and though he induced them to disperse peaceably, they formed a guard to watch the house; and Bettesworth complained that his attack upon the Dean had lowered his professional income by 1200*l.* a year. A quaint example of his popularity is given by Sheridan. A great crowd had collected to see an eclipse. Swift thereupon sent out the bellman to give notice that the eclipse had been postponed by the Dean's orders, and the crowd dispersed.

Influence with the people, however, could not bring Swift back to power. At one time there seemed to be a gleam of hope. Swift visited England twice in 1726 and 1727. He paid long visits to his old friend Pope, and again met Bolingbroke, now returned from exile, and trying to make a place in English politics. Peterborough introduced the Dean to Walpole, to whom Swift detailed his views upon Irish politics. Walpole was the last man to set about a great reform from mere considerations of justice and philanthropy, and was not likely to trust a confidant of Bolingbroke. He was civil but indifferent. Swift, however, was introduced by his friends to Mrs. Howard, the mistress of the Prince of Wales, soon to become George II. The Princess, afterwards Queen Caroline, ordered Swift to come and see her, and he complied, as he says, after nine commands. He told her that she had lately seen a wild boy from Germany, and now he supposed she wanted to see a wild Dean from Ireland. Some civilities passed; Swift offered some plaids of Irish manufacture, and the Princess promised some medals in return. When, in the next year, George I. died, the Opposition hoped great things from the change. Pulteney had tried to get Swift's powerful help for the *Craftsman*, the Opposition organ; and the Opposition hoped to upset Walpole. Swift, who had thought of going to France for his health, asked Mrs. Howard's advice. She recommended him to stay; and he took the recommendation as amounting to a promise of support. He had some hopes of obtaining English preferment in exchange for his deanery in what he calls (in the date to one of his letters[14]) "wretched Dublin in miserable Ireland." It soon appeared, however, that the mistress was powerless; and that Walpole was to be as firm as ever in his seat. Swift returned to Ireland, never again to leave it: to lose soon afterwards his beloved Stella, and nurse an additional grudge against courts and favourites.

The bitterness with which he resented Mrs. Howard's supposed faithlessness is painfully illustrative, in truth, of the morbid state of mind which was growing upon him. "You think," he says to Boling-broke in 1729, "as I ought to think, that it is time for me to have done with the world; and so I would, if I could get into a better before I was called into the best, and not die here in a rage, like a poisoned rat in a hole." That terrible phrase expresses but too vividly the state of mind which was now becoming familiar to him. Separated by death and absence from his best friends, and tormented by increasing illness, he looked out upon a state of things in which he could see no ground for hope. The resistance to Wood's halfpence had staved off immediate ruin, but had not cured the fundamental evil. Some tracts upon Irish affairs, written after the *Drapier's Letters*, sufficiently indicate his despairing vein. "I am," he says in 1737, when proposing some remedy for the swarms of beggars in Dublin, "a desponder by nature;" and he has found out that the people will never stir themselves to remove a single grievance. His old prejudices were as keen as ever, and could dictate personal outbursts. He attacked the bishops bitterly for offering certain measures which in his view sacrificed the permanent interests of the Church to that of the actual occupants. He showed his own sincerity by refusing to take fines for leases which would have benefited himself at the expense of his successors. With equal earnestness he still clung to the Test Acts, and assailed the Protestant Dissenters with all his old bitterness, and ridiculed their claims to brotherhood with Churchmen. To the end he was a Churchman before everything. One of the last of his poetical performances was prompted by the sanction given by the Irish Parliament to an opposition to certain "titles of ejectment." He had defended the right of the Irish Parliament against English rulers; but when it attacked the interests of his Church his fury showed itself in the most savage satire that he ever wrote, the *Legion Club*. It is an explosion of wrath tinged with madness:

> "Could I from the building's top
> Hear the rattling thunder drop,
> While the devil upon the roof
> (If the devil be thunder-proof)
> Should with poker fiery red
> Crack the atones and melt the lead,
> Drive them down on every skull
> When the den of thieves is full;
> Quite destroy the harpies' nest,
> How might this our isle be blest!"

What follows fully keeps up to this level. Swift flings filth like a maniac, plunges into ferocious personalities, and ends fitly with the execration—

> "May their God, the devil, confound them!"

He was seized with one of his fits whilst writing the poem, and was never afterwards capable of sustained composition.

Some further pamphlets—especially one on the State of Ireland—repeat and enforce his views. One of them requires special mention. The *Modest Proposal* (written in 1729) *for Preventing the Children of Poor People in Ireland from being a Burden to their Parents or Country*—the proposal being that they should be turned into articles of food—gives the very essence of Swift's feeling, and is one of the most tremendous pieces of satire in existence. It shows the quality already noticed. Swift is burning with a passion the glow of which makes other passions look cold, as it is said that some bright lights cause other illuminating objects to cast a shadow. Yet his face is absolutely grave, and he details his plan as calmly as a modern projector suggesting the importation of

Australian meat. The superficial coolness may be revolting to tender-hearted people, and has, indeed, led to condemnation of the supposed ferocity of the author almost as surprising as the criticisms which can see in it nothing but an exquisite piece of humour. It is, in truth, fearful to read even now. Yet we can forgive and even sympathize when we take it for what it really is—the most complete expression of burning indignation against intolerable wrongs. It utters, indeed, a serious conviction. "I confess myself," says Swift in a remarkable paper,[15] "to be touched with a very sensible pleasure when I hear of a mortality in any country parish or village, where the wretches are forced to pay for a filthy cabin and two ridges of potatoes treble the worth; brought up to steal and beg for want of work; to whom death would be the best thing to be wished for, on account both of themselves and the public." He remarks in the same place on the lamentable contradiction presented in Ireland to the maxim that the "people are the riches of a nation," and the *Modest Proposal* is the fullest comment on this melancholy reflection. After many visionary proposals he has at last hit upon the plan, which has at least the advantage that by adopting it "we can incur no danger of disobliging England. For this kind of commodity will not bear exportation, the flesh being of too tender a consistence to admit a long continuance in salt, although, perhaps, I could name a country which would be glad to eat up a whole nation without it."

Swift once asked Delany[16] whether the "corruptions and villanies of men in power did not eat his flesh and exhaust his spirits?" "No," said Delany. "Why, how can you help it?" said Swift. "Because," replied Delany, "I am commanded to the contrary—*fret not thyself because of the ungodly.*" That, like other wise maxims, is capable of an ambiguous application. As Delany took it, Swift might perhaps have replied that it was a very comfortable maxim—for the ungodly. His own application of Scripture is different. It tells us, he says, in his proposal for using Irish manufactures, that "oppression makes a wise man mad." If, therefore, some men are not mad, it must be because they are not wise. In truth, it is characteristic of Swift that he could never learn the great lesson of submission even to the inevitable. He could not, like an easy-going Delany, submit to oppression which might possibly be resisted with success; but as little could he submit when all resistance was hopeless. His rage, which could find no better outlet, burnt inwardly and drove him mad. It is very interesting to compare Swift's wrathful denunciations with Berkeley's treatment of the same before in the *Querist* (1735–'37). Berkeley is full of luminous suggestions upon economical questions which are entirely beyond Swift's mark. He is in a region quite above the sophistries of the *Drapier's Letters*. He sees equally the terrible grievance that no people in the world is so beggarly, wretched, and destitute as the common Irish. But he thinks all complaints against the English rule useless, and therefore foolish. If the English restrain our trade ill-advisedly, is it not, he asks, plainly our interest to accommodate ourselves to them? (No. 136.) Have we not the advantage of English protection without sharing English responsibilities? He asks "whether England doth not really love us and wish well to us as bone of her bone and flesh of her flesh? and whether it be not our part to cultivate this love and affection all manner of ways?" (Nos. 322, 323.) One can fancy how Swift must have received this characteristic suggestion of the admirable Berkeley, who could not bring himself to think ill of any one. Berkeley's main contention is, no doubt, sound in itself, namely, that the welfare of the country really depended on the industry and economy of its inhabitants, and that such qualities would have made the Irish comfortable in spite of all English restrictions and Government abuses. But, then, Swift might well have answered that such general maxims are idle. It is all very well for divines to tell people to become good, and to find out that then they will be happy. But how are they to be made good? Are the Irish intrinsically worse than other men, or is their laziness and restlessness due to special and removable circumstances? In the latter case is there not more real value in attacking tangible evils than in propounding general maxims and calling upon all men to submit to oppression, and even to believe in the oppressor's good-will, in the name of Christian charity? To answer those questions would be to plunge into interminable and hopeless controversies. Meanwhile, Swift's fierce indignation against English oppression might almost as well have been directed against a law of nature for any immediate result. Whether the rousing of the national spirit was any benefit is a question which I must leave to others. In any case, the work, however darkened by personal feeling or love of class-privilege, expressed as hearty a hatred of oppression as ever animated a human being.

NOTES

1. Letter to Pope, July 18, 1737.

2. *Catholic Reasons for Repealing the Test.*

3. *Letters on Sacramental Test* in 1738.

4. To Sir Charles Wigan, July, 1732.

5. To Lord Peterborough, April 21, 1726.

6. The ton of bronze, I am informed, is coined into 108,000 pence; that is, 450*l.* The metal is worth about 74*l.*

7. Simon, in his work on the Irish coinage, makes the profit 60,000*l.*; but he reckons the copper at 1*s.* a pound, whereas from the Report of the Privy Council it would seem to be properly 1*s.* 6*d.* a pound. Swift and most later writers say 108,000*l.*, but the right sum is 100,800*l.*—360 tons coined into 2*s.* 6*d.* a pound.

8. Monck Mason says only 300*l.* a year, but this is the sum mentioned in the Report and by Swift.

9. Letter I.

10. Letter II.

11. See, for example, Lord Stanhope's account. For the other view see Mr. Lecky's *History of the Eighteenth Century* and Mr. Froude's *English in Ireland.*

12. Letter IV.

13. "On the words Brother Protestants, &c."

14. To Lord Stafford, November 26, 1725.

15. *Maxims Controlled in Ireland.*

16. Delany, p. 148.

THE MYSTERIOUS STRANGER
(MARK TWAIN)

"*The Mysterious Stranger* and '3,000 Years Among the Microbes': Chimerical Realities and Nightmarish Transformations"
by Patricia M. Mandia, in *Comedic Pathos: Black Humor in Twain's Fiction* (1991)

INTRODUCTION

In this chapter from her study of Mark Twain's fiction, Patricia Mandia analyzes two of Twain's unfinished, posthumously published works—*The Mysterious Stranger* and "3,000 Years Among the Microbes"—in the context of postwar American dark humorists and the techniques they employ. Mandia argues that these stories, like the works of Vonnegut, Heller, and others, experiment with narrative form. For Mandia, Satan in *The Mysterious Stranger* offers the darkest and most humorously pessimistic of Twain's statements on human nature, morality, and our capacity to change. Mandia concludes that in these stories: "Twain fuses horror with humor, indicates that man has no free will, and ridicules man's follies without offering answers or standards because, since man does not possess the power to change, this would be futile."

Mandia, Patricia M. "*The Mysterious Stranger* and '3,000 Years Among the Microbes': Chimerical Realities and Nightmarish Transformations." *Comedic Pathos: Black Humor in Twain's Fiction.* Jefferson, N.C.: McFarland, 1991. 102–122.

"When I was a man, I would have turned a microbe from my door hungry. . . . The very littleness of a microbe should appeal to a person, let alone his friendlessness. Yet in America you see scientists torturing them, and exposing them naked on microscope slides, before ladies," Huck, a man who has been transformed into a cholera germ, points out in *3,000 Years Among the Microbes*.[1] In *The Mysterious Stranger*, Theodor Fischer fears that the beautiful image of Satan dissolving himself is only a dream. Theodor marvels, "You could see the bushes through him as clearly as you see things through a soap-bubble, and all over him played and flashed the delicate iridescent colors of the bubble" before Satan, lightly floating along, touches the grass and disappears.[2] As works of black humor, these stories have much in common. Although the humor in *Microbes* is whimsical at times, both stories intermingle cruelty and death with humor, present a deterministic universe, and include satire that does not attempt to reform. Most significantly, they make it difficult for the characters and the reader to distinguish between dreams which appear real and reality. In *Mysterious Stranger*, Twain goes so far as to suggest that there is no external reality, that life is a bad dream. Nihilistic and solipsistic, *Mysterious Stranger*, like contemporary black humor, offers laughter as the best weapon in an absurd world.

Mysterious Stranger and *Microbes*, written late in Twain's life, are more pessimistic and bitter in tone than such earlier works as *Huck Finn*.[3] Twain began *Mysterious Stranger* in 1898, after the failure of the Paige typesetting machine, the bankruptcy of his publishing firm, and the death of his daughter Susy. He wrote several versions of *Mysterious Stranger*, which he worked on intermittently, and was still writing this story when he began *Microbes* in 1905, after his wife's death.[4] Both were published posthumously. The tone of *Mysterious Stranger* is more despairing than that of *Microbes*. In *Mysterious Stranger*, Twain implies that there is no external reality. By suggesting that pain, suffering, and death are nothing more than events in a dream and that man has no free will, Twain attempted to assuage his feelings of guilt and pain over the losses he experienced. Perhaps the slightly lighter tone of *Microbes* may be attributed to the fact that the germ of this story appeared in his notebook as early as 1883, although this original idea is very pessimistic: "I think we are only the microscopic trichina concealed in the blood of some vast creature's veins, and it is that vast creature whom God concerns Himself about and not us."[5] Albert Bigelow Paine contends that *Microbes* contains some "fine and humorous passages," but that "its chief mission was to divert [Twain] mentally that summer during those days and nights when he would otherwise have been alone and brooding upon his loneliness."[6] Twain tired of it and never completed it, just as he never finished *Mysterious Stranger*.

Paine and Frederick Duneka pieced together *Mysterious Stranger* and published it in 1916. In 1909, just months before Twain died, Paine discloses that Twain pointed to a drawer full of manuscripts, one of which was *Mysterious Stranger*, and told him, "There are a few things there which might be published, if I could finish them; but I shall never do it, now"; Paine claims, however, that he found the final chapter of *Mysterious Stranger* among Twain's papers several years after his death and published it (*Notebook* 369). Twain wrote three distinct versions of this story and, according to William Gibson, he did write a draft of the conclusion for the third version. Gibson maintains, however, that Paine attached this ending to the first version, changed characters' names, and bowdlerized and eliminated parts of the manuscript to "create the illusion that Twain had completed the story."[7] But as James Cox points out, "Paine's posthumous edition of Mark Twain's last work is the closest thing to Mark Twain's intention that we shall ever have."[8] Because it is beyond the scope of this study to analyze all three unfinished manuscripts, Paine's edition, which is the most well-known and widely criticized version, will be examined here.

Perhaps the narrative structure of *Mysterious Stranger* and *Microbes* is loose because they were left uncompleted. More than likely, however, the rambling plots reflect a belief typically held by black humorists: life lacks coherence. The plot of *Mysterious Stranger* largely consists of a string of episodes in which Satan awes the narrator, Theodor Fischer, and two other boys, Nikolaus Bauman and Seppi Wohlmeyer, by performing such extraordinary feats as instantaneously starting a fire by blowing on a pipe, making a clay squirrel and dog come to life, and showing the boys the history of the human race. In *Microbes*, after being transformed into a cholera germ by a magician whose trick goes awry, Huck meets various other microbes and bacteria on his journeys inside of Blitzowski, the man whose body he inhabits. In the preface to this story, the "translator" of Huck's narrative admits that it is anything but tightly constructed: "His style is loose and wandering and garrulous and self-contented beyond anything I have ever encountered before, and his grammar breaks the heart" (*MIC* 162).

The mock-historical preface supposedly written by a human translating the original microbic into English and the mock-authentic footnotes supposedly written by Huck are evidence of the typical black humor device of obviously contriving form in order to emphasize that life is empty and meaningless beneath the metaphysical, scientific, and religious systems that man tries to impose on it. In black humorists' view, these systems are as ridiculous as the conspicuously contrived forms of their fiction. In addition, this technique distances the reader from the story by reminding him that he is reading fiction, not fact, thus enabling him to laugh at the humor he sees in the characters' plights. In the preface, the translator declares that he believes Huck's story is true, and he professes, "There is internal evidence in every page of it that its Author was conscientiously trying to state bare facts, unembellished by fancy" (*MIC* 161). And in one explanatory note, Huck says that 5,000 microbic years later the microbe no longer calls itself Microbe, but labels itself a Sooflasky. He translates that "Sooflasky" means "The Pet, The Chosen One, The Wonderful One, The Grand Razzledazzle, The Whole Thing, The Lord of Creation, The Drum Major, The Head of the Procession" (*MIC* 167). In a subtitle to *3,000 Years Among the Microbes*, Huck reveals that the notes were "Added by the Same Hand 7,000 Years Late" (*MIC* 161). In this way, Twain further attempts to enhance the authentic appearance of the manuscript.

Besides exhibiting structural techniques typically seen in contemporary black humor, *Microbes* and *Mysterious Stranger* evidence stylistic techniques, one of which is the inclusion of antiheroes in the story. In *Mysterious Stranger*, Satan is an outsider, a stranger who is very different from the others but, unlike antiheroes, his supernatural abilities give him the power to control his environment. A handsome boy, this Satan is the nephew of the legendary Satan. He humorously alludes to Satan's work down in hell when he discloses that he has "an uncle in business down in the tropics" (*MS* 48). The youthful Satan in *Mysterious Stranger* is all-knowing. At all times he knows what everyone is thinking. He declares, "Nothing goes on in the skull of man, bird, fish, insect, or other creature which can be hidden from me" (*MS* 85–86). A supernatural being, he is not governed by heredity and environment, as the others are.

Unlike Satan, Father Peter and Wilhelm Meidling are antiheroes. Father Peter is ostracized after calling the astrologer a charlatan; the outraged astrologer persuades the bishop to give Father Peter's congregation to Father Adolph. After the destitute Father Peter finds a large sum of money (gold coins conjured up by Satan) in his wallet, the astrologer accuses him of robbing him and has Father Peter incarcerated, leaving his niece, Marget, penniless and alienated. Her boyfriend, Wilhelm, an unsuccessful lawyer, wins Father Peter's case, much in the manner of Pudd'nhead Wilson. Instead of dreaming the solution, however, Wilhelm is possessed by Satan during the trial and magically realized that the coins Father Peter found could not belong to Father Adolf, who claimed to have had them two years ago, because the dates stamped on the coins are more recent than that. A typical antihero, Wilhelm succeeds because of Satan's intervention, not by his own efforts. And Father Peter is assured future happiness not by his own actions but by Satan who, believing that only insane people can be happy, intervenes and makes him insane.

Huck is a representative antihero in *Microbes*, as well. Environmental circumstances beyond his control change him from a man to a microbe. Huck says, "At first I was not pleased" (*MIC* 163). This understatement describing his feelings after the tragic transformation is darkly humorous in itself. As an outsider, Huck is ridiculed. When he finally finds the courage to tell some of his microbe companions that he was once a man who lived on the planet Earth, they laugh at him and call him a liar. His descriptions of the world's characteristics are outrageous to them. When he discloses, for instance, that the Earth is round and has continents and oceans, they say, "What a shape for a planet! Everybody would slide off," and they think that the oceans would spill off of the bottom of the planet (*MIC* 209–10). They look at this alien "sadly" and "reproachfully" because they believe he is lying (*MIC* 213). In the end, though, this antihero succeeds, at least in his own mind, when he believes his own lie that he found a gold mine in Blitzowski's molar.

In *Microbes*, Twain shows the reader that there are multiple realities and that one must accept different views. At first, Huck, new to their world, is afraid to introduce the microbes to a different reality, for fear that they will think he is mad, so he tells them that he is a native of the northwestern nerve in the back molar on the left side of Blitzowski's jaw. He confides that he has good reason to lie about being from this region: "To say I was an American and came of a race of star-bumping colissi who couldn't even see an average microbe without a microscope, would have landed me in the asylum" (*MIC*

190). What is normalcy to one is insanity to another, depending upon one's point of view. Huck, like Hank Morgan in *Connecticut Yankee*, has two views. Both of them see from two perspectives: Hank can view his world from the perspective of the sixth and the nineteenth century, and Huck can see from the perspective of a human being and a cholera germ. Huck expresses an awareness of his double perception when he says, "I could observe the germs from their own point of view. At the same time, I was able to observe them from a human being's point of view" (*MIC* 163).

Twain reveals that even though people's view is restricted because they have been limited to one perspective, the possibility exists that there are other perspectives and other realities. Life on Earth is real to humans, and life inside of a human body is real to Twain's microbes, who think of this body as the universe and can conceive of nothing existing outside of it. There are worlds within worlds in *Microbes*, and except for Huck and the reader, everyone's view is limited to what he can see within his own cosmos. The microbes myopically believe that Blitzowski is the only planet, and when Huck informs them that he is from a larger planet, Earth, one of them chides him: "Why, you muggins, there *isn't* any other. Lots of germs like to play with the *theory* that there's others, but you know quite well it's only a theory. Nobody takes it seriously" (*MIC* 205). The microbes do acknowledge that there are microbes within microbes. When the bacteriologist, himself a microbe, reveals this to Huck, he is astonished. Huck marvels that the "little old familiar microbes" he viewed under this scientist's microscope "were *themselves* loaded up with microbes that fed *them*," and he expresses amazement over their finding that below each "infester there is yet another infester that infests *him*—and so on down and down and down till you strike the bottomest bottom of created life—if there is one, which is extremely doubtful" (*MIC* 252 and 255).

Twain thus plants the idea in the reader's mind that the universe he inhabits is contained within another one, which is housed by yet another, and that this continues infinitely. In addition, he suggests that man's purpose is to foster parasites, to be their "universe," and man, in turn, is a parasite in a bigger universe. Each universe is absurd, diseased, and ultimately meaningless because its only contribution is that it sustains others that are like itself, only smaller.

Besides showing that there are multiple realities Twain, like other black humorists, establishes emotional distance between the reader and the characters, thus encouraging the reader to laugh at the humor present in inherently sad or tragic situations. Twain prevents one from excessively sympathizing with the characters in *Mysterious Stranger* by setting this story in a distant place (Austria) in the distant past (the winter of 1590).

The microscopic motif in *Mysterious Stranger* and *Microbes* also emotionally distances the reader from the characters and their suffering. In *Microbes*, the characters are so diminished that they are invisible to the naked human eye. And in *Mysterious Stranger*, Satan shows that man is as small, petty, and trivial to him as man also must be to God.[9] Time and space seem limitless in this story. In comparison to the immensity of space and time, man and his life indeed seem to be microscopic and unimportant. All Satan has to do is think of a destination, and instantly he is there. He provides the boys with panoramic visions of historical events that begin in the garden of Eden and end in the boys' present. Then he shows them the future in visions of destruction and war. The amount of time any one person's life lasts is infinitesimal when compared to the vast expanse of time with which Satan is acquainted. He tells the boys that man's "foolish little life is but a laugh, a sigh, and extinction" (*MS* 84). Satan confesses that he is only "amused" by man, "just as a naturalist might be amused and interested by a collection of ants" (*MS* 147). Like the naturalist, whose interest is scientific, Satan remains superior and detached.

Satan's violent destruction of the miniature people he created out of clay illustrates that it is impossible for him to care for paltry man and his trivial suffering. To entertain the boys, Satan makes 500 toy people, but when two of them quarrel Satan, annoyed, "crushed the life out of them with his fingers, threw them away, wiped the red from his fingers on his handkerchief, and . . . went right on talking, just as if nothing had happened" (*MS* 16–17). The boys are shocked. Nevertheless, enchanted by the "fatal music of his voice," they continue to listen to Satan's stories of his travels through other solar systems (*MS* 18). When the relatives and friends of the two dead miniature men sob and a miniature priest prays, Satan is irked by their noise and smashes them into the ground with a board, "just as if they had been flies" (*MS* 17). Later, he makes more living toy people, only to destroy them in a storm and earthquake which he creates for amusement. Satan's indifference is apparent when he reminds the crying boys, "They were of no consequence. . . . They were of no value. . . . It is no matter; we can make plenty more" (*MS* 22).

Primarily through Satan, Twain intermingles humor, cruelty, and death in *Mysterious Stranger*. Satan, for example, chuckles over the fact that he has sent the evil astrologer to the moon: "I've got him on the cold side of it, too. He doesn't know where he is, and is not having a pleasant time" (*MS* 93). Then he dryly remarks, "Still, it is good enough for him, a good place for his star studies" (*MS* 93). After Frau Brandt's daughter drowns, Satan alters one link in the chain of circumstances comprising her life so that instead of living in grief for 29 years, she will be burned at the stake in three days. Satan logically explains that she can only benefit from this: "She gets twenty-nine years more of heaven than she is entitled to, and escapes twenty-nine years of misery here" (*MS* 111). There is macabre humor in Theodor's statement that Satan "Did not seem to know any way to do a person a kindness but by killing him" (*MS* 111). Similarly, after Satan makes Father Peter insane, Theodor comments, "He didn't seem to know any way to do a person a favor except by killing him or making a lunatic out of him" (*MS* 141). And it is gruesomely humorous later when Theodor says after watching Satan quarrel with a foreign man and then vanish, "I was sorry for that man; sorry Satan, hadn't been his customary self and killed him or made him a lunatic" (*MS* 145). At this point in the story, Theodor seems almost as indifferent to human suffering as Satan.

Although some of the humor in *Microbes* is whimsical, much of it, too, is fused with dismalness. The humor, for instance, is light and fanciful when Huck says that he entertained the microbes by singing "Bonny Doon" and "Buffalo Gals Can't You Come Out To-night," and he explains, "Microbes like sentimental music best" (*MIC* 190). When Huck describes in a footnote a banquet he attended, the humor is still whimsical: "We had both kinds of corpuscles, and they were served up in six different ways, from soup and raw down to pie" (*MIC* 173). The humor darkens, however, when Huck discusses food later in a passage that echoes Jonathan Swift's "A Modest Proposal." He notes that when a noble microbe of the highest rank is ambling along and "munching on" a live "spring pectin" of the working class, "its cries and struggles made [Huck's] mouth water, for it was an infant of four weeks and quite fat and tender and juicy" (*MIC* 240). The satire on the nobility's greedy exploitation of the poor is grimly humorous. After the noble microbe shares a leg with him, Huck attests, "It seemed to me that I had never tasted anything better," and he points out that spring pectin are "quite choice when they are well nourished" (*MIC* 240).

The fact that death is imminent is treated comically when Huck offers a microbe acquaintance, Franklin, a bit of wisdom: "Carpe diem—quam minimum credula postero" which, Huck explains, is Latin for "Be thou wise: take a drink whilst the chance offers; none but the gods know when the jug will come around again" (*MIC* 183). Franklin likes this so much that he wants to "make an illuminated motto out of it and stick it up in his parlor like a God-Bless-Our-Home" (*MIC* 183). Grotesque humor results from the incongruity between the commonplace sign typically embroidered and hung in the parlor and Huck's ominous reminder.

Finally, the humor is sinister when Huck describes malignant cells. Ironically, the most destructive cells in Blitzowski's body, the cancer cells, are also the most beautiful, energetic, and intelligent. One of these cells, Catherine of Aragon, benefits from the disease because "it lifted her mentalities away above the average intellectual level of her caste, for the cancers are bright, and have always been so" (*MIC* 217). Huck admires Catherine, who is so petite and "very very pretty—pretty as a diatom" (*MIC* 217).

Like much contemporary black humor, the setting of *Microbes* is a wasteland. The action in this story takes place within the body of a ragged, dirty, diseased old tramp, Blitzowski. Although Hungary has sent the tramp to America to get rid of him, he is the microbes'"world, their globe, lord of their universe, its jewel, its marvel, its miracle, its masterpiece," and his veins are rivers of which the microbes are proud because of the numerous diseases that they so efficiently transport (*MIC* 163–64). From a human's point of view, however, "his body is a sewer, a reek of decay, a charnel house, and contains swarming nations of all the different kinds of germ-vermin" (*MIC* 164).

Similarly, the setting of *Mysterious Stranger*, Eseldorf, Austria, is a wasteland. At first glance, Eseldorf appears to be a land of idyllic, peaceful beauty where a "tranquil river, its surface painted with cloud forms and the reflections of drifting arks and boats," flows near a "far-reaching plain dotted with little homesteads nested among orchards and shade trees" (*MS* 1 and 2). The village "drowsed in peace" and was "infinitely content" (*MS* 1). But this description belies the ghastliness of the villagers. After the astrologer spreads the rumor that Father

Peter said "God was all goodness," Father Peter is excommunicated and alienated because, as all agree, "it was a horrible thing to say" (*MS* 4). The self-righteous residents of Eseldorf ("Assville") are always ready to condemn and destroy anyone who deviates from their standards. Witch-burning is one of their favorite sports. It becomes evident that killing people that they do not like has become increasingly popular when Theodor naïvely states:

> Of late years there were more kinds of witches than there used to be; in old times it had been only old women, but . . . it was getting so that anybody might turn out to be a familiar of the Devil—age and sex hadn't anything to do with it. (*MS* 61)

Ironically, Theodor unsuspectingly is a friend of Satan's.

Irony of fate also operates in *Mysterious Stranger* and *Microbes*; again Twain shows that man is controlled by heredity and environment.[10] Twain emphasizes that the way man is "made" determines his behavior. Theodor says that it is easy for people to lie because "it is the way we are made" (*MS* 42). Likewise, when discussing how one person's conception of beauty can be different from someone else's, Huck says, "It is the way we are made and we can't help it" (*MIC* 194). And when he thinks he has discovered gold in a molar Huck, musing over his new feelings of greed, says, "So suddenly as this I was changed like that! We *are* strangely made!" (*MIC* 279).

Born with the moral sense, man is the only creature who can distinguish between right and wrong. Yet man "inflict[s] pain for the pleasure of inflicting it," according to Satan (*MS* 53). Possessing the ability to choose right instead of wrong, "in nine cases out of ten he prefers the wrong" (*MS* 53).

Nevertheless, man is blameless, Twain would like to believe. Satan says that man is a mere machine, "a suffering-machine and a happiness-machine combined," and that some men are never happy because "sometimes a man's make and disposition are such that his misery-machine is able to do nearly all the business" (*MS* 83). Here, of course, Twain suggests that no one is responsible for his unhappiness, that man is like a robot operating according to the program that has been built into him. In *Microbes*, Huck indicates that man cannot control his mind, particularly his memory: "Memory is a curious machine and strangely capricious. . . . It is always throwing away gold and hoarding rubbish" (*MIC* 184). If man is a machine that cannot govern his emotions, thoughts, or deeds, then he cannot be held responsible for anything. Addressing the reader, Huck argues that man is not to be blamed for his hypocrisy:

> We can't help our nature, we didn't make it, it was made for us; and so we are not to blame for possessing it. . . . Let us not allow the fact to distress us and grieve us that from mommer's lap to the grave we are all shams and hypocrites and humbugs, seeing that we did not make the fact and are in no way responsible for it. If any teacher tries to persuade you that hypocrisy is not a part of your blood and bone and flesh, and can therefore be trained out of you . . . do not you heed him; ask him to cure himself first, then call again. (*MIC* 188)

Because these flaws are inborn and permanent, it would be futile to try to reform.

In *Mysterious Stranger*, Satan reveals that guilt over one's misdoings is ridiculous because everyone's actions are determined, rendering them blameless. Satan, having foreknowledge, can change the future. He knows that Nikolaus is supposed to save Lisa Brandt from drowning, that he will then catch a cold followed by scarlet fever, which will transform him into a deaf, dumb, and blind "paralytic log," and that this condition will last for 46 years until he dies (*MS* 91). By altering this chain of circumstances, Satan ensures that Nikolaus will arrive several seconds later than the predetermined time, that Lisa will be in deeper water by then, and that he will drown attempting to rescue her. After this happens, and the boy's mother blames herself for allowing him to leave the house that day, Theodor points out, "It shows how foolish people are when they blame themselves for anything they have done" (*MS* 107).

Except for Satan's intervention, future outcomes are impossible to change. Satan professes that a child's "first act determines the second and all that follow after," and that "nothing can change the order" of one's life "after the first event has determined it" (*MS* 87). Satan says of this first act, which takes place at an age left unspecified: "Man's circumstances and environment order it" (*MS* 87). Repeating one of Satan's lessons, Theodor says that everything is inevitable: "Of your own motion you can't ever alter the scheme or do a thing that will break a link" in the chain of circumstances (*MS* 107). And Satan explains that when one does drop a link in the chain, it is due to the fact that this, too, has been predetermined (*MS* 88–89).

Like Satan, Huck acknowledges the power of circumstance. "Circumstance," Huck says, "is master," and "we are his slaves" (*MIC* 198). He elaborates, "We seem to be free, but we go in chains—chains of training, custom, convention; association, disposition, environment—in a word, Circumstance—and against these bonds the strongest of us struggle in vain" (*MIC* 213). Because man is not free to change anything, including himself, it is useless to try.

Twain's pessimism permeates both stories because the satire in them does not attempt to reform. Because man's vices cannot be corrected, it would be pointless to provide standards, norms, or answers. The tone of both stories is mocking, particularly in *Mysterious Stranger* when Satan ridicules man. At the same time, however, the tone of this story is calm and resigned, perhaps because nothing can be done to alter anything. It is possible that Twain did not finish either novel because late in his life he came to the conclusion that even writing about the uselessness of attempting to reform anyone was in itself futile.

Like other black humor, these stories satirize polarities to reveal that there are no answers, that everything is flawed. Monarchy and democracy, for instance, are satirized in *Microbes*. The microbes in Blitzowski have been ruled by the royal Pus family for twenty-five hundred thousand years, and each king of the Pus lineage uses the name "Henry" (*MIC* 166). This "stern and noble race" which "by diplomacy and arms has pushed its frontiers far" is revered by the microbes who, in honor of their good work, "have come to speak of pus and civilization as being substantially the same thing" (*MIC* 167). In a similar vein, nobility is satirized when Huck discloses that they are all diseases. Speaking of one of these nobles, Huck confides, "He had a gentle way with him, and a kind and winning face, for he was a Malignant; that is to say, a Noble of the loftiest rank and the deadliest. . . . *He* was not aware that he was deadly; he was not aware that *any* Noble was deadly" (*MIC* 239). Conversely, Twain satirizes a possible remedy, democracy. There is a republic in Blitzowski's stomach, the Republic of Getrichquick. Getrichquick's "commerce, both domestic and foreign, is colossal"; it "imports raw materials from the North and ships the manufactured product" to the South (*MIC*

170). For years, Huck notes, Getrichquick selfishly cared only for its own prosperity and happiness. Later, when recounting a shooting that took place on Earth, Huck, who believes that the killer was justified in committing this deed, says that "the whole State joined in an effort to get the death-sentence commuted to a term in Congress or jail, I do not remember which it was," suggesting that congressmen endure punishment that is not better than being incarcerated (*MIC* 184).

In addition, Twain satirizes science and its antithesis, religion. Science and religion are examples of man's vain attempts to impose order on the chaos of life. Huck is a cholera germ that was once a scientist. He mentions that when he was human he was most interested in paleontology. Yet, in hopes of being turned into a bird, this scientist puts himself into the hands of a magician. The microbes who are scientists in Blitzowski are laughably narrow-minded. When Huck tries to enlighten them by describing life on Earth, they refuse to consider the possibility that anything he has said is true. Twain satirizes religion in this story when Catherine of Aragon recites an unintelligible religious doctrine of the Established Church of Henryland:

> The fealty due from the Ultimate in connection with and subjection to the intermediate and the inferential, these being of necessity subordinate to the Auto-Isothermal, and limited subliminally by this contact, which is in all cases sporadic and incandescent, those that ascend to the Abode of the Blest are assimilated in thought and action by the objective influence of the truth which sets us free. [*MIC* 226–27]

When Huck says that he does not understand what she has said, Catherine informs him, "We are not allowed to explain the text, it would confuse its meaning" (*MIC* 227). Twain indicates here that the Church encourages rote memorization, not understanding and thinking. Thinking is dangerous because it could lead to disagreement and subsequent rebellion against the Church.

Similarly, Twain satirizes Christianity in *Mysterious Stranger*. The villagers, believing that Satan, who uses the alias Philip Traum when he is around them, is studying for the ministry, attribute the attainment of high religious rank to physical attractiveness, not to spiritual goodness. It is darkly ironic when they say of Satan, "His face is his fortune—he'll be a cardinal some day" (*MS* 73). Twain's satire lapses into sarcasm later, when Satan notes that in contrast to the Greeks and Romans, Christians have developed such amazing weapons that people in the future "will confess that without Christian civilization war must have remained a poor and trifling thing to the end of time. . . . All the competent killers are Christians" (*MS* 118 and 114).

In *Microbes*, by proposing that man's purpose is to provide microbes with a place to reside, and that man may, in turn, be nothing but a microbe, Twain satirizes man's vanity, his conceited belief that he is the focal point of God's attention because he is so important.[11] Huck deflates man's feelings of self-importance when he says that man is possibly "himself a microbe, and his globe a blood-corpuscle drifting with its shining brethren of the Milky Way down a vein of the Master and Maker of all things" (*MIC* 182). Twain satirizes man's obsession with status and rank when he shows how ridiculous is the microbes' concern with these things. High-ranking microbes never ask such lowly workers as plumbers, carpenters, or cobblers to dinner, and microbe parents with the most status refuse to allow their daughters to marry any natives; instead they make the girls wait until "a foreign bacillus with a title comes along" (*MIC* 235). Describing the castes in Blitzowski, Huck notes that kings look down upon nobles, who look down upon commoners, and that at the lower end of the scale the burglar looks down upon the landlord, who finally looks down upon the real estate agent, who is at the bottom of the scale.

Twain even satirizes himself, the satirist, in *Microbes*. Huck, trying to recall the name of an author whose books he read long ago when he was human says, "Twain . . . Twain . . . what was his other name? Mike? I think it was Mike" (*MIC* 184). He claims that he read his books but does not "remember what they were about now . . . no, it wasn't books, it was pictures. . . . He was a Californian, and his middle name was Burbank; he . . . was finally hanged" (*MIC* 184). Twain satirizes his own feelings of self-importance here by showing that a writer's fame is fleeting.

Most importantly, like other black humorists Twain confuses appearance and reality to indicate the unreliability of reality.[12] In *Microbes*, Huck has difficulty distinguishing between dreams which appear real and reality. When his microbic acquaintances want to gather together Huck's stories about Earth and sell them, Huck, to divert their attention and make them forget this idea, lies about discovering a gold mine in a molar. But Huck gradually comes to believe his own lie. Like the Fosters in "The $30,000 Bequest," Huck forgets that his dreams of being wealthy are just dreams. Shortly after planting dreams of dental gold in the others' minds, he is aware that his imagination is starting to make the nonexistent gold seem real: "The mine was there, sure—pretty dreamy, yes, pretty dreamy, but there, anyway ... honest dentist's gold, 23 carats fine! ... In the alembic of my fancy ... my dream-gold was turning into the real metal, and my dream was turning into fact" (*MIC* 278). But as the gold becomes more and more real to him, he changes his original plans to share it with his friends until, at the end of the story, he concludes that he will keep it all and give them part of the amalgam and all of the cement. The dream has overpowered reality.

Additionally, the longer Huck is in Blitzowski's bloodstream, the more his past as a human seems a dream to him. His life in the tramp's body seems vivid and real in contrast to his past, which seems "far away and dim, very dim, wavering, spectral, the substantiality all gone out of it," and he can no longer visualize the faces of his human loved ones, who seem to be "mere dream-figures drifting formless through a haze" now (*MIC* 177).

Twain also intermingles dreams and reality in *Mysterious Stranger*. The possibility exists that this story is Theodor's dream. Satan's alias is Philip Traum. The name Traum, meaning "dream" in German, indicates that he is associated with dreams. Sleep and dream imagery pervade the novel. Eseldorf is in the middle of "Austria [which] was far from the world, and asleep"; it "drowsed in peace"; and "news from the world hardly ever came to disturb its dreams" (*MS* 1). While he sits with Satan upon a mountain, Theodor says of the scenery: "It was a tranquil and dreamy picture" (*MS* 82). When Satan makes himself and the boys invisible, Theodor insists, "It seemed almost too good to be true, that we were actually seeing these romantic and wonderful things, and that it was not a dream" (*MS* 25). Later, after Satan dissolves himself for the boys' entertainment, they "sat wondering and dreaming," and one of them says, "I suppose none of it has happened" (*MS* 29). And when Satan possesses the astrologer, who then juggles and walks a tightrope like an expert, the villagers walk "like persons in a dream" and wonder, "Was it real? Did you see it, or was it only I—and I was dreaming?" (*MS* 80 and 77–78). Satan imparts a feeling of lazy ecstasy to all who surround him. Theodor associates Satan with a "winy atmosphere" (*MS* 80).

Felix Brandt, the oldest serving-man in the Eseldorf castle, tells the boys stories which may influence Theodor to dream about Satan. Felix takes the boys down into the "haunted chamber in the dungeons of the castle" at night and recounts stories about ghosts, witches, enchanters, and "horrors of every kind," including "battles, murders, and mutilations" (*MS* 8 and 9). He encourages the boys not to be afraid of supernatural beings, because they mean no harm, and he confides that not only has he seen angels, but he has talked with them. Felix points out that angels wear clothes, not wings, and that they are always pleasant and cheerful. One night the boys go to a wooded hill after listening to the stories, and while they are mulling over Felix's description of such supernatural beings as angels and are comfortably lying on the grass, a youth strolls toward them. Perhaps at this point Theodor has fallen asleep and dreams that he sees this youth, Satan, who fits Felix's description. Satan is "friendly" and "handsome," he has "a pleasant voice," and he is wearing "new and good clothes," which he may have just created when he assumed the form of a human (*MS* 10). When the boys ask him who he is, he replies "an angel" (*MS* 13).

Whether Satan really appears in Eseldorf or is only a creature in Theodor's dream ultimately does not appear to matter. Most significantly, at the end of the story Satan speaks for Twain when he tells Theodor that life is nothing more than a dream:

> *Life itself is only a vision, a dream.* . . . *Nothing* exists; all is a dream . . . *Nothing exists save empty space—and you!* . . . And you are not you—you have no body, no blood, no bones, you are but a *thought*. I myself have no existence; I am but a dream—your dream, creature of your imagination. . . . There is no God, no universe, no human race, no earthly life, no heaven, no hell. It is all a dream—a grotesque and foolish dream. Nothing exists but you. And you are but a *thought*—a vagrant thought, a useless thought, a homeless thought, wandering forlorn among the empty eternities! (*MS* 149 and 151)

In his last work, Twain renounces external reality and proposes that life is a bad dream in which one imagines his own reality. This nihilistic, solipsistic conclusion reveals that the only reality that exists is produced by one's own mind. Twain moves beyond black humorists' contention that the universe is fragmented, pluralistic, without system, meaning, or design. He proclaims that there is no universe.

If there is no external reality, it cannot harm anyone, and one need not ever feel guilt or despair, because he does not physically exist and therefore could never have done harm to anyone else or even have known anyone else. In 1904, while writing the conclusion of *Mysterious Stranger*, Twain wrote a letter that echoes this conclusion. Lonely, in deep despair over his failed business ventures, and grieving over his loved ones who died, Twain insists that the past seven years have seemed "NON-EXISTENT" (Gibson 30). Additionally, in this letter Twain argues:

> There is *nothing*. ... There is no God and no universe.... There is only empty space, and in it a lost and homeless and wandering and companionless and indestructible *Thought*. And ... I am that thought. And God, and the Universe, and Time, and Life, and Death, and Joy and Sorrow and Pain only a grotesque and brutal *dream*, evolved from the frantic imagination of that insane Thought. [Gibson 30]

If life is a dream, as Twain suggests, then he cannot be blamed for his past mistakes. It is likely that his nihilistic views helped him to cope with his failures and losses.

The absurdities of life are accounted for and seem less absurd when one knows that life is a dream. Satan informs Theodor that his dreams are "frankly and hysterically insane—like all dreams" (*MS* 150). Then he enumerates parts of his dreams, which include a God "who mouths justice and invented hell," a God who "could have made every one of [his children] happy, yet never made a single happy one," a God who "with altogether divine obtuseness, invites his poor, abused slave to worship him!" (*MS* 150–51). Likewise, in his letter written during the same period, Twain argues that once one knows that life is a bad dream, "the absurdities that govern life and the universe lose their absurdity and become natural, and a thing to be expected"; everything becomes understandable, even "a God who has no morals, yet blandly sets Himself up as Head Sunday-school Superintendent of the Universe.... Taken as the drunken dream of an idiot Thought ... these monstrous sillinesses become proper and acceptable" (Gibson 30). After revealing that life is a dream, Satan advises Theodor to "dream other dreams, and better!" (*MS* 150).

But Twain's indication in *Mysterious Stranger* that life is a dream is not convincing, although he himself would have liked to believe that his late nightmarish years were unreal. This world must not be a dream; it must be real. The structural problem Twain faces in *Mysterious Stranger* is obvious: while Twain proposes in the story that life is a dream, the past life experiences Theodor narrates are based on fact.

Moreover, Theodor is more than a "thought"; he is a disillusioned old man looking back. At the beginning of the story it is clear that the narrator is older when he says of the Austrian winter of 1590, "I remember it well, although I was only a boy" (*MS* 1). And he is more sophisticated than a boy. It is apparent that he is an older man who has suffered the loss of many loved ones. Theodor says that when he knew that Nikolaus had little time left before he would drown, he recalled the wrongs he had done to his friend, and he was filled with remorse, "just as it is when we remember our unkindnesses to friends who have passed beyond the veil, and we wish we could have them back again, if only for a moment" to beg for their forgiveness (*MS* 96). He explains that his last days with Nikolaus "were days of companionship with one's sacred dead, and I have known no comradeship that was so close or so precious" (*MS* 101).

Like other black humorists, Twain offers laughter as the best weapon in an absurd world. If an absurd external reality does exist, the best way to abide it is to laugh at it. Satan indicates that if one does not have the good fortune of being insane like Father Peter, who obviously no longer lives in reality, he must have a sense of humor. Father Peter is "as happy as a bird" because he thinks he is Emperor (*MS* 138). Satan comments, "No sane man can be happy, for to him life is real, and he sees what a fearful thing it is" (*MS* 140). The best a sane man can do is laugh. Satan says that people have "one really effective weapon—laughter," and he wonders, "Will a day come when the race will detect the funniness of these juvenilities and laugh at them—and by laughing at them destroy them?" (*MS* 142).

Twain laughs at the absurdity of life in *Mysterious Stranger* and *Microbes*, but the humor is dark, especially in *Mysterious Stranger*. These stories represent some of the blackest humor Twain wrote. In both of them, Twain fuses horror with humor, indicates that man has no free will, and ridicules man's follies without offering answers or standards because, since man does not possess the power to change, this would be futile. Like contemporary black humorists, Twain suggests that there is no one correct answer anyway in this pluralistic universe. In *Microbes*, the characters have difficulty distinguishing between reality, and perceptions and dreams that appear real. Additionally, in this story Twain plants the notion in the reader's mind that there are multiple realities. The microbes believe that the human being they inhabit is reality, and human beings believe that their universe is reality. Twain suggests that this universe, in turn, may be contained within another, which is encased within another, in a never-ending series which is ultimately meaningless. In *Mysterious Stranger*, Twain offers laughter as the best coping mechanism in an absurd world. This world, he propounds, is not real, but a bad dream. Beset by tragedies in his life, he would have liked to believe that life is only a nightmare that appears real to the unenlightened.

NOTES

1. Mark Twain, *3,000 Years Among the Microbes, The Devil's Race-Track: Mark Twain's Great Dark Writings: The Best from Which Was the Dream? and Fables of Man*, ed. John S. Tuckey (Berkeley: University of California Press, 1980) 232; parenthetical references to *Microbes* will be abbreviated *MIC*.

2. Mark Twain, *The Mysterious Stranger* (New York: Harper and Brothers, 1916) 28; parenthetical references to *Mysterious Stranger* will be abbreviated *MS*.

3. Twain wrote "The Great Dark" during the same period when he was writing *Mysterious Stranger* and *Microbes* and, like them, it displays numerous elements typically used by black humorists. Unlike them, however, "The Great Dark" is nearly devoid of humor. In this unfinished story written during the 1890s and published posthumously, Mr. Edwards falls asleep after looking at a drop of water through his children's microscope. He dreams that he and his family are aboard a ship voyaging across the drop of water he had scrutinized through the microscope. The one-celled organisms he had viewed earlier are huge sea monsters in his dream, and they attack the passengers and crew. The story and Twain's notes that indicate how he intended to complete the plot are replete

with other disasters: they are lost because under the microscope there are no stars by which to steer; the crew mutinies; they chase phantom ships, but their distress signals are never seen; they enter the Great White Glare (the light from the microscope's reflector), and the intense heat evaporates their "sea"; they run out of provisions; most of the people aboard ship die, including all of Edwards' family, and their corpses are mummified by the heat. Although he dreams that his voyage took years, he has actually been dreaming for only a few minutes, and upon awakening Edwards sees that his family is still young and alive. His dream, however, has driven him mad, and he believes that their presence is a dream. One feature of black humor that this story exhibits is the confusion of dream and reality. In his dream, Edwards begins to believe that his past, his waking life, was a dream and that life on the ship is reality, and this delusion destroys him when he awakens and cannot stop grieving for the family he believes he lost on the ship. In addition, in the dream the lost ship, like the plots of much black humor, travels in a circle, illustrating that life is absurd and that people repeat the same mistakes. As in black humor, in "The Great Dark" the universe is indifferent, and the characters lost on a sea that dries up and becomes a wasteland, drift aimlessly. For a summary of Twain's notes outlining the conclusion of this story, see Bernard DeVoto, ed., *Letters from the Earth* (New York: Harper and Row, 1938) 226–27.

4. Twain indicates in a letter to Frederick Duneka (the secretary of his publisher, Harper and Brothers), 9 October 1905, *The Selected Letters of Mark Twain*, ed. Charles Neider (New York: Harper and Row, 1982), that he was working on both stories during the autumn of that year (298–99).

5. Mark Twain, *Mark Twain's Notebook*, ed. Albert Bigelow Paine (New York: Harper and Brothers, 1935) 170.

6. Albert Bigelow Paine, *Mark Twain: A Biography*, 3 vol. (New York: Harper and Brothers, 1912) 1238–39.

7. William M. Gibson, ed., *Mark Twain: The Mysterious Stranger Manuscripts* (Berkeley: University of California Press, 1969) 2–3; This book contains all three fragmentary versions of *The Mysterious Stranger*.

8. James Cox, *Mark Twain: The Fate of Humor* (Princeton: Princeton University Press, 1966) 272.

9. The Old Man in Twain's "Supplement A: *What Is Man?* Fragments," What Is Man? *And Other Philosophical Writings*, vol. 19 of *The Works of Mark Twain*, ed. Paul Baender (Berkeley: University of California Press, 1973), professes that God is indifferent to man. In a passage about God, written in 1898 when Twain was writing *Mysterious Stranger*, the Old Man compares men to microbes in a discussion that anticipates *Microbes*. In his opinion, it is as ludicrous to believe that God would send Christ to Earth to save man as it would be for a man to bother being "re-born as a microbe" in a drop of water, "reared as a microbe, crucified as a microbe ... and all this foolishness to 'save' the microbe species for the rest of time from the consequences of some inconsequential offence" (485). In this same passage, the Old Man tries to convince the Young Man that people are too small and insignificant for God to concern Himself with them: "I cannot conceive of myself caring for the compliments of the wiggling cholera-germs concealed in a drop of putrid water. I cannot conceive of myself caring whether they appointed microbe-popes and priests to beslaver me with praises or didn't" (485). Like Satan in *Mysterious Stranger*, Twain's God is indifferent.

10. Sherwood Cummings, in "*What Is Man?*: The Scientific Sources," *Essays on Determinism in American Literature*, ed. Sydney J. Krause (Kent: Kent State University Press, 1964), agrees that *Mysterious Stranger*, "written in the *What Is Man?* period, can be called a fictional restatement of the notion that men's lives are shaped by inexorable internal and external forces in which the human will plays no part" (114).

11. Likewise, Twain reveals in a letter to William Dean Howells, 12 May 1899, *The Selected Letters of Mark Twain*, ed. Charles Neider (New York: Harper and Row, 1982), that his purpose in writing *Mysterious Stranger* is to "tell what I think of Man, and how he is constructed, and what a shabby poor ridiculous thing he is, and how mistaken he is in his estimate of his character and powers and qualities and his place among the animals" (256).

12. Richard Hauck, in *A Cheerful Nihilism: Confidence and "The Absurd" in American Humorous Fiction* (Bloomington: Indiana University Press, 1971), attests that "by the time he came to write his darkest books, Twain was convinced that there is no test for reality, that not only is what man sees absurd but the position from which he sees is also absurd, unfixed, and not definable" (159).

RESERVATION BLUES
(SHERMAN ALEXIE)

"The Saddest Joke: Sherman Alexie's Blues"
by James A. Crank,
Northwestern State University

Native American author Sherman Alexie's first novel, *Reservation Blues* (1995), follows a ragtag band of musicians living on the Spokane Indian Reservation who inherit African American bluesman Robert Johnson's cursed guitar. The band, dubbed "Coyote Springs," rocket to local stardom before falling apart at a recording session in New York City. Throughout the novel, Alexie uses humor to articulate the possibility for beauty and joy even in the heartbreaking surroundings of the Native American reservation.

Critic Douglas Ford suggests that Alexie's goal in *Reservation Blues* is, in fact, an "act of recovery, excavating the traditions we would presume lost in a tide of postmodernity" (213). John Newton posits that the novel is an act of reclaiming "the Native American's own alienated image" (427) from the perspective of white America. Alexie's attempts to reclaim his cultural identity and its traditions through humorous critiques of the American (white) perspective on Native American culture, the lack of a responsible masculine influence on the reservation, and the ironies and contradictions of reservation life. Throughout *Reservation Blues*, Alexie's humor provides the same catharsis that Robert Johnson's blues gave to African Americans in the Jim Crow South: Through music and laughter, a culture can heal itself.

The most frequent subject of Alexie's humorous criticism is the misguided American imagination and its perspective on Native American culture. In the world of *Reservation Blues*, the white outsider's perspective on Native Americans is largely based upon television, film, and popular culture and not actual, meaningful contact between cultures. Alexie often points out the ridiculous disconnect between actual Native American life and the fantasies of mainstream America. When the band first begins to make music, Alexie notes that many white audiences flocked to the reservation not expecting to hear a rock band:

> White strangers had begun to arrive on the Spokane Indian Reservation to listen to this all-Indian rock and blues band. A lot of those New Agers showed up with their crystals, expecting to hear some ancient Indian wisdom and got a good dose of Sex Pistols covers instead. (40–41)

Though white culture looks to the Native American characters as fonts of wisdom and magic, it becomes clear that, in Alexie's novel, "Indian culture and people frequently embody rationality while the West spews easy, dangerous magic" (Belcher 7). Despite the flat, one-dimensional white American image of Native Americans, Alexie's characters in *Reservation Blues* are complex and unique. They do not exist as desperate savages or gentle sages. Alexie furthers his critique in a scene in which the band tries to come up with a suitable name. The lead singer, Thomas Builds-a-Fire, asks the members what name suits them best:

> "How about Bloodthirsty Savages?" Victor asked.
> "That's a cool name, enit?" Junior asked.
> "I was thinking about Coyote Springs," Thomas said.
> "That's too damn Indian," Junior said. "It's always Coyote this, Coyote that. I'm sick of Coyote."

Though Junior decides "Coyote Springs" is too "Indian," he is clearly in favor of the alternate stereotype, that of the vicious savage popularized by American pop culture and Western films. Later, Alexie offers an explanation for Thomas's band name that connects to the purpose of the novel. In Thomas's journal, Alexie notes that Coyote is both "a traditional figure in Native American mythology" and "a trickster whose bag of tricks contains permutations of love, hate, weather, chance, laughter, and tears, e.g. Lucille Ball" (48). Like the Coyote trickster, Alexie both represents the tradition of Native American culture and humorously criticizes the stereotype this tradition produces; in his guise as novelist, then, Alexie operates as both originator and critic of Native American tradition.

Alexie's funniest and harshest criticism surfaces in his satirical portrait of the white groupies and producers that follow Coyote Springs from concert to concert. In fact, Alexie names the two most prominent white groupies who follow the band after comic book characters from Archie Comics, Betty and Veronica. Just as the whites imagine Native Americans as caricatures, Alexie presents white culture as a homogenized and clichéd cartoon. Betty and Veronica follow Coyote Springs not because they enjoy their music but because they want a piece of their culture. Betty tells Chess, one of the lead singers of the group, "White people want to be Indians. You all have things we don't have. You live at peace with the earth. You are so wise" (168). However, when Betty and Veronica follow the band back to the squalid living conditions on the reservation, they suddenly change their mind about the sanctity of Native American culture. When they ask to be driven home, one of the backup singers attacks their naiveté:

> "Can't you handle it? You want the good stuff of being an Indian without all the bad stuff, enit? Well, a concussion is just as traditional as a sweatlodge.... What did you New Agers expect? You think magic is so easy to explain? You come running to the reservations, to all these places you've decided are sacred. Jeez, don't you know *every* place is sacred? You want your sacred land in warm places with pretty views. You want the sacred places to be near malls and 7-Elevens, too." (184)

Here, Alexie criticizes both white culture's perspective on Native culture and the "mainstream media's representation of Indians" (Andrews 147). Eventually, Betty and Veronica form their own band and steal the recording contract offered to Coyote Springs. Ironically, even though neither Betty nor Veronica is Native American, the record producers plan to advertise them as an all-Indian band. Through Betty

and Veronica, Alexie manifests the ridiculous way white culture transforms Native American culture into a safe commodity. The producer
tells his partner of Betty and Veronica,

> " ... these two women are part Indian.... I mean, they had
> some grandmothers or something that were Indian. Really. We
> can still sell that Indian idea. We don't need any goddam just-
> off-the-reservation Indians. We can use these women. They've
> been on the reservations.... These women have got the Indian
> experience down. They really understand what it means to be
> Indian. They've been there." (269)

In Alexie's world, being in close proximity to a people is just as
authentic as being born a member of their tribe. Native American
identity is a product that has been claimed by white America.

Alexie's humorous attack on white perception concludes with
the figures of the two record producers who sign Coyote Springs to
their label. Just as with Betty and Veronica, Alexie comments on their
function in his novel through their names. Phil Sheridan and George
Wright reference the historical figures of General Philip Sheridan and
Colonel George Wright, two of the central figures in the American
Indian Wars of the late 1800s. Both General Sheridan and Colonel
Wright were responsible for murderous actions against Native Americans. Sheridan ruthlessly killed off the bison of the Great Plains in
order to starve the Native Americans into submission; he is also
widely believed to have uttered the quotation, "The only good Indian
is a dead Indian." Colonel George Wright mercilessly attacked the
Spokane Indians in the 1850s and killed women and children alike.
Like their historical namesakes, the record producers are obsessed
with dominating Native American culture. When they first learn of
Coyote Springs, Sheridan and Wright write to the studio head, Mr.
Armstrong (a historical reference to General George Armstrong
Custer, who was killed at the Battle of Little Bighorn in June 1876),
"Overall, this band looks and sounds Indian. They all have dark skin.
Chess, Checkers, and Junior all have long hair. Thomas has a big
nose, and Victor has many scars" (190). Their perspective on Native
American identity is as superficial as Betty's and Veronica's: It is based
solely on physical attributes like skin color and hair length.

Once the band arrives at Cavalry Studios (another reference to the American Indian Wars), they lose their ability to make music. The once-friendly duo of Sheridan and Wright turn on the band and attack them: "My ass is on the line here, too. I brought you little shits here. You screwed me over" (228), Sheridan shouts at Victor. By the end of the scene, it's clear that Sheridan represents what one critic calls, "the historically hostile, dishonest, and violent approach mainstream America has taken toward Indians" (Grassien 95). Later, Checkers, one of the band's backup singers, is brutally attacked and possibly raped by Sheridan. As he approaches her in her hotel room, Sheridan completes the implied historical connection he has made: "You had a choice.... We gave you every chance. All you had to do was move to the reservation. We would have protected you. The U.S. Army was the best friend the Indians ever had" (236). When Checkers attempts to flee, Sheridan overpowers her and pushes her to the floor. He connects Coyote Springs with the epic struggle between Native American individuality and his need for dominance: "I don't want to hurt you," he tells her, "But it was war. This is war. We won. Don't you understand? We won the war. We keep winning the war. But you won't surrender" (237).

Though Alexie takes issue primarily with white culture's commodification and dominance of Native American culture, he also uses his humor to criticize the way in which Native Americans buy into the images and stereotypes that film, television, and popular culture promote. Early in *Reservation Blues*, Alexie tries to articulate the dichotomy between the way Native Americans are portrayed by popular culture and life on the reservation. In one scene, Thomas has a dream about television. In the dream he imagines the "little black-and-white television" he uses "to watch white people live." On the television, he searched

> ... for evidence of Indians, clicked the remote control until his hands ached. Once, on channel four, he watched three cowboys string telegraph wire across the Great Plains until confronted by the entire Sioux Nation, all on horseback. (70)

In his dream, Thomas notes that the Indians "argued amongst themselves, [and] whooped like Indians always do in movies and dreams."

Eventually, the cowboys lure the Indians to the telegraph wire by telling them, "*We come in friendship*" (71). Once they touch the wire, the Indians are all electrocuted. The dream reminds Thomas of how Victor and Junior tortured snakes on the reservation by throwing them against an electric fence. When Thomas interfered in their malicious game, Victor forced Thomas to either decide whether to electrocute himself or touch the snake. The dream makes Thomas think about his band mates and "what those snakes felt on the electric fence" (73). Through this dream sequence, Alexie suggests that popular culture's portrayal of Native Americans often perpetuates a culture of violence and humiliation.

In a similar way, Alexie humorously chastises the culture of degenerate masculinity that is perpetuated throughout the reservations. He notes that when "Indian women begin the search for an Indian man, they carry a huge list of qualifications.... But as the screwed-up Indian men stagger through their lives, Indian women are forced to amend their list of qualifications" (74–75). Emotionally stunted by reservation life, the men of Alexie's *Reservation Blues* are mostly immature and thoughtless alcoholics who shun responsibility and treat their women with disdain or ignorance. Victor, the band's lead guitarist, is shackled by his own immaturity and inability to communicate with women in any meaningful way. For example, as the band eats omelets one morning, "Victor wanted to say something profound and humorous about eggs but couldn't think of anything, so he farted instead" (74). Such childish behavior is representative of most of the men throughout the novel. Thomas's own father is an alcoholic man-child who has never taken responsibility for his family. In fact, Thomas had

> ... lost count of the number of times he saved his father, how many times he'd driven to some reservation tavern to pick up his dad, passed out in a back booth. Once a month, he bailed his father out of jail for drunk and disorderly behavior. That had become his father's Indian name: Drunk and Disorderly. (95)

The lack of responsible masculinity is an absence felt throughout *Reservation Blues*, and while Alexie presents it in a humorous way, the reality of the loss of masculinity causes a terrible emotional wound across the entire reservation. Without a responsible role model, the men of Alexie's world stagger through life with the same self-destructive attitude they inherited from their fathers. In one passage, Alexie chronicles the absurdity and irony of reservation men through Chess's list of boyfriends:

> Bobby, the beautiful urban Indian, transferred to the reservation to work for the BIA, who then left Chess for a white third-grade teacher at the Tribal School. Joseph, the journalist, who wrote a powerful story on the white-owned liquor stores camped on reservation borders and then drank himself into cirrhosis. Carl, the buck from Browning, who stashed away a kid or two on every reservation in the state, until his friends called him The Father of Our Country. (75)

These men flit in and out of the lives of the reservation women without providing any physical or emotional support; all Chess is left with, in the end, is the memory of them.

Though the reservation men may rage against the stereotypes of their culture, through their actions they end up playing roles created by white culture. For example, Victor's self-destructive behavior is largely the result of his dependence on alcohol and lack of a father. Unable to locate his identity through his family, Victor instead adopts the stereotype of Native Americans invented by white American culture. While Victor is addicted to alcohol, he is also addicted to "the shallow and cheap manifestations of white popular culture" (Evans 63); it is precisely because American culture sees all Native Americans as alcoholic savages that Victor's identity is tied up in his inexplicable brutality and constant drunken binges. After Coyote Springs fails to make it in New York, Alexie's description of Victor suggests that he is unable to separate his identity from the savage creation of American white culture:

> Victor roared against his whole life.... He had enough anger inside to guide every salmon over Grand Coulee Dam. He wanted to steal a New York cop's horse and go on the warpath. He wanted to scalp stockbrokers and kidnap supermodels. He wanted to shoot flaming arrows into the Museum of Modern Art. He wanted to lay siege to Radio City Music Hall. Victor wanted to win. Victor wanted to get drunk. (230)

Victor's entire conception of himself is based on stories told by other people. When asked whether Victor is a Christian, Thomas replies that all he knows "about religion [he] saw in *Dances with Wolves*" (145). Alexie humorously criticizes both Victor's lack of self-knowledge and mindless adoption of stereotypes. In the end, Victor becomes both "alienated from [his] American Indian culture as well as from America" (Gillan 91).

Finally, Alexie uses his humor to try to find joy in the difficult and impoverished conditions on the reservation. Throughout the novel, Alexie explores "the dilemmas of being an Indian on the reservation" (Bird 51). Though economically depressed, living in cheap government houses, and eating terrible food, the Native Americans on the reservation are not joyless. In fact, Father Arnold, a Catholic priest assigned to Wellpinit, is surprised by the reservation's constant mirth: "He was impressed by the Spokane's ability to laugh. He'd never thought of Indians as being funny. What did they have to laugh about? Poverty, suicide, alcoholism?" (36). *Reservation Blues* is, in some ways, an explanation of the inexplicable presence of joy and laughter on the reservation. Alexie takes child abuse, alcoholism, and self-destruction and mines them for humor. For example, Alexie's first sentence is a joke about the isolation of Native Americans on the reservation: "In the one hundred and eleven years since the creation of the Spokane Indian Reservation in 1881, not one person, Indian or otherwise, had ever arrived there by accident" (3). Through this joke, Alexie suggests both the loneliness and isolation of the Native American life on the reservation and the culture's life-affirming joy. While Alexie presents the reservation as an impoverished wasteland, *Reservation Blues* is still full of humorous observations on the difficulties of life on the reservation. For example, when Thomas encounters bluesman Robert Johnson, he thinks briefly of taking him to Indian Health Services for a checkup but remembers that "Indian Health only gave out dental floss and condoms, and Thomas spent his whole life trying to figure out the connection between the two" (6).

The reservation in Alexie's novel represents loss and sorrow. Late in the novel, Thomas worries that his tears will end up being "tribal," not individual. Alexie explains that "tribal tears [are] collected and fermented in huge BIA barrels. Then the BIA poured those tears into beer and Pepsi cans and distributed them back onto the reservation" (100). Here Alexie suggests that even the sorrow of Native

Americans is a commodity that is purchased daily on the reservation. The constant dark cloud over the reservation is the invisible hand of the American government. In Thomas's journal, he presents a parody of the Ten Commandments as "The Reservation's Ten Commandments as Given by the United States of America to the Spokane Indian." Among the commandments is an attack on the American government's welfare program:

> Remember the first of each month by keeping it holy. The rest of the month you shall go hungry, but the first day of each month is a tribute to me, and you shall receive welfare checks and commodity food in exchange for your continued dependence. (154)

For Alexie, the government's intrusion into the lives of Native Americans is full of absurd contradictions. In Thomas's ninth commandment, he writes, "You shall not give false testimony against any white men, but they will tell lies about you, and I will believe them and convict you." He continues, "You shall not commit adultery, but I will impregnate your women with illegitimate dreams" (155). This parody of both religion and American culture captures Alexie's vicious criticism of the duplicity of white America's patronizing of Native American culture. Though the government pretends to offer assistance to Native Americans, all white America really offers is contradiction, sorrow, and misery. Meanwhile, the truth of America's displacement and murder of Native Americans remains a skeleton in the closet throughout *Reservation Blues*:

> Thomas thought about all the dreams that were murdered here [on the reservation], and the bones buried just inches below the surface, all waiting to break through the foundations of those government houses built by the Department of Housing and Urban Development. (7)

Alexie attacks white America's relationship to Native American culture and uses his novel to expose the savageness of white America's past.

It is difficult to create humor out of sadness and loss, but in *Reservation Blues*, Alexie uses humor as a means of exposing hidden truths about his culture. Humor is more than a literary device for Alexie; it is a means of self-preservation. Alexie says of the importance of humor in relation to Native Americans, "Humor is self-defense on the rez. You make people laugh and you disarm them. You sort of sneak up on them. You can say controversial or rowdy things and they'll listen or laugh" (Grassien 2). Humor allows the opportunity for Alexie to dialogue with stereotypes and reservation idiosyncrasies. The blues allow the members of Coyote Springs to do the same. Humor and the blues both offer what critic Meredith James describes as "the ambivalence of suffering and the joy of survival" (77). Similarly, Daniel Grassian notes that the blues, like humor, are "a transformative medium" (87). It is precisely because Alexie's humor is so rich and powerful that the reader is able to understand the poignancy of the sorrow and isolation of the reservation. With its emphasis on sadness and sorrow, *Reservation Blues* is fashioned as an approximation of the blues; but in his humor, Alexie also expresses the blues' affirmation of the indomitable spirit of a culture.

WORKS CITED

Alexie, Sherman. *Reservation Blues*. New York: Warner Books, 1995.

Andrews, Scott. "A New Road and a Dead End in Sherman Alexie's *Reservation Blues*." *The Arizona Quarterly* 63.2 (Summer 2007), pp. 137–152.

Belcher, Wendy. "Conjuring the Colonizer: Alternative Readings of Magic Realism in Sherman Alexie's *Reservation Blues*." *American Indian Culture and Research Journal* 31.2 (Spring 2007), pp. 87–101

Bird, Gloria. "The Exaggeration of Despair in Sherman Alexie's 'Reservation Blues.'" *Wicazo Sa Review* 11.2 (Autumn 1995), pp. 47–52.

Evans, Stephen F. "'Open Containers': Sherman Alexie's Drunken Indians." *American Indian Quarterly* 25.1 (Winter 2001), pp. 46–72.

Ford, Douglas. "Sherman Alexie's Indigenous Blues." *MELUS* 27.3 (Fall 2002), pp. 197–215.

Gillan, Jennifer. "Home Movies: Sherman Alexie's Poetry." *American Literature* 68.1 (March 1996), pp. 91–110.

Grassian, Daniel. *Understanding Sherman Alexie*. Columbia: U of S.C. Press, 2005.

James, Meredith K. *Literary and Cinematic Reservation in Selected Works of Native American Author Sherman Alexie*. Lewiston: Edwin Mellen Press, 2005.

Newton, John. "Alexie's Autoethnography." *Contemporary Literature* 42.2 (Summer 2001), pp. 413–428.

WHITE NOISE
(DON DELILLO)

"The Dark Humor of *White Noise*"
by Joseph Dewey, University of Pittsburgh

"*White Noise* is about fear, death and technology. A comedy, of course."

—Don DeLillo

Initially, the comedy in *White Noise* can seem a bit elusive. After all, the narrator, 51 year-old Jack Gladney, is obsessed by death. He has been married five times. His oldest son is a moody 14 year-old with a receding hairline (most likely from exposure to a local chemical waste dump) who stays in his darkened bedroom and exchanges chess moves in the mail with a serial killer on death row (Gladney's wife fears someday the boy will shoot up a mall). Gladney's daughter relishes the smell of burning toast and sitting in her own filthy bath water; his stepdaughter wears a visor to protect herself from ultraviolet waves and, fascinated by carcinogens and diseases, lugs about a *Physicians' Desk Reference* (she volunteers to be a dead body in a neighborhood disaster simulation drill). Gladney's youngest, his stepson Wilder, although already a toddler, has yet to show any interest in talking, his vocabulary inexplicably stalled at 25 words, and at one point he goes on a seven-hour crying jag.

Gladney teaches at an upscale private university, the College-on-the-Hill. In his Department of American Environments, pretentious academics are constantly preoccupied with pointless departmental turf wars and unironically study things like cereal boxes, commercial jingles, comic books, and the implications of James Dean's death. Gladney has built an international reputation in Hitler Studies, a field he invented. In packed classes, he entrances students with vintage footage of Hitler's spellbinding rallies. His accompanying lectures are uncomplicated by any moral outrage over the Holocaust. The college itself overlooks the dreary town of Blacksmith, a nondescript postindustrial urban sprawl that teeters on environmental disaster. Odd-colored, noxious clouds hang about the streets, and residents suffer from watery eyes, nausea, headaches, and a stubborn metallic taste. Nevertheless, despite such an atmosphere of impending calamity, the locals docilely cluster every night before their televisions, hoping for grainy disaster footage or live feeds from newly unearthed backyard mass graves to stimulate their long-flatlined routines. "Every disaster made us wish for more, for something bigger, grander, more sweeping" (64).

That routine is upended one January night when a derailed tank car releases a massive, slow-moving black cloud of insecticide derivative, Nyodene D, that compels an evacuation of Blacksmith. Gladney is exposed to the contaminant when, during the panicked evacuation with his family, he must stop briefly to pump gas. Although a cadaverous evac medic gives Gladney a maddeningly vague prognosis, Gladney is certain he must now confront not the idea of his death, but its reality.

It is at this point that Gladney begins to piece together evidence that, sometime earlier, his wife, Babette, who unbeknownst to him had long been afflicted with similar death anxieties, had volunteered to help test an experimental psychopharmaceutical, Dylar, designed to suppress that portion of the brain that generates the fear of death. Gladney subsequently learns that Babette was compelled to negotiate with a maverick drug researcher named Willie Mink after the company decided testing on humans was too risky—a negotiation in which she had swapped sex for the drug samples. Though shaken by the revelations of adultery, Gladney is more interested in securing the drug, even though his wife insists it did not work (it merely impaired her memory and triggered bouts of déjà vu). On the advice of a rather sinister colleague, Gladney decides to take control of death, to kill rather than simply die. Empowered, he takes a loaded revolver, steals a car, and heads to a seedy motel to confront his wife's seducer (and, in the process, secure samples of Dylar). In the ensuing showdown (the researcher, his career now in shambles, is nearly catatonic from over-dosing on his own untested drug), both men end up shot. Gladney, with the wounded researcher in tow, drives to a nearby clinic under the care of Catholic nuns. As one ancient nun treats Gladney's wound, she shatters Gladney's comforting assumptions about the afterlife by vehemently asserting the absurdity of angels and God and heaven. We then leave Gladney some weeks later waiting to check out (literally, he is in line at a supermarket), refusing to return his doctor's calls, apparently resigned now to die.

Funny stuff.

Clearly, if DeLillo were a traditional psychological realist using narrative to illuminate the complicated struggles of recognizable characters caught up in recognizable dilemmas, the book would be decidedly un-funny, even tragic. That *White Noise* is howlingly funny testifies to DeLillo's far more ambitious sensibility, his use of narrative not to excavate private lives but rather to take the measure of an entire culture. Like caustic cultural anatomists from Mark Twain to Kurt Vonnegut, from Herman Melville to Matt Groening, DeLillo uses character and situation to indict an era with evident glee and snarky wit. Here DeLillo lampoons, in turn, know-it-all scientists and doctors; pretentious academics; religious hypocrites enthralled by endtimes; fanatical consumers who dream in commercial jingles and murmur product names in their sleep; glassy-eyed television zombies terrorized by those moments when the screen darkens and they must face the banality of their lives; techno-addicts convinced that science can control nature itself; and supermarket drones who parse tabloids for evidence of the supernatural. DeLillo deploys the full range of satire's most devastating effects: exaggeration, farce, understatement, juxtaposition, wit, parody, burlesque, irony, sarcasm. In this, *White Noise* is one of the most accomplished American satires since Joseph Heller's *Catch-22* and Saul Bellow's *Herzog* a generation earlier.

As the object of satire, Gladney is less a character and more a premise—specifically a test case in the causes and effects of contemporary death anxiety. Gladney never achieves multidimensionality. He is never entirely convincing as a loving father, a cuckolded husband, or a troubled professional at midlife. We learn nothing of Gladney's upbringing, his education, the traumas of his previous marriages, his relationship with his children and stepchildren, the roots of his thanatophobia. Instead of a traditional plot, DeLillo presents a quirky episodic narrative, short chapters that resist linkage and drift one into the next (in class, Gladney argues that all plots move inevitably death-ward—it is then not surprising that his first-person narrative would resist such momentum). And readers must deal with a kind of offbeat non-ending: Gladney goes shopping. We are left without a tying up of the considerable loose ends: Gladney still faces an uncertain medical prognosis and a shattered marriage and now, presumably, charges of grand theft auto and attempted murder.

Gladney works best as a philosophical posture, his psychological circuitry narrowed to how he handles his anxiety. Gladney startles awake at night in death sweats; he peruses obituary columns handicap-ping his own odds against the ages of those listed; he clings to Babette, her satisfying girth, her rigorous exercise regimen, her cheerful faith in good posture and healthy eating as an antidote to his own anxieties. He is determined to live within a kind of happy drift. When he stops at an abandoned cemetery outside Blacksmith, Gladney decides, "May the days be aimless. Let the seasons drift. Do not advance the action according to a plan" (98). Certain that death happens only to people when they are alone, Gladney clings to crowds, in lecture halls, shop-ping malls, grocery stores, or even at home within his reassuringly large family (he even finds comfort when the ATM accepts his bank card). He cannot be alone with Jack Gladney. His appropriation of Hitler itself stems from his sense of Hitler as a larger-than-death figure who coolly trafficked in death on an unprecedented scale. Within that commanding aura, Gladney draws a kind of secondhand invulner-ability. In fact, for 15 years, Gladney has hidden behind an alternative persona he has fashioned: Professor J. A. K. Gladney, a sustained piece of performance art complete with costuming. On campus, he wears black academic robes and heavy-framed dark glasses. He knows he is a fraud. Indeed, he cannot even speak German; he is struggling to learn elementary German in advance of hosting an international conference of Hitler scholars. He describes himself as "... the false character that follows the name around" (17). When in a hardware store a colleague "with a dangerous grin" (82) spots Gladney without his regalia, the colleague dismisses Gladney as a "big, harmless, aging, indistinct sort of guy" (83). Terrorized by his sudden exposure, Gladney calms himself by commandeering his family to a nearby mall and sponsoring a massive shopping spree, the accumulating packages with their feel of stability acting as a bunker to protect his exposed self. Fending off death by hiding in crowds, binge shopping, and sporting academic robes is comic, yes, but the fear that sustains such desperation is unsettling. As DeLillo himself explained, "We ourselves may almost instantaneously use humor to offset a particular moment of discomfort or fear, but this reflex is so deeply woven into the original fear that they almost become the same thing" (DeCurtis 296).

Gladney is a kind of cautionary character. An Every-American of the late twentieth century post-industrial post-Christian hyper-mediated consumer capitalist technoculture. Gladney's exposure to the Nyodene cloud and his futile pursuit of Dylar represent a contemporary American culture that has lost touch with the complicated gift of the awareness of mortality. Disconnected from the religious sensibility that for centuries had offered solace, DeLillo argues, contemporary American culture has placed its faith in science, specifically in the comforting illusion that death is correctable. In turn, late twentieth-century Americans like Gladney have lost touch with the density of the everyday, both its beauty and its terror, the appreciation of which DeLillo presents as the last vestige of the spiritual sensibility otherwise made ironic in the post-Enlightenment era. As DeLillo himself noted, "In *White Noise* in particular, I tried to find a kind of radiance in dailiness.... This extraordinary wonder of things is somehow related to the extraordinary dread, to the death fear we try to keep beneath the surface of our perceptions" (quoted in DeCurtis 283). Rather than engage the everyday, Americans surrender to an artificial environment constructed and sustained by the media, specifically here by television, that offers secondhand experiences as real enough. The novel's title in fact refers to this oppressive electronic landscape; white nose is the fusion of random sound waves into a single steady signal without high or low pitches, a nearly imperceptible background drone. It is DeLillo's archmetaphor for the wash of media noise that so easily distracts us from engaging the business of living and, ultimately, the reality of dying (the novel's working title was *Panasonic*, Greek for "all sounds").

Not surprisingly, *White Noise* is noisy. Academics in Gladney's department dissect pop culture in lengthy conversations edged with hip cynicism. We listen to extended passages of Gladney's own accomplished lectures (including a hilarious dueling lecture with another colleague in which Hitler and Elvis are compared). The Gladney clan engages in delicious conversations in the family station wagon or around the kitchen table—quirky, disjointed dialogues full of clichés and nonsequiturs. During the tense evacuation, we listen to a confusion of conflicting misinformation, news updates, cryptic technical jargon, emergency evacuation procedures, weather bulletins, and panicked rumors. Babette volunteers to read to the blind and the elderly, often using stacks of supermarket tabloids. The narrative is bombarded by commercial jingles and advertising slogans. Product names abound; telephones ring incessantly; talk radio blathers.

But DeLillo's primary focus is the reach of television, a "primal force ... sealed-off, timeless, self-contained, self-referring.... like a myth being born right there in our living room" (51). The disembodied voice of the Gladney television is nearly constant, like some unnamed offstage character. When a plane loses power and nearly goes into a tailspin, deplaning passengers, far from being relieved, complain bitterly that their experience was all for nothing: There was no media coverage. When young Wilder watches his mother being interviewed on television, he makes no distinction between image and reality: He strokes the screen and murmurs contentedly, and, when the program ends, he cries softly, missing his mother. Gladney's narrative voice is periodically interrupted by the names of commercial products, disruptions that suggest how the media noise has seeped subliminally into his consciousness. At the evacuation camp, Gladney is calmed watching his sleeping daughter, who peacefully murmurs, "*Toyota Celica*" (155), an indication of the gentle brainwashing of commercial television. But Gladney finds the chanted words "gold-shot with looming wonder" (155) tap a feeling of unforced transcendence that, we recognize, darkly parodies authentic spirituality. In sum, this relentless sonic assault creates a cultural (and narrative) environment that renders irrelevant the search for consequence, the possibility of depth to the unfolding experience of living and dying; characters' perceptions are dulled, their awareness flattened. As Gladney's exasperated father-in-law asks, "Were people this dumb before television?" (249).

No character more embodies the insidious threat of the contemporary culture of trivialization, the easy persuasion of depthlessness, and the grosser satisfactions of the immediate world than Murray Jay Siskind. Within DeLillo's satire, of course, that means that Murray is at once the funniest and darkest character. Murray is a Manhattan sportswriter in grateful exile from the city to teach a course on "living icons" in Gladney's department. Casually forsaking the complications of identity, Murray is a consummate performer: His stiff little beard seems pasted on; he puffs a pipe and wears corduroy jackets because they suggest professor to him; he admits to working on his vulnerability, a posture he argues women find appealing. Stoop-shouldered, with dense eyebrows and wisps of hair (horn-like) about his ears, so recently released from the brutal heat of New York City, Murray is a Mephistophelean figure who tempts Gladney to accept the shallowest expressions of life.

Although Jewish, he offers no outrage over Gladney's presentation of Hitler; rather he is fascinated by Gladney's flattened, one-dimensional Hitler and seeks Gladney's counsel on how to develop a similar program centered on Elvis. In classes, Murray encourages students to relax into the pull of television; he shows horrific movie car crashes, arguing that they are cathartic, evidence of American optimism. Early on, Murray is "immensely pleased" by a local tourist trap, The Most Photographed Barn in America. Tourists gather at a nondescript barn that has earned its celebrity simply by being photographed; these pilgrim-tourists (on the day Gladney visits, 40 cars and a bus) do not actually see the barn (the thing itself is irrelevant) but rather see the familiar image from billboards and postcards, thus "taking pictures of taking pictures" (13). A crowd abdicating curiosity and original experience to embrace the generic is for Murray a "religious experience" (12). When Gladney later meets Murray in a grocery store—Murray is filling his cart with generic food—Murray expounds on how the store's fluorescent calm and ample shelves recharge the souls of the weary consumers, likening a shopping trip to the Tibetan concept of the transitional state of the soul's spiritual rebirth after death. "Here we don't die, we shop. But the difference is less marked than you think" (38). Murray is unpleasantly sensual, attached to things, their feel and odors. He openly leers at Gladney's wife, even sniffs her hair. At the evacuation camp, he negotiates (without consequence) with three stranded hookers to have them perform the Heimlich maneuver on him.

But it is only after Gladney's exposure that Murray emerges at his darkest (and most humorous). Murray, a master manipulator of language (his conversations are sardonic, epigrammatic), argues to an anxious Gladney that fear of death is inevitable. During a looping walk around campus, Murray convinces the gullible Gladney to take control of death. The scene is rendered almost entirely in dialogue—thus we feel the verbal suction of Murray's persuasive argument. Knowledge of death, he argues, inevitably reduces life to quivering anxiety. We must therefore repress our fear of death and, in the process, indulge the fabulous escapism of constructing extravagant afterlife alternatives. As Murray explains:

> "[T]here are two kinds of people in the world. Killers and diers. Most of us are diers.... But think what it's like to be a killer. Think how exciting it is, in theory, to kill a person in direct confrontation. If he dies, you cannot. To kill him is to gain life-credit. The more people you kill, the more credit you store up." (290)

Despite its evident absurdity and its troubling distance from moral accountability (Murray cautions Gladney it is merely a theory exchanged between academics), the tidy logic appeals to a terrified Gladney.

His temptation complete, Gladney begins to carry a gun (a "little bitty thing that shoots real bullets" [253], the gift of his dying father-in-law). Although another colleague, a neurochemist named Winnie Richards, who looks into Dylar, counsels Gladney to forget the drug—that people need the parameter of death to give a "precious texture to life, a sense of definition" (228)—Gladney coldly dismisses her as a "true enemy" (230). He relishes the power of the tiny gun (it only has three bullets). But when he decides to play killer by murdering Willie Mink, like those tourists' pictures of a picture, Gladney's plot is secondhand, fashioned from the clichés of countless films noirs about wronged husbands: He will steal his neighbor's car, drive in the middle of the night to an appropriately seedy motel, shoot his wife's lover three times in the gut, put the gun in the man's hand to make it appear a suicide (the absurdity of a three-shots-to-the-gut suicide apparently escaping Gladney), leave the clichéd faked suicide note in lipstick on the bathroom mirror, pilfer whatever Dylar he can find, then make the clichéd clean getaway. The perfect crime. Quickly, the plot collapses into farce. Willie Mink is hardly a significant adversary. He is slumped in front of the television; he drools, barely able to form a sentence. He embodies the threat of Dylar, the implications of losing the awareness of death: He is entirely disconnected from experience; he cannot distinguish words from things. When Gladney tests him and says, "Plunging aircraft," the pathetic Mink assumes the appropriate fetal position.

The farcical High Noon showdown when both he and Willie Mink end up shot exposes Gladney to the very essence of the death experience he has been so desperately dodging: the eruption of chance, the absurdity of control, the muddle of accident, the intervention of bad luck, the reality of pain (he is stung by the gunshot to his wrist). But does he learn? His plot in shambles, Gladney simply improvises another movie. In this one, he plays the redeemed hero, fancying himself suddenly full of epic pity and compassion, even giving the wounded Willie Mink mouth-to-mouth, before driving both of them to the emergency room. Of course, Gladney is no more convincing as noble hero than he was as vicious killer—it is another shabby bit of performance art, another persona engendered and sustained by a weak man still unable to engage experience without elaborate dodges. In the early morning, Gladney simply returns the stolen car—although we assume it is bloodsoaked—strolls home, checks in on his sleeping children, and then goes to the kitchen for coffee. "There was nothing to do but wait for the next sunset, when the sky would ring like bronze" (321).

And so we close Gladney's narrative. Is this the punchline or is it the slender promise of character reformation? Does Gladney's interest in the sunset signal a new awareness, a willingness to engage mortality, or is it another escape into another elaborate distraction? Despite the presumed intimacy of first-person narration, Gladney never makes explicit what the shooting teaches him. The closing chapter is in fact a triptych of unrelated scenes in which Gladney is only a marginal presence. In one, young Wilder careens down a busy highway on his trike; in another, crowds of locals gather nightly at a highway overpass to watch the striking colorations of the sunset, most likely the lingering effects from the Nyodene cloud; and in the third, Gladney discovers that the supermarket shelves have been unexpectedly rearranged.

Such a end leaves deliberately unanswered what Gladney has "learned." As with most objects of American satire, from Twain's Widow Douglas to Groening's Homer Simpson, Gladney is not especially burdened with the expectation of experiencing a clarifying epiphany. Does the pretentious, shallow fraud Jack Gladney finally glimpse what we have known all along: the absurdity of ignoring the reality of death? We learn only that Gladney has decided not to inquire about his test results, indeed not to pursue additional medical tests, and that Mylex-suited men still sweep the neighborhoods. If the premise of DeLillo's unsettling humor has come from the extravagant strategies Gladney uses to skirt death, redemption can come only from confrontation, from the expansion into awareness. DeLillo offers the reader—if not Gladney—the rediscovery of depth that represents the best chance at redemption against the inauthenticity and shallowness of life within the postindustrial, materialistic, hypermediated culture.

Accordingly, each of the three closing scenes suggests elements of the death experience that has so terrified Gladney. Wilder's harrowing ride across the busy highway underscores both the play of chance (Wilder survives without a scratch) and the risk of living without awareness—the unexamined aimlessness that offers the comforting illusion of indestructibility that Gladney so resolutely endorsed early on. Gathering to watch the "atmospheric weirdness" of the sunsets suggests a willingness to confront the terrifying sublimity, the awe and dread, of endings. And the supermarket reorganization exposes the illusion of control, the hard reality of our vulnerability and how, amid such confusion, persists the need for easy comfort. Panicking shoppers wander in "fragmented trance," "sweet-tempered people taken to the edge" (326). But as they move inevitably (as we all must) toward checkout, they are drawn by the racks of tabloids and their tantalizing faux-promises, "tales of the supernatural and the extraterrestrial. The miracle vitamins, the cures for cancer, the remedies for obesity" (326).

These, then, are the lessons of *White Noise*. But does Gladney make his peace with such insights? Does he finally break through into authenticity? Does he accept intimacy with his own person, that fragile and vulnerable self? We are left exactly where DeLillo as satirist, indeed as a novelist of ideas, wants us to be: perplexed rather than comforted, suspended among choices, challenged by confrontation, shaken by the implications of an awareness that his own character resists. That, of course, is the ascendant vision that has been at the heart of satire's dark humor since Aristophanes: to dare the reader to accept an intimacy with a dense and complicated reality, the gift of insight that is, finally, clear sight. We are to move beyond simply laughing at the characters and do what they will not: reject the shallow contemporary pseudolife of escape into cheap wonder worlds of dazzling spectacle and entrancing surfaces and accept the irresistible momentum toward mystery—toward a death that cannot be wished away in a life that will always be done too soon.

WORKS CITED

Cowart, David. *Don DeLillo: The Physics of Language*. Athens: University of Georgia Press, 2003.

DeCurtis, Anthony. "'An Outsider in This Society': An Interview with Don DeLillo." *South Atlantic Quarterly* 89 (1990): 280–319.

DeLillo, Don. *White Noise*. New York: Viking, 1984.

Dewey, Joseph. *Beyond Grief and Nothing: A Reading of Don DeLillo*. Columbia: University of South Carolina Press, 2006.

Ferraro, Thomas J. "Whole Families Shopping at Night!" in Lentricchia, 15–38.

Keesey, Douglas. *Don DeLillo*. New York: Twayne, 1993: 130–150.

Lentricchia, Frank. "Tales of the Electronic Tribe" in *New Essays on "White Noise"* ed. Lentricchia. New York: Cambridge University Press, 1991: 87–113.

Osteen, Mark. *American Magic and Dread: Don DeLillo's Dialogue with Culture* Philadelphia: University of Pennsylvania Press, 2000.

WHO'S AFRAID OF VIRGINIA WOOLF?
(EDWARD ALBEE)

"Dark Humor in Edward Albee's *Who's Afraid of Virginia Woolf?*"
by Kate Falvey, New York City College of Technology

Who's Afraid of Virginia Woolf?—Edward Albee's mordant, horrifically comic anatomization of an American marriage, has become an iconic cultural touchstone since its controversial 1962 Broadway premiere. Its humor is multilaycred and thematically integral, routing the almost unbearable emotional ferocity of its characters into an absurdist pronouncement on the true fragility of our most obdurate psycho-social beliefs. George and Martha, an upper-middle-class academic couple, are the central players in this depiction of the night side of our civil natures; the couple epitomizes marriage itself—the institutional bedrock of postwar American life. As such, the play is a discomfiting, audience-implicating social satire, an evisceration of our own most basic and sacred tenets. The scathing verbal skirmishes of the game-playing protagonists, with their cheap shots and deadly accuracy, creates a kind of set piece in which language itself is center stage. The humor is broad, campy, sardonic, playful, full of quips, wisecracks, and pop culture references. With savage brio George and Martha let loose their awful witticisms and boozy insults while the audience is drawn into their illness and intimacy, fascinated and appalled, as if observing a tragic accident, gradually becoming aware that such voyeurism is itself a very dangerous cat-and-mouse game.

By the time the three-act *Virginia Woolf* opened on Broadway to much acclaim and infamy, Albee had already earned an international reputation as an innovative new American dramatist, a formidable successor to such luminaries as Eugene O'Neill, Arthur Miller, and Tennessee Williams. He is credited with creating a distinctly American kind of absurdism, influenced by such European playwrights as Samuel Beckett, Eugene Ionesco, Jean Genet, and Harold Pinter. His searing one-act plays—*The Zoo Story* (1958, first staged in 1959 at the Provincetown Playhouse with Beckett's *Krapp's Last Tape*), *The Sandbox* (1959), and *The American Dream* (1960)—expose American pieties and platitudes with irreverent, biting wit. *Who's Afraid of Virginia Woolf* is constructed in three acts, "Fun and Games," "Walpurgisnacht," and, tellingly, what was the original title of the play, "The Exorcism." The plot hinges on the increasing vehemence with which George and Martha attack each other, first in marital exasperation and with sadomasochistic familiarity, then, when Martha breaks a sacred trust, in deadly earnest—the final target being the couple's shared imagined son. George and Martha, a middle-aged couple living in the ironically named college town of New Carthage, return home in the middle of the night from a booze-ridden faculty party given by Martha's father, the college president, whose success Martha pointedly contrasts with what she deems George's embarrassing failures: "In fact, he was sort of a . . . a FLOP! A great . . . big . . . fat . . . FLOP!" (84). Martha surprises George by announcing that she has invited Nick and Honey, a new faculty couple, for a visit, even though, as George protests, "it's after two o'clock in the morning" (10). The older couple commences to bait each other and their guests in games George titles, "Humiliate the Host," "Hump the Hostess," "Get the Guests," and, finally, "Bringing Up Baby."

As Albee's Act Two title makes plain, the hazy drunkenness of the characters and their oddly off-kilter wee-hour revels are ominously suggestive of the eerie borderland between the living and the dead. Critic Robert Brustein calls the intricate games George and Martha play a "comedy of concealment" reminiscent of Pirandello and Genet (29). The borders between revelation and concealment, between comedy and tragedy, are artfully blurred. The play runs for over three hours, making the intensity of the action as fraught and draining for the audience as it is for the characters. Through the course of the night, no one remains unscathed. Nick's overweening ambition and amorality,

Honey's vacuity, and the dodgy foundations of their marriage will be revealed. "It will be dawn soon. I think the party's over," George says in the harrowing final act, after he has killed off the 21-year-old son he and Martha gave imaginative birth to, an "exorcism" of their demonically false rendering of their real need for fulfillment (237). The dawn is coming as the play ends, providing a much-needed ray of "liberating" hope after all the "fun and games"—the helter-skelter barrage of comically delivered indignities that cease, in aggregate, to be funny.

The desperate games, the play-acting, the barbed puns and scathing witticisms that George and Martha use to defy, demean, toy with, and, paradoxically, support each other fuse into an exposé of the uses and limits of language itself. The language plays on the life-denying/life-sustaining act of playing: The words sneer and spin into a kind of colossal theatrical pun. In the theater of life, the games we play, the acts we perform, demonstrate the constant interplay between fact and fiction, reality and illusion, substance and ephemera, the need for comic consolation and the recognition that we often laugh inanely or futilely, as a rash or involuntary response to rage or suffering. Our interpersonal, self-deluding games are as silly as they are sinister, ameliorating as they are disquieting. As George and Martha bait each other and their unwitting but culpable guests, the audience laughs as much out of shock and, perhaps, shame, as we do out of genuine appreciation for Albee's verbal dexterity. There are one-liners aplenty, mostly pitched by George with perfect comic timing. George, while waiting for his unexpected guests to arrive, quips: "What did they do ... go home and get some sleep first, or something?" In Act One, when Honey wants to "put some powder on [her] nose," George asks Martha to "show her where we keep the ... euphemism?"; when taking drink orders, he inquires: "Martha? Rubbing alcohol for you?"

The seriocomic tone is immediately introduced in the title, a play on Frank Churchill's popular song "Who's Afraid of the Big Bad Wolf?" from the 1933 Walt Disney animated classic *The Three Little Pigs*. In a 1966 *Paris Review* interview, Albee claimed to have spied the phrase written in soap on a mirror in a Greenwich Village saloon, a story that at once deflates his own cleverness and underscores the high-brow/low-brow mix that pervades the play's action: "And of course, who's afraid of Virginia Woolf means who's afraid of the big *bad* wolf . . . who's afraid of living life without false illusions. And it did strike me as being a rather typical university intellectual joke" (103). *Virginia Woolf*, however, is nightmarishly far removed from the gleeful "tra la la's" of the three little pigs' naïve refrain. It is as if the audience, along with the young academic couple, Nick and Honey, has been summoned to George and Martha's command performance—or ritual dance of death. *Virginia Woolf* has often been likened to Strindberg's *Dance of Death* (1900)—an earlier work about torturous marital games. Robert Brustein calls Albee's play, "a Strindbergian battle royal" (29) and Marion A. Taylor suggests that "Virginia Woolf" is a kind of camped up version of the Strindberg play. This is comedy close to the bone—a grim and nasty assault on complacency and self-delusion—comedy as a glittering and necessary facet of tragedy. According to Mel Gussow, Albee sees "a lot of [James] Thurber in Virginia Woolf" (161). The Eliot Nugent/Thurber play *The Male Animal* (1939) is another comedy about a strained marriage in an academic setting that uses "Who's Afraid of the Big Bad Wolf?" as a mocking self-defense, just as George does with "Who's Afraid of Virginia Woolf?" at the end of Act One's bitter "Fun and Games." Gussow cites the acerbically comic Thurber stories "The Breaking up of the Winships" (1936) and "Afternoon of a Playwright" (1961) as being particularly relevant to *Virginia Woolf*. Thurber's playwright, Bernard Hudley, says: "I'm trying to outline a drawing-room comedy of horror . . . but a note of hope, even of decency, keeps creeping into it" (cited in Gussow 162).

It is clear from the outset that George and Martha's interdependency is shaped by their verbal sniping and their shared jokes, which are like habitual relational tics. The obvious layers of meaning in their banter provide dramatic tension: What will be revealed? Who will be left standing? At the same time, their exchanges are often used to release tension. In Act One, for example, Martha recalls the hilarity of the "Who's Afraid of Virginia Woolf" song that was such a hit at her father's party. She taunts George for his lukewarm reaction to what she says was "a real scream" (12). The seemingly innocuous exchange swiftly turns ugly with Martha hurling a stripped-bare insult: "You make me puke!" (13). The threat of full-scale abusiveness—which will erupt later in the play—is tamed within a cozy marital jokiness, and the two almost immediately reconcile:

George (With boyish pleasure ... a chant): I'm six years younger than you are.... I always have been and I always will be.
Martha (Glumly): Well ... you're going bald.
George: So are you. (Pause ... they both laugh) Hello honey. (15)

As the play progresses, the joke of the title sounds a refrain and darkens significantly. In Act One, after their guests arrive, Martha reprises her attack after again singing "Who's Afraid of Virginia Woolf?" (usually staged with the tune to "Here We Go Round the Mulberry Bush," which is in the public domain):

Martha: [...] I really thought I'd bust a gut laughing. George didn't like it.... George didn't think it was funny at all.
George: Lord, Martha, do we have to go through this again?
Martha: I'm trying to shame you into a sense of humor, angel, that's all. (25)

Or her sense of humor is used as a flimsy cover for her real mission of shaming her husband, who, in her self-loathing, she despises for having the effrontery, she admits in Act Three, to love her:

"George who is good to me, and whom I revile ... ; who can make me laugh, and I choke it back in my throat ... ; who keeps learning the games we play as quickly as I can change the rules.... who has made the hideous, the hurting, the insulting mistake of loving me and must be punished for it. George and Martha: sad, sad, sad." (191)

The play opens with Martha imitating the oft-imitated Bette Davis, with lines from the 1949 film *Beyond the Forest*: "What a dump." Since Albee envisioned Davis in the role of Martha and since the work in progress was even referred to as "Betty Wolfe" by Albee's friend, playwright Terrence McNally (Gusow 155), Martha doing Bette comically riffs on the theme of role-playing, with the audience only partially in the know. Martha berates George because he can't recall the title of the Bette Davis movie. Pressed, he guesses wrong, sparking a derisive response from Martha: "*Chicago* was a thirties musical, starring little Miss Alice Faye. Don't you know *anything?*" (5). Martha's taunt has uneasy implications and will pervade the escalating savagery of their games. George and Martha contrive to one-up each other as their games grow more treacherous, their "in-jokes" more lacerating and strained. More significantly, this double-edged verbal swordplay makes the language a kind of character or, more accurately, George and Martha take the shape of the words slung to fill their hollowness—words that both obscure and help clarify what Virginia Woolf famously refers to as "moments of being"—moments of acute consciousness—that are dulled by the "cotton wool of daily life" ("Sketch" 72).

In her well-known 1964 essay "Notes on Camp," Susan Sontag defines the "camp sensibility" in 58 "notes." Note 41 states that "[t]he whole point of Camp is to dethrone the serious. Camp is playful, anti-serious. More precisely, Camp involves a new, more complex relation to 'the serious.' One can be serious about the frivolous, frivolous about the serious." In *Virginia Woolf*, the rarefied, insular world of academia is parodied and undermined, with its petty power struggles, arrogance, and hankering after trivialities. Once again, borders are fuzzy: The intellectual elite are portrayed as mean-spirited, vulgar, ineffectual boors. Brenda A. Silver notes, "At this level, the title becomes an academic or intellectual joke, made possible by the happy conjunction of [Virginia Woolf's] name with the animal in the fairytale and the Disney song" (30). In the college town of New Carthage, Martha's "daddy," the college president, holds sway and George lays waste his powers. Albee embeds academic and theatrical references in his play, just as he does references to Hollywood movies. Echoes of T.S. Eliot's "The Waste Land" ("To Carthage then I came. . . ." (II. 307–308)) with its reference to Chapter 3 of Augustine's *Confessions* at once underscore the emptiness of the characters' lives and poke fun at academic reference-making. Albee also pays tribute to playwrights whom he admires, like Beckett and Tennessee Williams, directly referencing, for example, *A Streetcar Named Desire* in Act Three when George stands in the doorway with a bunch of snapdragons and says "in a hideously cracked falsetto": "Flores; flores para los muertos" (195). This is his weirdly macabre prelude to the revelation of his and Martha's own barrenness and his destruction of their sham child.

George is a minor academic, a historian, who has disappointed Martha and Daddy by not aspiring to be successor to the president.

He is "*not* the History Department, but is only *in* the History Department" (50), he says, as he wearily parries Martha's attempt at a timeworn thrust. George, with his intellectual dexterity and sardonic wit, wastes his talent with pointless minutiae. His one attempt at creative mastery is a book about a young man who accidentally kills his mother with a shotgun and his father in an automobile accident. He tells this horror story to Nick, and Martha reveals in Act Two that her father quashed George's bid for publication:

> "And Daddy said ... Look here, kid, you don't think for a second I'm going to let you publish this crap, do you?.... And you want to know the clincher? ... Georgie said ... but Daddy.... I mean ... ha, ha, ha, ha ... but, *Sir*, it isn't a *novel* at all ... No, sir.... this isn't a novel at all ... this is the truth ... this really happened ... TO ME!" (135–137)

In Act One, Martha's emasculating mockery of her husband results in him pointing a shotgun at her. "POW!!!" he says as he pulls the trigger. The stage direction reads: "Pop! From the barrel of the gun blossoms a large red and yellow Chinese parasol." In Act Two this sight gag transmogrifies into George's cry of "I'LL KILL YOU!" and his grabbing Martha by the throat (137).

Albee has been impatient with the repeated critical insinuations that, because he is gay, George and Martha must be stand-ins for a gay couple: "I've had to close down a number of productions that tried to do that play with four men. It doesn't make any sense; it completely distorts the play" (Farr 40). If his intention is to hold a mirror to the complex daily hypocrisies we all perpetuate and contend with, then angling the play toward a uniquely gay perspective would narrow his purpose. He deliberately means to bring George and Martha Washington to mind through the names of his central protagonists, thereby ensuring the critical symbolic link to American life. When the play first opened, many critics and theatergoers were aghast at the violent "obscenity" of the dialogue, the blatant sexuality, and the profane use of language. Though the jury selected *Who's Afraid of Virginia Woolf?* to receive the 1963 Pulitzer Prize, the trustees of Columbia University who served as the Pulitzer's advisory board refused to award the prize that year. The play won both the 1963 Tony Award for Best Play and the 1962–1963 New York Drama Critics' Circle Award for Best Play.

The 1966 film version, directed by Mike Nichols, was nominated for eight Academy Awards and won five of them, including a best actress award for Elizabeth Taylor, who played Martha.

WORKS CITED

Albee, Edward. "Which Theatre is the Absurd One?" Book Section. *New York Times*. February 25, 1962. http://www.nytimes.com/books/99/08/15/specials/albee-absurd.html

———. *Who's Afraid of Virginia Woolf?* New York: Atheneum, 1973.

Armacher, Richard E. *Edward Albee*. Boston: Twayne Publishers, 1982.

Ardolino, Frank. "Nugent and Thurber's *The Male Animal* and Edward Albee's *Who's Afraid of Virginia Woolf?*" *Explicator* 61.2 (Winter 2003): 112.

Bloom, Harold, ed. *Edward Albee*. New York: Chelsea House, 1987.

Brustein, Robert. "Albee and the Medusa Head." *New Republic* 147.18 (3 November 1962): 29–30.

Camus, Albert. *"The Myth of Sisyphus" and Other Essays*. New York: Vintage, 1991.

Davis, Walter A. "The Academic Festival Overture: *Who's Afraid of Virginia Woolf?*" *Get the Guests: Psychoanalysis, Modern American Drama, and the Audience*. Madison: University of Wisconsin Press, 1994. 209–263.

Duplessis, Rachel Blau. "In the Bosom of the Family: Contradiction and Resolution in Edward Albee." *Minnesota Review* 8 (1977): 133–145.

Eby, Clare Virginia. "Fun and Games with George and Nick: Competitive Masculinity in *Who's Afraid of Virginia Woolf?*" *Modern Drama* 50.4 (Winter 2007): 601–619.

Esslin, Martin. "Introduction." *Penguin Plays: Absurd Drama*. Ed. Martin Esslin. New York: Penguin, 1965. http://www.samuel-beckett.net/AbsurdEsslin.html

Falk, Eugene. "*No Exit* and *Who's Afraid of Virginia Woolf?*: A Thematic Comparison." *Studies in Philology* 67.3 (July 1970): 406–417.

Farr, Richard. "Interview with Edward Albee." *Progressive* 60:8 (August 1996): 39–41.

Flanagan, William. "Edward Albee: The Art of the Theatre." *The Paris Review* 39 (Fall 1966): 92–121.

Hayman, Ronald. *Edward Albee*. New York: Frederick Ungar Publishing, 1973.

Gussow, Mel. *Edward Albee: A Singular Journey*. New York: Simon & Schuster, 1999.

Kolin, Philip C., ed. *Conversations with Edward Albee*. Jackson: University Press of Mississippi, 1988.

Meyer, Ruth. "Language: Truth and Illusion in *Who's Afraid of Virginia Woolf?*" *Educational Theatre Journal* 20.1 (March 1968): 60–69.

Sontag, Susan. "Notes on 'Camp.'" *Partisan Review* 31 (Fall 1964): 515–530.

Richardson, John Adkins. "Dada, Camp, and the Mode Called Pop." *The Journal of Aesthetics and Art Criticism* 24.4 (Summer 1966): 549–558.

Roudane, Matthew Charles. "Who's Afraid of Virginia Woolf?": *Necessary Fictions, Terrifying Realities*. Boston. Twayne, 1990.

Silver, Brenda R. "What's Woolf Got to Do with It? Or, the Perils of Popularity." *Modern Fiction Studies*. 38:1 (Spring 1992) 20–60.

Taylor, Marion A. "Edward Albee and August Strindberg: Some Parallels Between the *Dance of Death* and *Who's Afraid of Virginia Woolf?*" *Papers in English Language and Literature* 1 (Winter 1965) 59–71.

Wasserman, Julian N. "The Pitfalls of Drama: The Idea of Language in the Plays of Edward Albee." *Edward Albee: An Interview and Essays*. Ed. Julian N. Wasserman. Houston, Texas: University of St. Thomas Press, 1983. 29–53.

Woolf, Virginia. "A Sketch of the Past." *Moments of Being*. Ed. Jeanne Schulkind. New York: Harvest Books. 1985.

"THE YELLOW WALLPAPER"
(CHARLOTTE PERKINS GILMAN)

"'Too Terribly Good to Be Printed':
Charlotte Gilman's 'The Yellow Wallpaper'"
by Conrad Shumaker,
in *American Literature* (1985)

INTRODUCTION

In his essay on Charlotte Perkins Gilman's "The Yellow Wall-paper," Conrad Shumaker observes that, though the story has been widely praised for its accurate portrayal of mental illness and its critique of patriarchal bias in nineteenth-century society, few have recognized its technical mastery and use of dark humor. Shumaker finds many ironies in Gilman's characterization of the protagonist's husband, John, and his faith in "common sense," an irrational and dogmatic view of the world that decries both irrationality and dogmatism. The end of Gilman's story exposes such ironies in such a way that, for Shumaker, is both comic and terrifying.

In 1890 William Dean Howells sent a copy of "The Yellow Wall-paper" to Horace Scudder, editor of the *Atlantic Monthly*. Scudder

Shumaker, Conrad. "'Too Terribly Good to Be Printed': Charlotte Gilman's 'The Yellow Wallpaper.'" *American Literature* 57.4 (December 1985).

gave his reason for not publishing the story in a short letter to its author, Charlotte Perkins Stetson (later to become Charlotte Perkins Gilman): "Dear Madam, Mr. Howells has handed me this story. I could not forgive myself if I made others as miserable as I have made myself!"[1] Gilman persevered, however, and eventually the story, which depicts the mental collapse of a woman undergoing a "rest cure" at the hands of her physician husband, was printed in the *New England Magazine* and then later in Howells' own collection, *Great Modern American Stories*, where he introduces it as "terrible and too wholly dire," and "too terribly good to be printed."[2] Despite (or perhaps because of) such praise, the story was virtually ignored for over fifty years until Elaine Hedges called attention to its virtues, praising it as "a small literary masterpiece."[3] Today the work is highly spoken of by those who have read it, but it is not widely known and has been slow to appear in anthologies of American literature.

Some of the best criticism attempts to explain this neglect as a case of misinterpretation by audiences used to "traditional" literature. Annette Kolodny, for example, points out that though nineteenth-century readers had learned to "follow the fictive processes of aberrant perception and mental breakdown" by reading Poe's tales, they were not prepared to understand a tale of mental degeneration in a middle-class mother and wife. It took twentieth-century feminism to place the story in a "nondominant or subcultural" tradition which those steeped in the dominant tradition could not understand.[4] Jean F. Kennard suggests that the recent appearance of feminist novels has changed literary conventions and led us to find in the story an exploration of women's role instead of the tale of horror or depiction of mental breakdown its original audience found.[5] Both arguments are persuasive, and the feminist readings of the story that accompany them are instructive. With its images of barred windows and sinister bedsteads, creeping women and domineering men, the story does indeed raise the issue of sex roles in an effective way, and thus anticipates later feminist literature.

Ultimately, however, both approaches tend to make the story seem more isolated from the concerns of the nineteenth-century "dominant tradition" than it really is, and since they focus most of our attention on the story's polemical aspect, they invite a further exploration of Gilman's artistry—the way in which she molds her reformer concerns into a strikingly effective work of literature. To be sure, the polemics are important. Gilman, an avowed feminist and a relative of Harriet Beecher Stowe, told Howells that she didn't consider the work to be "literature" at all, that everything she wrote was for a purpose, in this case that of pointing out the dangers of a particular medical treatment. Unlike Gilman's other purposeful fictions, however, "The Yellow Wallpaper" transcends its author's immediate intent, and my experience teaching it suggests that it favorably impresses both male and female students, even before they learn of its feminist context or of the patriarchal biases of nineteenth-century medicine. I think the story has this effect for two reasons. First, the question of women's role in the nineteenth century is inextricably bound up with the more general question of how one perceives the world. Woman is often seen as representing an imaginative or "poetic" view of things that conflicts with (or sometimes complements) the American male's "common sense" approach to reality. Through the characters of the "rational" doctor and the "imaginative" wife, Gilman explores a question that was—and in many ways still is—central both to American literature and to the place of women in American culture: What happens to the imagination when it's defined as feminine (and thus weak) and has to face a society that values the useful and the practical and rejects anything else as nonsense? Second, this conflict and the related feminist message both arise naturally and effectively out of the action of the story because of the author's skillful handling of the narrative voice.

One of the most striking passages in Gilman's autobiography describes her development and abandonment of a dream world, a fantasy land to which she could escape from the rather harsh realities of her early life. When she was thirteen, a friend of her mother warned that such escape could be dangerous, and Charlotte, a good New England girl who considered absolute obedience a duty, "shut the door" on her "dear, bright, glittering dreams."[6] The narrator of "The Yellow Wallpaper" has a similar problem: from the beginning of the story she displays a vivid imagination. She wants to imagine that the house they have rented is haunted, and as she looks at the wallpaper, she is reminded of her childhood fancies about rooms, her ability to "get more entertainment and terror out of blank walls and plain furniture than most children could find in a toy store."[7] Her husband has to keep reminding her that she "must not give way to fancy in the least" as she comments on her new surroundings. Along with her vivid imagination she has the mind and eye of an artist. She begins to study the wallpaper in an attempt to make sense of its artistic design, and she objects to it for aesthetic reasons: it is "one of those sprawling, flamboyant patterns committing every artistic sin" (p. 13). When her ability to express her artistic impulses is limited by her husband's prescription of complete rest, her mind turns to the wallpaper, and she begins to find in its tangled pattern the emotions and experiences she is forbidden to record. By trying to ignore and repress her imagination, in short, John eventually brings about the very circumstance he wants to prevent.

Though he is clearly a domineering husband who wants to have absolute control over his wife, John also has other reasons for forbidding her to write or paint. As Gilman points out in her autobiography, the "rest cure" was designed for "the business man exhausted from too much work, and the society woman exhausted from too much play."[8] The treatment is intended, in other words, to deal with physical symptoms of overwork and fatigue, and so is unsuited to the narrator's more complex case. But as a doctor and an empiricist who "scoffs openly at things not to be felt and seen and put down in figures," John wants to deal only with physical causes and effects: if his wife's symptoms are nervousness and weight loss, the treatment must be undisturbed tranquility and good nutrition. The very idea that her "work" might be beneficial to her disturbs him; indeed, he is both fearful and contemptuous of her imaginative and artistic powers, largely because he fails to understand them or the view of the world they lead her to.

Two conversations in particular demonstrate his way of dealing with her imagination and his fear of it. The first occurs when the narrator asks him to change the wallpaper. He replies that to do so would be dangerous, for "nothing was worse for a nervous patient than to give way to such fancies." At this point, her "fancy" is simply an objection to the paper's ugliness, a point she makes clear when she suggests that they move to the "pretty rooms" downstairs. John replies by calling her a "little goose" and saying "he would go down to the cellar if she wished and have it whitewashed into the bargain" (p. 15). Besides showing his obviously patriarchal stance, his reply is designed to make her aesthetic objections seem nonsense by fastening on concrete details—color and elevation—and ignoring the real basis of her request. If she wants to go downstairs away from yellow walls, he will take her to the cellar and have it whitewashed. The effect is precisely what he intends: he makes her see her objection to the paper's ugliness as "just a whim." The second conversation occurs after the narrator has begun to see a woman behind the surface pattern of the wallpaper. When John catches her getting out of bed to examine the paper more closely, she decides to ask him to take her away. He refuses, referring again to concrete details: "You are gaining flesh and color, your appetite is better, I feel really much better about you." When she implies that her physical condition isn't the real problem, he cuts her off in midsentence: "I beg of you, for my sake and for our child's sake, as well as for your own, that you will never for one instant let that idea enter your mind! There is nothing so dangerous, so fascinating, to a temperament like yours. It is a false and foolish fancy" (p. 24). For John, mental illness is the inevitable result of using one's imagination, the creation of an attractive "fancy" which the mind then fails to distinguish from reality. He fears that because of her imaginative "temperament" she will create the fiction that she is mad and come to accept it despite the evidence—color, weight, appetite—that she is well. Imagination and art are subversive because they threaten to undermine his materialistic universe.

Ironically, despite his abhorrence of faith and superstition, John fails because of his own dogmatic faith in materialism and empiricism, a faith that will not allow him even to consider the possibility that his wife's imagination could be a positive force. In a way John is like Aylmer in Hawthorne's "The Birthmark": each man chooses to interpret a characteristic of his wife as a defect because of his own failure of imagination, and each attempts to "cure" her through purely physical means, only to find he has destroyed her in the process. He also resembles the implied villain in many of Emerson's and Thoreau's lectures and essays, the man of convention who is so taken with "common sense" and traditional wisdom that he is blind to truth. Indeed, the narrator's lament that she might get well faster if John were not a doctor and her assertion that he can't understand her "because he is so wise" remind one of Thoreau's question in the first chapter of Walden: "How can he remember his ignorance—which his growth requires—who has so often to use his knowledge?" John's role as a doctor and an American male requires that he use his "knowledge" continuously and doggedly, and he would abhor the appearance of imagination in his own mind even more vehemently than in his wife's.

The relationship between them also offers an insight into how and why this fear of the imagination has been institutionalized through assigned gender roles. By defining his wife's artistic impulse as a potentially dangerous part of her feminine "temperament," John can control both his wife and a facet of human experience which threatens his comfortably materialistic view of the world. Fear can masquerade as calm authority when the thing feared is embodied in the "weaker sex." Quite fittingly, the story suggests that America is full of Johns: the narrator's brother is a doctor, and S. Weir Mitchell—"like John and my brother only more so!"—looms on the horizon if she doesn't recover.

As her comments suggest, the narrator understands John's problem yet is unable to call it his problem, and in many ways it is this combination of insight and naiveté, of resistance and resignation, that makes her such a memorable character and gives such power to her narrative. The story is in the form of a journal which the writer knows no one will read—she says she would not criticize John to "a living soul, of course, but this is dead paper"—yet at the same time her occasional use of "you," her questions ("What is one to do?" she asks three times in the first two pages), and her confidential tone all suggest that she is attempting to reach or create the listener she cannot otherwise find. Her remarks reveal that her relationship with her husband is filled with deception on her part, not so much because she wants to hide things from him but because it is impossible to tell him things he does not want to acknowledge. She reveals to the "dead paper" that she must pretend to sleep and have an appetite because that is what John assumes will happen as a result of his treatment, and if she tells him that she isn't sleeping or eating he will simply contradict her. Thus the journal provides an opportunity not only to confess her deceit and explain its necessity but also to say the things she really wants to say to John and would say if his insistence on "truthfulness," i.e., saying what he wants to hear, didn't prevent her. As both her greatest deception and her attempt to be honest, the journal embodies in its very form the absurd contradictions inherent in her role as wife.

At the same time, however, she cannot quite stop deceiving herself about her husband's treatment of her, and her descriptions create a powerful dramatic irony as the reader gradually puts together details the meaning of which she doesn't quite understand. She says, for instance, that there is "something strange" about the house they have rented, but her description reveals bit by bit a room that has apparently been used to confine violent mental cases, with bars on the windows, a gate at the top of the stairs, steel rings on the walls, a nailed-down bedstead, and a floor that has been scratched and gouged. When she tries to explain her feelings about the house to John early in the story, her report of the conversation reveals her tendency to assume that he is always right despite her own reservations:

> . . . there is something strange about the house—I can feel it.
>
> I even said so to John one moonlight evening, but he said what I felt was a *draught*, and shut the window.
>
> I get unreasonably angry with John sometimes. I'm sure I never used to be so sensitive. I think it is due to this nervous condition. (p. 11)

As usual, John refuses to consider anything but physical details, but the narrator's reaction is particularly revealing here. Her anger, perfectly understandable to us, must be characterized, even privately, as "unreasonable," a sign of her condition. Whatever doubts she may have about John's methods, he represents reason, and it is her own sensitivity that must be at fault. Comments such as these reveal more powerfully than any direct statement could the way she is trapped by the conception of herself which she has accepted from John and the society whose values he represents. As Paula A. Treichler has pointed out, John's diagnosis is a "sentence," a "set of linguistic signs whose representational claims are authorized by society," and thus it can "control women's fate, whether or not those claims are valid." The narrator can object to the terms of the sentence, but she cannot question its authority, even in her own private discourse.[9]

To a great extent, the narrator's view of her husband is colored by the belief that he really does love her, a belief that provides some of the most striking and complex ironies in the story. When she says, "it is hard to talk to John about my case because he is so wise, and because he loves me so," it is tempting to take the whole sentence as an example of her naiveté. Obviously he is not wise, and his actions are not what we would call loving. Nevertheless, the sentence is in its way powerfully insightful. If John were not so wise—so sure of his own empirical knowledge and his expertise as a doctor—and so loving—so determined to make her better in the only way he knows—then he might be able to set aside his fear of her imagination and listen to her.

The passage suggests strikingly the way both characters are doomed to act out their respective parts of loving husband and obedient wife right to the inevitably disastrous end.

Gilman's depiction of the narrator's decline into madness has been praised for the accuracy with which it captures the symptoms of mental breakdown and for its use of symbolism.[10] What hasn't been pointed out is the masterly use of associations, foreshadowing, and even humor. Once the narrator starts attempting to read the pattern of the wallpaper, the reader must become a kind of psychological detective in order to follow and appreciate the narrative. In a sense, he too is viewing a tangled pattern with a woman behind it, and he must learn to revise his interpretation of the pattern as he goes along if he is to make sense of it. For one thing, the narrator tells us from time to time about new details in the room. She notices a "smooch" on the wall "low down, near the mopboard," and later we learn that the bedstead is "fairly gnawed." It is only afterwards that we find out that she is herself the source of these new marks as she bites the bedstead and crawls around the room, shoulder to the wallpaper. If the reader has not caught on already, these details show clearly that the narrator is not always aware of her own actions or in control of her thoughts and so is not always reliable in reporting them. They also foreshadow her final separation from her wifely self, her belief that she is the woman who has escaped from behind the barred pattern of the wallpaper.

But the details also invite us to reread earlier passages, to see if the voice which we have taken to be a fairly reliable though naive reporter has not been giving us unsuspected hints of another reality all along. If we do backtrack we find foreshadowing everywhere, not only in the way the narrator reads the pattern on the wall but in the pattern of her own narrative, the way in which one thought leads to another. One striking example occurs when she describes John's sister, Jennie, who is "a dear girl and so careful of me," and who therefore must not find out about the journal.

> She is a perfect and enthusiastic housekeeper, and hopes for no better profession. I verily believe she thinks it is the writing which made me sick!
>
> But I can write when she is out, and see her a long way off from these windows.

There is one that commands the road, a lovely shaded winding road, and one that just looks off over the country. A lovely country too, full of great elms and velvet meadows.

This wallpaper has a kind of sub-pattern in a different shade, a particularly irritating one, for you can only see it in certain lights, and not clearly then.

But in the places where it isn't faded and where the sun is just so—I can see a strange, provoking, formless sort of figure, that seems to skulk about behind that silly and conspicuous front design.

There's sister on the stairs! (pp. 17–18)

The "perfect and enthusiastic housekeeper" is, of course, the ideal sister for John, whose view of the imagination she shares. Thoughts of Jennie lead to the narrator's assertion that she can "see her a long way off from these windows," foreshadowing later passages in which the narrator will see a creeping woman, and then eventually many creeping women from the same windows, and the association suggests a connection between the "enthusiastic housekeeper" and those imaginary women. The thought of the windows leads to a description of the open country and suggests the freedom that the narrator lacks in her barred room. This, in turn, leads her back to the wallpaper, and now she mentions for the first time the "sub-pattern," a pattern which will eventually become a woman creeping behind bars, a projection of her feelings about herself as she looks through the actual bars of the window. The train of associations ends when John's sister returns, but this time she's just "sister," as if now she's the narrator's sister as well, suggesting a subconscious recognition that they both share the same role, despite Jennie's apparent freedom and contentment. Taken in context, this passage prepares us to see the connection between the pattern of the wallpaper, the actual bars on the narrator's windows, and the "silly and conspicuous" surface pattern of the wifely role behind which both women lurk.

We can see just how Gilman develops the narrator's mental collapse if we compare the passage quoted above to a later one in which the narrator once again discusses the "sub-pattern," which by now has become a woman who manages to escape in the daytime.

> I think that woman gets out in the daytime!
>
> And I'll tell you why—privately—I've seen her!
>
> I can see her out of every one of my windows!
>
> It is the same woman, I know, for she is always creeping, and most women do not creep by daylight.
>
> I see her on that long road under the trees, creeping along, and when a carriage comes she hides under the blackberry vines.
>
> I don't blame her a bit. It must be very humiliating to be caught creeping by daylight!
>
> I always lock the door when I creep by daylight! (pp. 30–31)

Here again the view outside the window suggests a kind of freedom, but now it is only a freedom to creep outside the pattern, a freedom that humiliates and must be hidden. The dark humor that punctuates the last part of the story appears in the narrator's remark that she can recognize the woman because "most women do not creep by daylight," and the sense that the journal is an attempt to reach a listener becomes clear through her emphasis on "privately." Finally, the identification between the narrator and the woman is taken a step further and becomes more nearly conscious when the narrator reveals that she too creeps, but only behind a locked door. If we read the two passages in sequence, we can see just how masterfully Gilman uses her central images—the window, the barred pattern of the paper, and the woman—to create a pattern of associations which reveals the source of the narrator's malady yet allows the narrator herself to remain essentially unable to verbalize her problem. At some level, we see, she understands what has rendered her so thoroughly powerless and confused, yet she is so completely trapped in her role that she can express that knowledge only indirectly in a way that hides it from her conscious mind.

In the terribly comic ending, she has destroyed both the wallpaper and her own identity: now she is the woman from behind the barred pattern, and not even Jane—the wife she once was—can put her back. Still unable to express her feelings directly, she acts out both her triumph and her humiliation symbolically, creeping around the room with her shoulder in the "smooch," passing over her fainting husband on every lap. Loralee MacPike suggests that the narrator has finally gained her freedom,[11] but that is true only in a very limited sense. She is still creeping, still inside the room with a rope around her waist. She has destroyed only the front pattern, the "silly and conspicuous" design that covers the real wife, the creeping one hidden behind the facade. As Treichler suggests, "her triumph is to have sharpened and articulated the nature of women's condition,"[12] but she is free only from the need to deceive herself and others about the true nature of her role. In a sense, she has discovered, bit by bit, and finally revealed to John, the wife he is attempting to create—the woman without illusions or imagination who spends all her time creeping.

The story, then, is a complex work of art as well as an effective indictment of the nineteenth-century view of the sexes and the materialism that underlies that view. It is hard to believe that readers familiar with the materialistic despots created by such writers as Hawthorne, Dickens, and Browning could fail to see the implications. Indeed, though Howells' comment that the story makes him "shiver" has been offered as evidence that he saw it as a more or less conventional horror story, I would assert that he understood quite clearly the source of the story's effect. He originally wrote to Gilman to congratulate her on her poem "Women of Today," a scathing indictment of women who fear changing sexual roles and fail to realize that their view of themselves as mothers, wives, and housekeepers is a self-deception. In fact, he praises that poem in terms that anticipate his praise of the story, calling it "dreadfully true."[13] Perhaps the story was unpopular because it was, at least on some level, understood all too clearly, because it struck too deeply and effectively at traditional ways of seeing the world and woman's place in it. That, in any case, seems to be precisely what Howells implies in his comment that it is "too terribly good to be printed."

The clearest evidence that John's view of the imagination and art was all but sacred in Gilman's America comes, ironically, from the author's own pen. When she replied to Howells' request to reprint the story by saying that she did not write "literature," she was, of course, denying that she was a mere imaginative artist, defending herself from the charge that Hawthorne imagines his Puritan ancestors would lay at his doorstep: "A writer of story-books!—what mode of glorifying God, or being serviceable to mankind in his day and generation—may that be? Why, the degenerate fellow might as well have been a fiddler!"[14] One wonders what this later female scion of good New England stock might have done had she been able to set aside such objections. In any case, one hopes that this one work of imagination and art, at least, will be restored to the place that Howells so astutely assigned it, alongside stories by contemporaries such as Mark Twain, Henry James, and Edith Wharton.

NOTES

1. Quoted in Charlotte Perkins Gilman, *The Living of Charlotte Perkins Gilman: An Autobiography* (1935; rpt. New York: Arno, 1972), p. 119.

2. *The Great Modern American Stories: An Anthology* (New York: Boni and Liveright, 1920), p. vii.

3. Afterword, *The Yellow Wallpaper* (Old Westbury, N.Y.: Feminist Press, 1973) p. 37.

4. "A Map for Rereading: Or, Gender and the Interpretation of Literary Texts," *New Literary History*, 11 (1980), 455–56.

5. "Convention Coverage or How to Read Your Own Life," *New Literary History*, 13 (1981), 73–74.

6. Gilman, *Living*, p. 24.

7. *The Yellow Wallpaper* (Old Westbury, N.Y.: Feminist Press, 1973), p. 17. Page numbers in the text refer to this edition.

8. Gilman, *Living*, p. 95.

9. "Escaping the Sentence: Diagnosis and Discourse in 'The Yellow Wallpaper,'" Tulsa Studies, in *Women's Literature*, 3 (1984), 74.

10. See Beate Schöpp-Schilling, "'The Yellow Wallpaper': A Rediscovered 'Realistic' Story," *American Literary Realism*, 8 (1975), 284–86; Loralee MacPike, "Environment as Psychopathological Symbolism in 'The Yellow Wallpaper'" *American Literary Realism*, 8 (1975), 286–88.

11. MacPike, p. 288.

12. Treichler, p. 74.

13. Quoted in Gilman, *Living*, p. 113.

14. *The Scarlet Letter* (Columbus: Ohio State Univ. Press, 1962), p. 10.

❧ *Acknowledgments* ❧

Bradley, A.C. "The Rejection of Falstaff." *Oxford Lectures on Poetry,* 2nd Ed. 1909. New York: MacMillan, 1917. 247–275.

Cowan, Louise. "Aristophanes' Comic Apocalypse." *The Terrain of Comedy.* Ed. Louise Cowan. Dallas, Texas: Dallas Institute of Humanities, 1984, 61–88. Copyright by The Pegasus Foundation. Reprinted by permission.

Esslin, Martin. "The Theatre of the Absurd." *Theatre in the Twentieth Century.* Ed. Robert W. Corrigan. New York: Grove Press, 1956. 229–244. Copyright by Grove Press.

Mandia, Patricia M. "*The Mysterious Stranger* and *3,000 Years Among the Microbes*: Chimerical Realities and Nightmarish Transformations." *Comedic Pathos: Black Humor in Twain's Fiction.* Jefferson, N.C.: McFarland, 1991. 102–122. Copyright by Patricia M. Mandia. Reprinted by permission.

Nagel, James. "*Catch-22* and Angry Humor: A Study of the Normative Values of Satire." *Studies in American Humor* 1.2 (1974): 98–105. Copyright by James Nagel. Reprinted by permission.

O'Neill, Patrick. "The Comedy of Entropy: The Contexts of Black Humour." *Canadian Review of Comparative Literature* 10.2 (June 1983): 145–166.

Rowe, W. Woodin "Observations on Black Humor in Gogol and Nabokov." *The Slavic and East European Journal.* 18. 4 (Winter 1974): 392–399. Reprinted by permission.

Shumaker, Conrad. "'Too Terribly Good to Be Printed': Charlotte Gilman's 'The Yellow Wallpaper.'" *American Literature* 57.4 (December 1985). Reprinted by permission.

Stephen, Leslie. "Wood's Halfpence." *Swift.* 1882. London: MacMillan, 1898. 145–165.

Index

A

absurd
  black humor and, 94–95, 99
  defined, 31
  Falstaff and, 161–162
  laughter at the, 214–215
absurd drama, 29–46, 98
Acharnians (Aristophanes), 10–12, 17
Act Without Words (Beckett), 41
Ada (Gogol), 130
Adamov, Arthur, 29–32, 34, 36, 40,
  43
Aeschylus, 18–19
Albee, Edward
  absurdism of, 242
  Who's Afraid of Virginia Woolf,
    241–248
Alexie, Sherman, *Reservation Blues,*
  219–228
alienation, 32–33
allegory, 44–45
Amédée (Ionesco), 36
American culture, 52–53, 55, 233,
  238, 253
amiable humor, 87–88
angry comedy, 51–53, 55
antiheroes, 200–201
anti-novel, 61–62
anti-plays, 30
anxiety, 34

apocalyptic vision, 26n14
  of Aristophanes, 6–10, 20–24
  in *Cat's Cradle,* 58–63
Apollinaire, Guillaume, 36–37, 43
Arachne and Pallas (fable), 184
archetype, 6
Arendt, Hannah, 24
Aristophanes, 1–28
  Acharnians, 10–12, 17
  apocalyptic vision of, 6–10, 20–24
  Birds, 17–18, 20–24
  chorus of, 24
  comedy of, 2–9
  comic heroes of, 7–10, 23
  Frogs, 17–19
  Lysistrata, 10, 15–17, 51
  Peace, 10, 12–15, 17–18, 20, 24
  peace depicted by, 10–17, 20
  social satire of, 8–9
  Wasps, 24
Aristotle, 61, 86
Artaud, Antonin, 37–38, 40
Auden, W. H., 51
audience, in Theatre of the Absurd,
  32–33, 42–44
avant-garde, 41

B

Bakhtin, Mikhail, 4–5
Bald Soprano, The (Ionesco), 30, 39

265

Balliett, Whitney, 47
Barrault, Jean-Louis, 38–39
Barth, John, 83, 129
beast imagery, 24, 42
Beckett, Samuel, 29–32, 36, 41, 83, 93
    on dianoetic laugh, 95–96
    Waiting for Godot, 30, 40, 42, 43
    Watt, 91
benign humor, 87–90, 95, 97
Bergin, Thomas G., 109, 112
Bergson, Henri, 69, 123
Berkeley, George, 194–195
Bermel, Albert, 124
Bernhard, Thomas, 83
Birds (Aristophanes), 17–18, 20–24
Birthday Party, The (Pinter), 115
black humor, 51
    conceptual model of, 90–97
    defined, xv–xvi, 80–81, 85–86, 88
    historical development of, 81–90
    North American, 81–83
    reader response to, 84, 91
    tradition of, 97–100
Black Humor (Friedman), 82
bodily functions, 129–131, 134
bodily humor, 69–70
Book of Mormon, The, 62
Books of Bokonon, The, 62
Borges, Jorge Luis, 83
Bradbrook, Muriel, 2
Brecht, Bertolt, 32–33
Breton, André, 37, 83–84, 85, 89
Brustein, Robert, 242
Burgess, Anthony, *Clockwork Orange*, 67–77
Byron, Lord, 87

C

Calvino, Italo, 62, 83
camp, 246
caricature, 49–50

carnival, 4–5
Catch-22 (Heller), 47–56, 99
    caricature in, 49–50
    genre classification, 48–49
    madness in, 53–54
    normative values of, 51–53
    as satire, 48–56
Cat's Cradle (Vonnegut), 57–63
Cazamian, Louis, 90
Céline, Louis-Ferdinand, 82
chaos, 95
Chaucer, xv
Chesterton, G. K., xv
chorus, in Aristophanes' plays, 24
Christianity, 209–210
circumstance, 208
circus, 41
clichés, 140–143
Clockwork Orange, A (Burgess), 67–77, 99
Cold War, 58, 62
collective unconscious, 34–35
comedy. *See also* humor
    angry, 51–53, 55
    defined, 105–106
    medieval view of, 106
    of menace, 124
    purpose of, 76–77
    "rule of three," 117
comic heroes, of Aristophanes, 7–10, 23
comic imagination, 23–25
comic violence, 121
Commedia (Dante), 23
contemporary culture, 233–235, 238
corporeal functions, 129
Cortazar, Julio, 83
Cowan, Louise, 106
Cox, James, 199
Critchley, Simon, 57
cruelty, 38
Cubism, 36

D

Dance of Death (Strindberg), 244
dancing jack technique, 123
Dante, 17, 23–24
 Divine Comedy, 105–113
 Inferno, 106–107, 109–112, 173
 intentions of, 106
 Paradiso, 113
 Purgatorio, 106–107, 112–113
dark humor. *See* black humor
Davis, Bette, 245
Dead Souls (Gogol), 131, 132–133
death, 133–134, 235–239
Defense, The (Nabokov), 130
DeLillo, Don
 use of satire by, 231
 White Noise, 229–239
Denniston, Constance, 48
depth psychology, 41
derisive humor, 87–89, 95
Despair (Nabokov), 129
devil, 110–111
dialogue, in Theatre of the Absurd,
 40, 41–42
dianoetic laugh, 95–96
"Diary of a Madman, The" (Gogol),
 129–130
Dikaiopolic (*Acharnians*), 10–12
Dionysus, 2–4, 7, 18, 19, 22
disembodied voices, 36
disorientation, 96, 99
Divine Comedy (Dante), 105–113
doctors, 128
Don Quijote, 87, 91
drama
 absurd, 29–46
 Greek, 2–3
Drapier's Letters (Swift), 185–191
dreams, 39, 210–214
duality, 24–25
Dumbwaiter, The (Pinter), 115–124
 characters in, 115–119

 as farce, 119–124
 use of pauses in, 118–119
Duneka, Frederick, 199

E

eating, 14
Eliot, T.S.
 "Love Song of J. Alfred Prufrock,
  The," 171–178
 "Waste Land, The," 246
emotional distance, between reader
 and characters, 202–203
empathy, 75
Endgame (Beckett), 36
English oppression, of Irish, 182–195
Enlightenment, 89
entertainment, superficial, 143–146
entropic humor, 79–100
Esslin, Martin, 98
Euelepides (*Birds*), 20–21
Euripides, 18–19
exaggeration, 93
experimentalism, 97–98

F

Falstaff, xv–xvi, 87, 91, 149–169
 character of, 160–169
 cowardice of, 163–165
 flaws of, 166–167
 humor of, 160–163
 ludicrousness of, 159–160
 in *Merry Wives*, 150
 rejection of, 151–159, 167–168
 sympathy for, 159, 165, 168–169
farce, 110–111, 119–124
Faulkner, William, 74–75
Felix Hoenikker (*Cat's Cradle*), 60–61
feminist literature, 252
festive imagery, 12–15
Fish, Stanley, 74

food imagery, 12–15, 130
Fool (*King Lear*), xv
Ford, Douglas, 219
free will, 70–72
Freud, Sigmund, 85, 87, 88
Friedman, Bruce Jay, 82
Frogs (Aristophanes), 17–19
Frye, Northrop, 6, 49, 51, 93, 98
futility, 32

G

Genesis, 58, 59
Gibson, William, 199
Gilman, Charlotte Perkins
    autobiography, 253
    "Yellow Wallpaper, The," 251–262
God, death of, 94–95
Gogol, Nikolai, 127–135
Gone With the Wind (Mitchell),
    146–147
"Good Man Is Hard to Find, A"
    (O'Connor), 139–147
Government Inspector, The (Gogol),
    128, 131
Grass, Gunter, 83
"Great Dark, The" (Twain), 215n3
Greek drama, 2–3
Grimes, Linda Sue, 171–172
grotesque
    in black humor, 91–95, 99
    in *Inferno*, 112

H

Hadas, Moses, 3
Hamlet, 177
Hauck, Richard, 218n12
Hazard, Paul, 90
Heller, Joseph, *Catch-22*, 47–56
Henninger, Gerd, 83, 85–86, 89–90,
    94

Henry (*Henry IV*)
    character of, 156–158, 167
    rejection of Falstaff by, 151–159,
        167–168
Henry IV (Shakespeare), 149–169
heroes
    antiheroes, 200–201
    Aristophanic, 7–10, 23
Hillman, James, 3
hospitals, 128
Howells, William Dean, 251, 261
Hudley, Bernard, 244
human condition, 32
human isolation, 32, 34
human nature, contradictions of, 68
humor, 100. *See also* comedy
    amiable, 87–88
    benign, 87–90, 95, 97
    biting, 142–143
    black. *see* black humor
    bodily, 69–70
    crisis of, 89–90
    cultural healing and, 219, 227–228
    derisive, 87–89, 95
    metahumor, 95–97
    theories of, 86–89

I

Iago, xv
images, 6
    ubiquitous, 50
imagination
    comic, 23–25
    fear of, 254–256
incest, 130
incongruity, 90–91, 93, 175
Inferno (Dante), 23–24, 106–107,
    109–112, 173
insanity, 53–54, 130, 134, 258–261
Ionesco, Eugene, 29–32, 34–36, 39
    on anxiety, 34

on black humor, 100
Lesson, The, 40
New Tenant, The, 41
on reality, 42
Rhinoceros, 43
Ireland, 182–184
copper coinage, 185–190
English oppression of, 182–195
irony, xv, 92–93, 107, 206

J

Jack or the Submission (Ionesco), 30
Jarry, Alfred, 35–36, 97
jazz, xii–xiii
Johnson, Robert, 219
Joyce, James, 39
Jung, C. G., 5–6

K

Kafka, Franz, 38–39, 85, 88, 93, 99, 100
Keillor, Garrison, 171–172
Kennard, Jean F., 252
Kerenyi, Carl, 2, 3, 7
kernan, Alvin, 50
Knox, Ronald, 88
Kolodny, Annette, 252

L

labeling, inaccurate, 131–132, 133
La Grande et la Petite Manouevre
(Adamov), 36
language
clichés, 140–143
in Theatre of the Absurd, 39–42
use of, by O'Connor, 140–141
in *Who's Afraid of Virginia Wolf*,
243, 246
La Parodie (Adamov), 32
laughter, 86–87, 100, 214–215

Legion Club (Swift), 193
Les Mamelles de Tirésias
(Apollonaire), 36–37
Lesson, The (Ionesco), 40
literary influence, xii
liturgical comedy, 2
Logical Positivism, 41
Lolita (Nabokov), 128, 130–132
"Love Song of J. Alfred Prufrock,
The" (Eliot), 171–178
Lysistrata (Aristophanes), 10, 15–17, 51

M

MacPike, Lorale, 260–261
madness, 53–54, 130, 258–261
Márquez, Gabriel García, 62, 83
marriage, 241, 244
masculinity, 224–225
materialism, 261
meaning, in Theatre of the Absurd,
42–43
media noise, 233
medieval carnival, 4–5
medieval drama, 2
Melville, Herman, 61
Menippean satire, 98
Meredith, George, 62–63
Merry Wives of Windsor, The
(Shakespeare), 150
metafiction, 62, 97
metahumor, 95–97
metaphors, xi–xiii
military, 54
Milne, Victor, 48
Milton, John, 74
mimesis, 61
Mitchell, Margaret, 146–147
Modest Proposal, A (Swift), 84, 93,
193–195
morality play, 147
moral order, 33–34

Morgann, Maurice, 163–164
Mormonism, 62
multiple realities, 40–43, 201–202
Murray, Gilbert, 27n26
Mysterious Stranger, The (Twain),
    197–218
    antiheroes in, 200–201
    black humor in, 198, 204, 214–215
    characters in, 203
    dreams in, 211–214
    irony in, 206
    narrative structure, 199
    publication of, 199
    satire in, 208–210
    setting, 205–206
    tone of, 198

N

Nabokov, Vladimir, 127–135
narrator, 131, 134
Native American culture, 219–228
New Tenant, The (Ionesco), 41
Newton, John, 219
Nietzsche, Friedrich, 87
nihilism, 212–213
nonsense verse, 98

O

O'Connor, Flannery
    "A Good Man Is Hard to Find,"
        139–147
    language use by, 140–141
Old Comedy, 2–5
Opora (*Peace*), 12–13
Orphism, 26n16
Otto, Rudolf, 6–10
Otto, Walter, 2, 3

P

Paine, Albert Bigelow, 198–199

Pale Fire (Nabokov), 133–134
Paolo Paoli (Adamov), 31
Paradise Lost (Milton), 74
Paradiso (Dante), 113
Parker, Douglas, 15
parody, 96, 99, 227
pataphysics, 97
Paulson, Ronald, 55
peace, 10–12, 15–17, 20
Peace (Aristophanes), 10, 12–15,
    17–18, 20, 24
pedophilia, 130
Peisthetairos (*Birds*), 20–22
pessimism, 182, 208
physical comedy, 69–70
Ping-Pong (Adamov), 30, 40, 43
Pinter, Harold
    The Birthday Party, 115
    The Dumbwaiter, 115–124
Plato, 8, 86
poetical reality, 40–41
polarities, 208–209
political corruption, 182
popular culture, 145–147, 233–235,
    238
pratfall, 75–76
predetermination, 207–208
primordial experiences, 5–6
Prometheus, 21–22
pure theatre, 31
Purgatorio (Dante), 106–107, 112–113
Pynchon, Thomas, 83

Q

Queneau, Raymond, 83
Querist (Berkeley), 195

R

racism, 146
reader, emotional distance of, 202–
    203

realism, 61–62
reality
    as mental construct, 82–83
    multiple, 40–43, 201–202
    unreliability of, 210–214
referential mania, 130
regeneration, 11–12
religion, 209
religious drama, 2
religious faith, 33
Reservation Blues (Alexie), 219–228
    characters in, 220–221
    degenerative masculinity in,
        224–225
    parody in, 227
    plot, 219
rest cure, 254
retributive justice, 107–108
reversal words, 128–129
Rhinoceros (Ionesco), 43
Richter, Jean Paul, 87
Roth, Philip, 49
"rule of three," 117

S

Sade, Marquis de, 84–85, 89
Saint John the Divine, 7
Satan, 198, 203–204, 206–211
satire, 92, 99
    of Aristophanes, 8–9
    Catch-22 as, 48–56
    in *Cat's Cradle*, 62–63
    characteristics of, 50–51
    of DeLillo, 231
    elements of, 49
    Menippean, 98
    normative values of, 51–53
    Swift on, 62
    of Twain, 208–210
Scholes, Robert, 97, 98
Schulz, Max F., 82–83, 127
science, 209

Scudder, Horace, 251–252
self-mockery, 173–174, 177–178
sexual imagery, 14, 15, 129–132
Shakespeare, William, xii, 98
    dark humor of, xv–xvi
    Henry IV, 149–169
    impartiality of, 156
sickness, 128
"Signs and Symbols" (Nabakov),
    130
Silver, Brenda A., 246
slapstick, in *A Clockwork Orange*,
    67–77
Smith, Joseph, 62
Solomon, Eric, 48
Solomos, Alexis, 4
Sontag, Susan, 246
"Sorocincy Fair, The" (Gogol), 130
soul, 22–23, 133
Sound and the Fury, The (Faulkner),
    74–75
spiritual conditions, 17
storytelling, superficial, 143–146
Strindberg, August, 39, 244
suicide, 133–134
surrealism, 37–38, 98
Swift, Jonathan, 89, 90
    Drapier's Letters, 185–191
    on Ireland, 182–184
    Legion Club, 193
    madness of, 194
    Modest Proposal, 84, 93, 193–195
    pessimism of, 182
    political issues and, 185–193
    popularity of, 190–191
    on satire, 62
    use of irony by, xv

T

taboo, 130, 133, 134
Tati, Jacques, 41
Tave, Stuart, 87, 88

television, 234
Théâtre Alfred Jarry (Artaud), 37–38
Theatre and Its Double, The (Artaud), 38
Theatre of the Absurd, 29–46, 98
 action in, 41–42, 44
 allegory and, 44–45
 audience in, 32–33, 42–44
 characteristics of, 36, 38
 vs. conventional theater, 43–44
 dialogue, 33
 dream element in, 39
 erosion of dramatic convention and, 33–34
 explicitness of, 36
 "Great Dark, The," 215n3
 language in, 39–42
 meaning in, 42–43
 tradition of, 35–39
 world portrayed in, 32–33
themes, xi–xiii
Theoria (*Peace*), 12
Thomson, Philip, 93–94
"3,000 Years Among the Microbes (Twain), 198–218
 antiheroes in, 201
 black humor in, 198, 204–205
 characters in, 203
 dreams in, 210–211
 irony in, 206
 multiple realities in, 201–202
 narrative structure, 199–200
 satire in, 208–210
 setting, 205
 tone of, 198–199
topos, xi
tragedy, 3, 94
Treichler, Paula A., 257
Trial, The (Kafka), 38–39
trope, xi–xii
Trygaios (*Peace*), 12–14, 20
Twain, Mark, 87

"3,000 Years Among the Microbes, 198–218
Mysterious Stranger, The, 197–218
 nihilism of, 212–213
 pessimism of, 208

U

Ubu Roi (Jarry), 35–36
Ulysses (Joyce), 39
unintented action, 72–73

V

verisimilitude, 61
violence
 comic, 121
 response to, 71–75
 slapstick, 67–77
Virgil, 109–112
Vonnegut, Kurt, 83
 Cat's Cradle, 57–63
 as satirist, 62–63
 themes touched by, 58

W

Waiting for Godot (Beckett), 30, 40, 42, 43
Wasps (Aristophanes), 24
"Waste Land, The" (Eliot), 246
Watt (Beckett), 91
White Noise (DeLillo), 229–239
 black humor in, 231, 238–239
 characters in, 229–235
 death theme in, 235–239
 dialogues in, 233–234
Whitman, Cedric, 9
Who's Afraid of Virginia Woolf (Albee), 241–248
 black humor of, 243–244
 language in, 243, 246

wine, 10–12
Wittgenstein, Ludwig, 41
women, role of, 253
Wood, William, 185–187, 190
Worcester, David, 49

Y

"Yellow Wallpaper, The" (Gilman),
  251–262

criticism of, 252–253
fear of imagination in, 254–256
husband in, 254–258
madness in, 258–261
narrator, 253–254, 256–261
publication of, 251–252

Z

Zeus, 21–22

Bloom's literary themes. Dark humor.

DATE			